Being Feminist, Being Christian

Being Feminist, Being Christian

Essays from Academia

Edited by
Allyson Jule and Bettina Tate Pedersen

First published in 2006 by
PALGRAVE MACMILLAN™
175 Fifth Avenue, New York, N.Y. 10010 and
Houndmills, Basingstoke, Hampshire, England RG21 6XS
Companies and representatives throughout the world.

PALGRAVE MACMILLAN is the global academic imprint of the Palgrave Macmillan division of St. Martin's Press, LLC and of Palgrave Macmillan Ltd. Macmillan® is a registered trademark in the United States, United Kingdom and other countries. Palgrave is a registered trademark in the European Union and other countries.

ISBN-13: 978-0-230-60644-9
ISBN-10: 0-230-60644-X

Library of Congress Cataloging-in-Publication Data

Being feminist, being Christian : essays from academia / edited by Allyson Jule and Bettina Tate Pedersen.
    p. cm.
Includes bibliographical references and index.
ISBN 1-4039-7295-8 (cloth)
ISBN 0-230-60644-X (pbk)
    1. Feminist theology. 2. Feminism—Religious aspects—Christianity.
I. Jule, Allyson, 1965–. II. Pedersen, Bettina Tate, 1960–

BT83.55.B44 2006
230.082—dc22   2005055232

A catalogue record for this book is available from the British Library.

Design by Newgen Imaging Systems (P) Ltd., Chennai, India.

First PALGRAVE MACMILLAN paperback edition: April 2008

10 9 8 7 6 5 4 3 2 1

Printed in the United States of America.

There is neither Jew nor Greek, slave nor free, male and female, for you are all one in Christ Jesus.

—*Galatians 3:28*

CONTENTS

ACKNOWLEDGMENTS

This book arose from conversations at the Western Regional Conference on Christianity and Literature (CCL) in March 2004 at Point Loma Nazarene University in San Diego. Thus, we are grateful to the Western Regional CCL and its organizers and sponsors for allowing space for such discussions to arise. We are also indebted to the Wesleyan Center for Twenty-first Century Studies at Point Lama Nazarene University for its financial support of several of the contributors' ongoing research.

It is no small thing to feel the encouragement of others. In this way, Maxine Hancock's encouragement has mattered greatly to this project. We have also been helped enormously by Cheryl Wall and her keyboarding skills, by the librarians at our respective institutions, as well as by the editors and staff at Palgrave in New York. Of course, the contributors themselves are owed a great deal because of their hard work on various drafts. We believe the collection is a direct result of their fine scholarship. A very special thanks goes to the artist, Jenni Lin, for the use of her thought-provoking collage on the cover.

This book is dedicated to the contributors' families, friends, and students who support and propel our work by asking, challenging, and living out the tough questions.

Introduction: Being Feminist, Being Christian

ALLYSON JULE AND BETTINA TATE PEDERSEN

In the aftermath of 9/11 what soon became an uncomfortable realization was the role religion played in the event. The hijackers involved in the suicide mission were quickly and clearly identified as religious fundamentalists. New discussions began on street corners, at family dinner tables, on the Internet, and in academic conferences. How massive a role did religion play in propelling the events of 9/11; what role might religion play in the twenty-first century if ideas thought to be ancient and outdated (like religion) could emerge with the added help and power of modern technology; and what, ultimately, could be said about such religious enactments in a postmodern milieu of radical relativism? Since 9/11, we have continued to experience the deadly mix of extremist religion and technology. From around the world there are regular reports of violence as a direct result of religious devotion. As the twenty-first century opens, it is clear that the task of understanding and responding to religious extremists is paramount.

For some people, religion continues to be a source of radicalism and extremism, but for others, it serves to enrich life with meaning, purpose, and peace of heart and mind. For some, religion is a very public identifier, while for others it is a private and personal reality, something protected from public display or public scrutiny. For some working, as we do, in academia, religion is regarded at best as completely irrelevant and outmoded, producing naive and unsophisticated views about the world, or at worst as narrow-minded and superstitious, producing the radical, extremist, and lethal acts of 9/11—and elsewhere. In all the various responses to religion there is a continuum of experience and thinking.

Both of us grew up in "traditional" two-parent homes (one in the United States and one in Canada), where church attendance and participation were significant factors. We also became academics, both committed to scholarship, and both educated to the doctoral level at secular institutions. In addition, we grew up during the mid-twentieth century and experienced much of our intellectual formation in the last decade of that century, a time when religion in Western society was on the wane and something seen as old-fashioned and out of sync with intellectual life. The 1960s and 1970s were decades of liberalism in both the United States and Canada. All areas of influence felt the effect of postmodern diversity and a widening of opportunity for many as a direct result. Ideas of modernism were giving way to the postmodern world, one where various individual experiences and opinions were encouraged and promoted. This widening of experience certainly included a widening of experience and opportunity for women.

In the 1960s and 1970s, feminism experienced a vibrant, almost frenzied focus as it profiled the female experience to be seen as dynamic and long misunderstood as lesser than the male experience. During our childhoods, women claimed more freedoms than ever before: the birth control pill allowed for greater control over child-bearing, divorce became legal and accepted, and new ways of being a woman emerged in the workplace and in the home. Women went into various careers in record numbers, and they continued to pursue these careers amidst their domestic roles or in reaction to them. Academic life also opened up for many women, and, hence, both of us grew up seeing our own life course as one of choice: we could pursue any field of scholarship we were interested in, our human potential being unrestricted because of our gender, and we both did. Bettina studied English Literature and Women's Studies; Allyson studied Applied Linguistics and Education. In our academic study, we have both searched out and examined women's lives. Whether in the reading and analyzing of fictional or nonfictional accounts written by and about women, or in the study and analyzing of women's use of language or silence in classroom or other spaces, we have been drawn to explore the lives of women.

Working as two academics who are also Christians, and working in academic disciplines that study and deal with human issues, situations, and responses, it was inevitable that we would confront the basic question of how our intellectual lives and commitments as academics and how our spiritual lives and commitments as Christians would come together. This coming together has, of course, happened and continues to profoundly shape all the deep textures of our lives: thinking, spiritual journeying, writing, research, teaching, mentoring students, living as spouses with dual primary careers, mothering, and living in relationships with our extended families, professional communities, and church congregations. This book is itself an expressing of that "coming together," a way for us to continue to connect the two most powerful guiding ideologies of our lives: Christianity and feminism. Both have been strong forces in our lives, and both were hard to ignore while growing up when and where we each did—Bettina in the United States and Allyson in Canada. Still, we grew up sensing Christianity and feminism as distinct. Being Christian and being feminist were too different to be seen together; indeed, they even appeared antithetical. We have come to see this separation more as a sign of the times in which we grew up than as a true ideological opposition. That is to say, Christianity and feminism were not and are not as far apart as we grew up believing they were. This discovery has been of critical importance in both our personal and professional lives. The post-9/11 world has altered a number of things for many of us, but no shift is more significant than the new under-standing of religion and society in a current intersection: the impact of religious identity and experience cannot be ignored nor separated from seemingly other pursuits and beliefs, like feminism.

While what is at issue for us in this book is the importance this shift represents in our own lives and work, this same shift is becoming significant for the wider academic world as well. In the Spring 2005 issue of *Feminist Studies*, Jacqueline de Vries reviews several recent studies by feminist historians that illustrate a more considered acknowledgment and examination of the important role religion, specifically Christianity, has played historically: "[A]fter decades of both benign and hostile neglect, feminist historians have rediscovered Christianity as an important site in the historical construction of gender" (135). As work of current feminist historians indicates, "feminist analysis has shifted away from paradigms emphasizing victimization and oppression above all else, opening up possibilities for less reactionary, more nuanced assessments of religion and its relationship to women's roles, self-definitions, and emancipation" (137) and some "adamantly [resist] the postmodernist tendency to reduce religious fervor to mere performance or symptom of some other (perhaps sexual or political) dynamic" (149). De Vries's review also highlights an emerging consensus among these feminist historians that religion not only influenced and shaped the lives of women, but it also provided the grounds and motivations for much of their political activism (143, 153), commitment to social transformation (140), and reworkings of conceptions of the Divine (138, 146). Though all the contributors here are not feminist historians per se, our work is part of a broader stream of scholarship giving careful consideration to the relation of intellectual and spiritual lives.

While recognizing the role and importance of religion may be viewed as a shift in the current postmodern sensibility, those of us, for whom our religious communities and commitments are central, know well that we live our lives in a dynamic relation to the world and to the spiritual life at one and the same time. Oftentimes this knowledge can result in a type of double life, a reality that feels, on the one hand, that ideologies such as Christianity and feminism seem to exist separately, and on the other, that both are inextricably linked. We have lived much our lives in the dynamic of Christianity's and feminism's relation to one another, some-times more and sometimes less consciously aware of how the two have unquestionably shaped our lives. This kind of multiple life is also rou-tinely described and theorized on many levels of feminist discourse. Women's lives are multiple, mixed, and multifarious. This observation is repeatedly confronted in examining the lives of women in history who at times seem to be challenging the status quo of their situations and at other times to be conforming to it. The same is true of contemporary women generally speaking and is reflected in the essays of this collection, many of which speak to the conflicting calls and commitments of cur-rent women's lives.

When we met in March 2004 at the Western Regional Conference on Christianity and Literature (a subdivision of the Modern Language Association) held that year at Point Loma Nazarene University in San Diego, we were both slotted to speak one after the other on the topic of Christian feminism. We had never met before, but it was instantly clear that we shared a passion for Christianity alongside a passion for femi-nism. Through our intellectual and personal journeys we had come to the conclusion that both could live in unison with each other and that both did in our own lives. It was clear that we no longer saw the two concepts as separate or antithetical but rather as deeply connected and profoundly informing our lives. From this first meeting grew a friend-ship and from the friendship grew the idea for this book: we connect feminist academia with Christianity. We knew of anthropological stud-ies connecting Christianity with feminism and/or the treatment of women and other such related topics, but often such writing appeared to us to be done by those outside the faith or by those no longer believers, having abandoned Christain faith for the sake of a stronger pull to feminism. We also knew of the work of feminist theologians, but that work is often not broadly accessible to students, church communities, or general or secular public populations. What we felt was missing for us as academics, as women, and as Christians was a community of thinkers who saw Christianity and feminism as worthy pursuits and not antithetical ones: as commitments that could, and perhaps should, exist concurrently, or at the very least be in vital conversation with one another. We believe we might have been helped earlier in our own education and lives had we known of such thought as working in tandem. We know, too, that there are many women and men in colleges, universities, and churches today who would also be helped and encouraged by such scholarship.

Like others of our time, we grew up surrounded by a stubborn myth at work in Western society: that one's faith undermines one's thought and scholastics, that one cannot believe *and* think. If one is a "Christian," then one must adhere to certain performances of that identity; if one is a "feminist," then one cannot have a dynamic religious faith because religious faith is too patriarchal and demeaning to women. To be a woman inside Christianity necessitates the role of submitting while to be a woman committed to feminist ideas necessitates a role of assertiveness or aggression. Perhaps 9/11 served as a painful catalyst in the wider secular society for further and deeper recognition of the power of religious belief, but it offered no new information to the thousands of women who have lived and continue to live with the material realities of religious ideologies that delimit, constrict, and paralyze their lives and their expressions. This is a painful manifestation of the human situation for which we have come to care greatly and to invest our lives in transforming. The contributors to this collection represent individuals who see themselves as Christian believers and yet also work in academic circles, connected at various intersections with feminist theory and practice in their everyday lives as scholars. All see feminism and Christianity as compatible though this compatibility is often marked with struggle, pain, and ambiguity.

This collection of essays explores myriad ways in which such compatibility is expressed and, in so doing, takes up questions important to current feminist inquiry. The work of these contributors also participates in the kind of "spiritual work" described and embodied in Gloria Anzaldua's *Borderlands/La Frontera: The New Mestiza*. Here Anzaldua articulates the conflicted and painful labor of living in multiple worlds simultaneously and of creating a self that blends strands of those worlds into something new:

> The new *mestiza* copes by developing a tolerance for contradic-
> tions, a tolerance for ambiguity. She learns to be an Indian in
> Mexican culture, to be Mexican from an Anglo point of view. She
> learns to juggle cultures. She has a plural personality, she operates in
> a pluralistic mode—nothing is thrust out, the good the bad and the
> ugly, nothing rejected, nothing abandoned. Not only does she
> sustain contradictions, she turns the ambivalence into something
> else. . . . The work takes place underground—subconsciously. It is
> work that the soul performs. (79)

Though Anzaldua writes about the very particular situation of the
mestiza, what she has to say about the creation of a blended and multiple
self or identity resonates deeply with the work of the contributors in this
collection. Her words illustrate that spiritual work is not reserved exclusively for religious domains. Courageous and radical as *Borderlands/La
Frontera* unquestionably was in 1987, it nonetheless also illustrated that it
is often easier to speak and write of matters of race and gender than of
religion.

This collection of essays attempts to speak of religion, in our case
Christianity, and its intersection with feminism. While these essays share
a common view that feminism and Christianity are not categorically or
fundamentally antithetical, they do not all handle the questions or issues
of this intersection in the same ways. The variations, even potential
disagreements, represented between these essays point to the intricacies
of the issues feminism seeks to address and so reflect the depth and
complexity of the wider discourse of feminist theory itself. Also, since
the contributors come from a variety of academic disciplines, we have
allowed the different style formats of those disciplines to remain
throughout the collection.

The essays that begin the collection discuss current experiences and
expression and preview many of the issues, questions, and predicaments
taken up in more focused and detailed scholarly analysis in the essays that
follow. Chapters one and two are our own essays. Bettina's article
explores some of her experiences growing as an evangelical Christian
and eventually becoming a committed feminist as well. Allyson's
article attempts to connect her Catholic childhood with her current life as
a feminist linguist. In both these more personal articles, we put
forward our current position and some of its genesis concerning the
working together of Christianity and feminism and why we see both as

connected rather than disconnected ideologies, each inflecting the other's key messages. Chapter three, Linda Beail's article, "Blessed Mother or Material Mom: Which Madonna Am I?," explores the contradictory and competing icons of motherhood, their inadequacies for representing and embodying women's actual lives, and their failure to productively challenge a debilitating patriarchal status quo.

Chapters four and five both explore feminist theory and key feminists in explaining and even defending the feminist mandate to Western society. Elizabeth Powell's article, "In Search of Bodily Perspective: A Study of Simone de Beauvoir and Luce Irigaray," explores and extends the discussion of feminist philosophy to connect specifically with the role of "other" as one experienced and propelled by women, and to examine the immanence/transcendence or essentialist/constructivist divide. Diane Leclerc's article, "Two Women Speaking 'Woman': the Strategic Essentialism of Luce Irigaray and Phoebe Palmer" is reprinted from *Wesleyan Theological Journal* 35.1 (Spring 2000) and is representative of Leclerc's larger work within Wesleyan theological discourse. It examines the ideas of Lucy Irigaray and Phoebe Palmer's use of a strategic essentialism as a way of authorizing her voice as a woman and the specific role of women as "object."

Chapter six, "Speaking Out: Feminist Theology and Women's Proclamation in the Wesleyan Tradition" is Lisa Bernal Corley's and Carol Blessing's joint essay on the lives of eighteenth- and nineteenth-century women working within the early Wesleyan and emerging Methodist movement and on current feminist theologians. Their essay documents the negotiations these early women preachers made within a dominantly patriarchal discourse and the connections between those negotiations and modern feminist theology. On a similar track chapter seven, Holly Faith Nelson's "Nascent Christian Feminism in Medieval and Early-Modern Britain," examines how women of faith in those periods found meaningful ways to maneuver around and resist patriarchy. They reconfigured notions of the Divine and found voice within the "radical Protestant discourse" that emerged in early-modern Britain. Their lived experience connected with feminist ideas long before the twentieth century added its own particular issues.

Chapter eight, Christopher Noble's "Biblical Literalism and Gender Stability: A Christian Response to Gender Performance Theory," discusses issues of biblical literalism and progressive revelation of scripture in conjunction with measured but hopeful alternatives suggested by contemporary gender performance theory. His essay brings a Christian perspective into conversation with some of the most recent iterations of feminist theorizing.

This collection rests ultimately on the belief that faith can be united with contemporary theoretical insights from academia for the health of one's faith and the ongoing redemption of the world. The contributors talk through various issues of feminism in ways that make the book a useful addition to the subject and illustrate that Christians need not fear a reasoned and thoughtful conversation with feminist theory. There is a host of literature connecting feminist theology to Christianity, but we feel this collection offers a space for a wider discussion and debate for twenty-first-century Christian scholars. How do we move forward with the lessons of the past toward meaningful new ways to be both feminist and Christian? What important questions arise when we bring together the commitments and insights of feminism and Christianity, and how do we address those questions in thoughtful and considered ways? What intellectual and behavioral shifts ought to be made in one's life as a result of a consciousness that is shaped by feminism and by Christianity? This collection is one response we are making to these very questions.

Our own experiences have shaped our thinking, yes, but our thinking has also shaped our experiences. It is our shared hope that this collection offers some assurance to our readers that there are others who rigorously connect Christianity and feminism. For Christians who care deeply about their faith, there is room in feminist theory for a religious position; likewise, for those who care deeply about feminism (in equal rights and opportunities for women in society, and in foundational notions of gender and identity) there is also space in Christianity for you. We invite you, our reader, to engage with us in this varied and complex search for what it means to be a committed, thinking feminist Christian or Christian feminist at this time in history.

Bibliography

Anzaldua, G. (1987). *Borderlands/La Frontera: The new Mestiza*. San Francisco: Aunt Lute Books.
de Vries, J. (2005). "Rediscovering Christianity after the postmodern turn." *Feminist studies*. 31.1 (Spring): 135–155.

CHAPTER ONE

Christian Feminist or Feminist Christian: What's Feminism Got to Do with Evangelical Christians?

BETTINA TATE PEDERSEN

Introductory Anecdotes

Not too many days before the end of a recent spring term, one of my students, who was about to graduate, was lingering in the office hallway waiting to see my colleague across the way who was busy at the time. Since my door was open and he had time to spare, he stuck his head into the doorway and asked, "Dr. Pedersen, why are you a feminist?" Now perhaps the prompt for his questions was the little card I keep posted on my bulletin board outside my office door that reads "I'll be a post feminist in the post patriarchy," or perhaps it was the quote from *Jane Eyre* posted there too that reads, "I am no bird; and no net ensnares me: I am a free human being with an independent will" (Brontë 266); or perhaps it was the fact that this young man had taken one of my literature classes during his college career and so been exposed to women writers and the questions those writers raised about gender. Whatever the nudge that provoked his question, I was glad to be asked it and given a chance to respond. My response was more spontaneous and easy than it sometimes is, and I said to him, "I'm a feminist because I am firmly committed to the full flourishing of women everywhere; who wouldn't be committed to that vision?"

We just had time to begin a conversation in which I could elaborate on what I meant by "flourishing" and why I thought that such flourishing was consistent with living out my Christian commitment when my colleague opened his door and indicated to my former student that he could now come in. Even though I did not have a chance to continue or conclude that conversation, I know that it is just part of an ongoing conversation I have with all the students I teach. More importantly, I am deeply grateful that he asked the question at all, because it tells me he is thinking about the very word, "feminist," and about the supposed contradictions between being a feminist and a Christian. While his question reveals that he takes for granted I am a Christian, what gives him pause enough to provoke a question is the "feminist" part of my claimed identity.

This student interchange contrasts somewhat with another routine kind of student conversation I often experience or observe working as a professor in a small, Christian, liberal arts college; it's the conversation with the "I'm-not-a-feminist-but" student. (Interestingly, I have begun to notice this same phrase cropping up in the feminist scholarship I read as well, so I know that my experience is not isolated or idiosyncratic to my Christian liberal arts college context, though I do think the label as a definition for one's position or one's identity has particular significance and currency in my context.) I generally move between a frustrated, even exasperated reaction and a more tolerant response to this kind of self-definition or positioning. My frustration almost always stems from the fact that I understand more deeply than do my students that the privilege and opportunity that characterize their daily lives as college-age individuals in the United States is utterly predicated on the lives and struggles of the women and men who have labored before them to make the very kind of lives they enjoy possible. In particular, to women college students who say, "I'm not a feminist but . . . ." I immediately want to point out two obvious realities: first, they are attending college and now actually outnumber their male counterparts in university; and second, they generally feel free and encouraged to speak their minds. Of course there are many more features that characterize their geographical, cultural, and historical situatedness, but these two obvious facts alone constitute a powerful contradiction to the phrase and position of "I'm-not-a-feminist-but," and it is generally the beginning of an antithesis they do not yet see.

I should also add here that the students who announce their resistance to the term "feminist" or to feminism in general often do so out of a deep fear of feminism. This fear typically arises from very little, if any, actual reading or study of feminist theory or praxis. It is a fear grounded largely in impressions, assumptions, and ignorance about feminism and arising, as near as I can tell, from their families, their churches, their peers, and caricatures in the mass media. This fear is also, for many of them, tantamount to a fear of conflict: conflict with peers by whom they want to be accepted or conflict with parents and/or mentors from whom they want approval.

The other response I have, the more tolerant one, arises out of my own history and similarity to the "I'm-not-a-feminist-but" students themselves. Though I am two decades older than most of the students I teach, and now have a very different consciousness about feminism than I did when I was an undergraduate in a small, Christian, liberal arts college, I would have to admit that my own feminist consciousness was just as underdeveloped and unrecognized as theirs is now. Being honest about this part of my own history reminds me that the pace of consciousness raising and social change is astonishingly slow and, if my own experience is a reliable indicator of the North American Evangelical Christian demographic, that little has changed in the feminist consciousness of that Christian community in the last 20 years despite the wide sweeping, complex, and thorough development in feminist theory and praxis over those same decades. The similarity between my former position and my students' current one also reminds me that people can and do change as a result of consciousness raising and education; that a teacher often learns as much or more than her/his students; and that there is a profound spiritual dimension to the dynamic of a life committed to feminist liberation and to Christian redemption. The humility, forgiveness, patience, passion, and endurance required to engage in this life journey, however, are not easy disciplines to develop or sustain.

Claiming the Name "Feminist"

This anecdotal information about my interactions with students regarding the term "feminist" has confirmed an intuition I had in moving, as I chose to do, from a teaching position in a large, secular state university to one in a small, Christian, liberal arts university. My intuition was that claiming the term "feminist" in this context would be a noticeable and important stance and would be a necessary expression of female liberation, even though it might appear to many current movements within feminism, such as womanism and third world feminism, as outmoded and inadequate. Even before I was offered and accepted my current teaching position, my hunch was confirmed. During the interview process I had a scheduled private luncheon with some of the literature majors I would be teaching. The luncheon was designed to facilitate candid conversation between the students and me, and it did just that. During that lunch one student very kindly, I believe, informed me that using the term feminist, calling myself a feminist, on this campus would cause me some difficulty. My sense was that he felt I might not understand this fact of the campus community, and he would be helping me out to warn me accordingly. I worked to receive his suggestion graciously and stopped short of pressing the situation into a teachable moment to help him see that my choice to use the term was deliberate and thoroughly intentional for the very effects from which he was trying to protect me.

Still to be candid myself, though I had chosen to use the term intentionally, I was rather nervous about what the full range of consequences might be in making that choice at a Christian school. Nevertheless, I was not willing to give up the term or to distance myself from it, and making that choice kept me, and, I believe, my students and colleagues as well, confronting the relationship between feminism and faith. Questions such as "Can a Christian be a feminist?" or "Why claim the name feminist in a Christian context?" or "Is a feminist position consistent with a biblical position?" are just some of the questions that arise from an intentional self-identification as "feminist," and articulating some of my responses to them is, of course, at the heart of this essay.

In my view, taking up the term feminism helps us construct a more, rather than less, historically grounded perspective because it compels us to clarify what it is, exactly, that we mean by the term: that is, to survey the development of the term, to participate in its construction, and to understand its ongoing evolution. To ask and try to answer—what feminism means to the generation of students I teach; what it means to the women and men of my generation and cultural demographic; what it means and meant to my parents' or even grandparents' generation— allows me to see much more clearly the legacies and historical connections I have to feminism.

To many, if not most, of the students I teach in my context, feminism is either a dead issue of their mothers' era, a battle already fought and won, so "get over it;" an overanalysis or mountain-making of molehills endeavor; or a thoroughly anti-Christian ideology in its rejection of the "man as head" paradigm for relationships and in its associations with abortion rights activists and lesbian women, politics, and agendas. To women and men of my generation it resonates with the political activism of the 1970s especially—the movement to ratify the Equal

Rights Amendment (ERA), the formation of the National Organization of Women (NOW), marches featuring lots of placards and perhaps some bra burning, the legalizing of abortion (*Roe v. Wade,* January 22, 1973), the sexual revolution and the increased sexual freedom women especially gained. To women and men of my parents' generation, it, named specifically as feminism, resonated as social upheaval and a challenge to the status quo; whereas unnamed, it included such extremes as the huge influx of women into the workforce as a result of WWII, and the feisty woman I had often heard my mother speak of—the woman who must "[h]ave spunks and do battle for [her]self" (69) as Jean Rhys writes in *Wide Sargasso Sea*. To women and men from the latter half of the nineteenth century through the 1920s roughly, it meant predominantly the suffrage movement, but even then issues of the status, position, and conditions of life for married women; women's control over their own bodies and reproductive capabilities; and interpretations of biblical texts that reified a patriarchal status quo and oppression were challenged.[1]

Now what is gained by mapping out some meanings and hallmarks of feminism over the last hundred years or so in this very sketchy generational way? For me and from my particular historical situatedness, I observe two things: one, that a number of changes have occurred that profoundly shape the kind and the quality of life I enjoy as a woman living today; and two, that many things have remained the same. Women today attend colleges and universities in the largest numbers in history. A recent National Public Radio broadcast entitled "Women Outnumber Men among College Graduates," and citing the researcher, Tom Martinson, Senior Scholar at Dell Institute for the Study of Opportunities in Higher Education, stated that in college graduation ceremonies in the spring of 2005, 200,000 more degrees were granted to women than to men (May 17, 2005). Young women students can look around their classrooms and see themselves surrounded by many other women students. Certainly I was not alone as a woman in the classes that I took either as an undergraduate or as a graduate student. In fact, it has been during the first two decades of my adult life that women in the United States have begun earning more Bachelor's degrees, than men ("Women Outnumber . . ." May 17, 2005).

Research studying the behavior of women in college and university classes, however, clearly shows that women students are still more silent and passive than their male peers and that their professors and instructors continue to call on male students more frequently than they do on women students. Women now can and do have careers of all kinds; indeed, my career as a university professor is one immediate example of this fact; yet, there remains a glass ceiling, myriad forms of systemic discrimination that privilege male professional advancement, and the violence of sexism in the workplace as well as on the street. Women have been voting for almost a century now; we have mobility without the chaperones our nineteenth-century and earlier foremothers required; we can dress rationally and for comfort if we choose; we have increased control over our reproductive lives, choosing if and when we want to become pregnant as well as whether or not we want to carry conceptions to term. Still, we have yet to see a woman president of the United States; battery remains the leading cause of injury for women; sex trafficking is a thriving global business, honor killings and mutilations abound, and female genital mutilation and rape continue worldwide.

The positives I just enumerated are some of the very reasons why many of my students want to dismiss feminism as an outmoded ideology and praxis. Yet a move to dismiss feminism because it has accomplished some of what it set out to do is curious to say the least. To grant these "accomplishments" we would have to acknowledge that each and every one of them is a legacy of the feminist struggles of all the remembered and forgotten women and men on whose labors we now live out our lives. To deny identification with the term "feminism" but to speak and to enjoy the politics and privileges that are available only because of feminist movement, agitations, sacrifice, and costly commitment seems to me to express an enormity of arrogance and self-importance as well as historical disregard. The widely quoted dictum of George Santayana, "Those who do not remember history, are doomed to repeat it" seems a particularly appropriate admonition here. To distance myself from the term and the history of feminism ruptures me from the community of women and men whose struggles created the very grounds upon which I live out my life as a woman of the twentieth and twenty-first centuries.

This maneuvering around the term is not the only problematic consequence of a refusal to associate with the term or history of feminism. If we dismiss the term or ideology because improved (somewhat more egalitarian) conditions exist in some measure and in some places, we fail to understand the depth of feminism's critique, and we risk losing sight of the very conditions and manifestations of sexist oppression that a feminist critique has helped us to see. As any feminist scholar or activist today will tell you, sexist oppression still exists, even thrives, and much work remains before a world in which women are safe and can flourish, reaching their fullest potential as human beings, dawns on us all.

The work of two such feminists, Jean Kilbourne and Kathleen Barry, remind us of the persistence of sexist oppression. Kilbourne's focused analysis of advertising's images of women in *Killing Us Softly III* (2000), which was first published in 1979 and is now in its third version, is a stunning and moving critique of the routine milieu of advertising that utterly infiltrates and defines modern life in the United States. Kilbourne relates the common response many modern consumers make when they are confronted with the sexist dimensions of her analysis of advertising—that they are simply not affected by advertisings' images, that they just don't pay attention to advertising. She notes that the modern person is confronted with 3,000 ads per day and will spend the equivalent of three years of her or his lifetime watching commercials. These two facts alone defy the logic of the claim that one is unaffected by such a pervasive medium. Moreover and apart from such statistical research claims, the anecdotal behavior that virtually any North American citizen can cite about the way we dress and groom ourselves, the products we buy, the values we hold for what is beautiful, successful, and important is enough to give us all pause about how much or little we might claim to be influenced by advertising.

In addition, Kathleen Barry, writing about the sexual objectification of women in her *Female Sexual Slavery*, published first in 1979 and reprinted in 1984, concurs with the underlying observations of Kilbourne's analysis. Barry notes that

> a major cause of sex slavery is the social-sexual objectification of women that permeates every patriarchal society in the world. Identifying women first as sexual beings who are responsible for the sexual services of men is the social base for gender-specific sexual slavery. As most women know, being sexually harassed while walking alone down a street, or sitting in a bar or restaurant without a man, is a poignant reminder of our definition as sexual objects. Spurning those advances and reacting against them are likely to draw indignant wrath from the perpetrator, suggesting the extent to which many men assume the sexual objectification of *any* women as their right. Under such conditions, sexual slavery lurks at the corners of every woman's life. (103 in 1979 ed.; 121 in 1984 ed.)

In her more broad sweeping analysis of the forms of sexist oppression worldwide Barry makes this stunning statement about the overwhelming yet concealed presence of sexist oppression in all the deep textures of women's lives today:

> Sex-is-power can be cast into many forms including denying or demanding female response. Both replace mutuality with

domination. Sexual domination acted out in one-to-one relationships is the basis for the cultural domination of women and female
sexual slavery. Because such domination is expressed in separate,
personal, private sexual experiences, and because on that level there
is no visibility of collective action, the generalized abuse of women
from the sex-is-power ethic has been seen only as individual
acts. . . . because it is invisible to social perception and because of
the clandestine nature of its practices, it is presently impossible to
statistically measure the incidence of female sexual slavery. But
considering the arrested sexual development that is understood to
be normal in the male population, and considering the numbers of
men who are pimps, procurers, members of syndicate and free-lance
slavery gangs, operators of brothels and massage parlors, connected
with sexual exploitation entertainment, pornography purveyors,
wife beaters, child molesters, incest perpetrators, johns (tricks) and
rapists, one cannot help but be momentarily stunned by the enormous male population participating in female sexual slavery. The
huge number of men engaged in these practices should be cause for
declaration of a national and international emergency, a crisis in
sexual violence. But what should be cause for alarm is instead
accepted as normal sexual intercourse. (220 in 1979 ed.; 259–260 in
1984 ed.)[2]

Research that produces claims such as those of Barry's are often dismissed
as examples of "male bashing," "lesbian paranoia," or "boys will be boys."
A more benevolent, but still dismissive response is, "But I'm not like that;
I'm not involved in those sorts of activities, and I don't support people
who are." Any of these responses, seem to me, to leave the door to sexist
oppression firmly wedged open because none of them position the
responder as a person—female or male—who is committed to the active,
conscious, and vigilant business of eradicating the least to the most
egregious grounds and forms of sexist oppression.

For my purpose in this essay, to address the question of the relationship between feminism and faith, my critique of a reluctance or refusal
to use the term feminist is important beyond the development of a
proper understanding and appreciation of history. Claiming the term
"feminist" raises yet another question for those of us who call ourselves
Christian. That question might be phrased obviously as "Are
Christianity and Feminism compatible ideologies or identities?" which is
simply another way of asking the question another student posed to me,
"Can a Christian be a feminist?" But perhaps an even more subtle but

important way of framing that question would be to ask, "If feminism and Christianity are compatible, do I frame my identity as a Christian feminist or as a feminist Christian?" Either arrangement suggests a certain kind of relationship to or negotiation with naming oneself "feminist."

To frame my identity as a Christian feminist foregrounds the Christian end of the polarity and tends to privilege the Christian perspective or identity as a corrective to the feminist perspective or identity. To prefix "feminism" with Christian implies syntactically and semantically that there is little if anything inherently "Christian" about feminism, or that there are important differences between species of feminism—feminism versus Christian feminism versus third world feminism versus lesbian feminism, for example. Any one of these syntactically and semantically qualifying moves carries with it the risk either of a prescriptive and delimiting politics or an insipid and innocuous generality. These are the syntactic and semantic stakes that bell hooks is addressing with her critique of "lifestyle feminism" in her book *Feminism is for Everybody*. She defines "lifestyle feminism" as a largely idiosyncratically shaped set of practices, politics, and beliefs that any number of individual women or men might list as characteristics that make them feminists or proponents of feminism. She notes the following:

> Lifestyle feminism ushered in the notion that there could be as many versions of feminism as there were women. Suddenly the politics was slowly removed from feminism. And the assumption prevailed that no matter what a woman's politics, be she conservative or liberal, she too could fit feminism into her existing lifestyle. Obviously this way of thinking has made feminism more acceptable because its underlying assumption is that women can be feminists without fundamentally challenging and changing themselves or the culture. (5–6)

Her last comment, about being feminist without fundamental personal or cultural change is what worries me most about framing my identity in terms of Christian feminism; indeed, entertaining feminism only in terms of a "Christianized" version of it seems to move too comfortably in the direction of a patriarchal status quo, both inside and outside the Christian church. Too often, in my view, that "Christian" perspective paints in too broad a stroke the very grounds and forms of sexist oppression as "sin," communicating an obvious denunciation and distancing that works to insulate the Christian from confronting the manifest forms of that "sin" or sexist oppression that must be squarely confronted and eradicated. To announce oneself as against sin needs the further interrogations of what such an "against" actually means, what kind of sin is that oppression exactly, and where is it found—is it sin of the "us in the church" or just sin of the "them outside it"? In other words, I am unsatisfied with the semantic and syntactic trick of sanitizing a perspective or ideology by prefixing it with an adjectival "Christian" in place of doing the hard work of critical thinking, analysis, self-examination, and effecting change. My discomfort here is of a piece with hooks' critique of a "lifestyle feminism" that really has no teeth and no commitments.

If, on the other hand, we frame an identity as feminist Christian, where the grammatical and substantive corrective is to the "Christian" dimension of identity or ideology, perhaps we gain a more rigorous and honest examination of the sin of sexist oppression and the Christian individual's accountability to that examination. How might reframing the identity as feminist Christianity help us see this oppression and our response to it differently? Virginia Woolf suggests in *A Room of One's Own* (1929) that pronouncing truth about difficult subjects is virtually impossible; all one can do is share one's own journey. She writes, "At any rate, when a subject is highly controversial—and any question about sex is that—one can not hope to tell the truth. One can only show how one came to hold whatever opinion one does hold" (4). It is in this same spirit that I share some responses to these questions with my own autobiographical anecdotes.

Autobiographical Anecdotes

For as long as I can remember I have understood myself and my identity to be Christian. Christian for me meant that I was part of a holiness tradition arising from the Wesleyan/Methodist revival of the Anglican church in the eighteenth century. From that revival movement arose the practice and eventual institutional denomination of Methodism, and from Methodism arose the early-twentieth-century holiness movements. The Church of the Nazarene developed out of these movements, and it was into a Nazarene family I was born as a third generation Nazarene. Sometimes I think being a Nazarene is a little like being Jewish. It's an ethnicity. Even though I'm attending a Presbyterian church at the present, I still consider myself a Nazarene, theologically a Wesleyan, as opposed to a Reformed tradition Christian. The theological distinction here is important because it has shaped the grounds out of which my own feminist commitments have arisen. Its importance is twofold: one, in developing my understanding of a Christian's calling to be engaged with the world, and two, in forming my understanding of the role of scripture and tradition as loci of authority in living out the Christian life.

Growing up in the Nazarene family and churches that I did instilled in me the unqualified responsibility I had as a Christian to involve myself in the redemption of the world by working to improve the social realities of people's lives. I don't ever remember hearing the famous John Wesley axiom from the "Preface" to his and Charles Wesley's *Hymns and Sacred Poems* (1739), "The gospel of Christ knows of no religion, but social; no holiness but social holiness" (321) before my adult years, but its message was everywhere present in the Christian values I was taught and that I observed in my family and church. This commitment to a social engagement with the world also carried with it an understanding that human agency played a pivotal role in one's Christian life: as a result of a Christian's engagement with the world, other people might also be brought to a knowledge of and relationship with Christ. Further, a Christian was called to exercise her or his own agency in living out the spiritual discipline of service to the world. In my Wesleyan tradition, there was no such privileged position as the elect. One's relationship to Christ and his redeeming work in the world was first made possible by God's grace and second by an individual's response to that grace. I have heard one of my colleagues, professor of Theology and author,[3] Michael Lodahl, describe the relationship between God's grace and human agency by recalling John Wesley's emphasis on the "means of grace." These are the practices of faith (ritualistic acts of prayer, scripture reading, receiving the Eucharist, Sunday worship, visiting the poor, and so on) through which God may meet us, but these are not the things we must do in order to "get" God or God's grace; rather, engaging in these practices of faith place one in the position to be open to God and to receiving God's grace. Human beings are moved by their affections and those affections need to be shaped by the spiritual disciplines, the habitual embodied practices of the life of a committed Christian.

The second aspect of my Wesleyan heritage and religious milieu was the understanding and place of scripture. I have come to understand the importance of the way one views scripture—and more importantly the way one views the authority of scripture—in shaping the way one responds to secular knowledge. If one is shaped by and chooses a position on scripture that derives predominantly from the Protestant Reformation of Martin Luther, seeing the scripture as *scriptura sola* (scripture alone) in establishing authority in the life of the believer, then one can tend more easily and more profoundly toward a fundamentalist understanding of scripture that reads the Bible more literally, and consequentially less allegorically, analogically, or metaphorically. If one takes a literal reading stance toward scripture, then the interpretive practices of situating a particular biblical passage in its historical or its cultural context can seem to undermine or erase the biblical authority of that passage, and for some readers the biblical authority of the entire scriptures in turn.

Conversely, if one comes from a religious tradition that recognizes the beliefs and practices of the church down through history as having an authority that should also be brought to bear on one's interpretations of scripture, then it is easier and more legitimate to use (or, perhaps more accurately, to recognize that one always already does use) interpretive strategies that take history, culture, author, audience, translators, possible interpolations, and one's own precise position or situatedness into account without eradicating scriptural authority. Elaine Storkey's and Margaret Hebblethwaite's *Conversations on Christian Feminism: Speaking Heart to Heart* gives a very accessible summary of the difference between Christian traditions (Evangelical for Storkey, Catholic for Hebblethwaite) that accord more versus less weight to the role of tradition in interpreting scripture:

> The great Reformation controversy was between *scriptura sola* (scripture alone, the Protestant position) or scripture and tradition (the Catholic position). We [Catholics] would see tradition as being deeply interwoven into the production of the biblical text in the first place. Then tradition continues in the ongoing history of the people of God, and in the ongoing interpretation of the biblical text. So that the scriptures come to us through tradition.
>
> Then the canon of the scriptures is established through the authority of the church. They did not drop down from heaven like the ten commandments written on stone on Mount Sinai. Therefore the Bible cannot be given an authority above tradition, because tradition has actually produced the Bible. The two go completely in hand.
>
> And that affects the way we look at texts from scripture today. You know the phrase which I always associate with evangelicals: "The Bible says . . ." [a]s though it was always one voice, one coherent teaching. Catholics would be suspicious of that kind of language.[4] Though we do it ourselves in our own way, in having our favourite bits: "Thou art Peter and upon this rock I will build

my church." . . . So for Catholics it would be a matter of taking the history of the people of God as sacred—because it is the history of salvation—and the Book is the record of that salvation history. It gets its sanctity out of being the officially authorized version of that story—the canon. But it is an ongoing story, it continues today. (125)

More specifically to the point of a Wesleyan theological view, Lovett H. Weems, Jr. has given a useful summary of "what has become known as [Wesley's] Quadrilateral," the four influences on Christian doctrine and theology. These are "scripture, tradition, experience, and reason [and they] constitute the main sources and guidelines for Christian theology. The four are interdependent and no one can be subsumed by another. Although there is a primacy that goes with scripture, all four guidelines should instruct all our theological reflection" (12).

This tension surrounding reading and interpretive strategies as applied to scripture is perhaps most recently a legacy of the influence of German Higher Criticism that came to bear on England's intellectual Christians in the nineteenth century. In my work as a Victorianist, it is certainly a legacy I deal with rather routinely in my scholarly work and especially in my teaching. It has also been an important influence on the shape of literary studies of the twentieth century, and consequently on the shape of my intellectual coming of age and professional life. As a literary scholar and teacher, trained in contemporary literary theory, I have little difficulty recognizing that any act of reading, scripture or otherwise, is always already an interpretive act. This is to say that virtually no act of reading or interpretation[5]—and the two are effectively synonymous—is objective, purely truthful, uninfluenced, or impartial in any absolute sort of way. Indeed, if we follow Stanley Fish's reader-response theory, a contemporary literary theory largely responsible, along with Deconstruction, for the thorough unhinging of the notion that any reading can express with any sort of totality or finality the ultimate meaning of a text, then we accept that reading is always already an act of interpretation, and an act that is profoundly shaped by the interpretive communities that conduct the acts of reading.[6]

Having drawn the distinction I just did between a Wesleyan and a Reformed understanding of scripture, I do not mean to suggest that all readers of scripture who come from or choose a Reformed Theology position read the Bible as literalists or fundamentalists. Rather, the distinction was made in the effort to lay out some of the grounds for my own views of scripture and its authority because they are central to my feminist identity and commitments. If, in fact, tradition is to be considered along with scripture when determining authority for reading, interpretation, and embodied practice, then situating a biblical passage in its historical and cultural context does not simultaneously undermine or erase biblical authority. Understanding scriptural authority in this way, it seems to me, is absolutely crucial in dealing with the biblical passages that require the most careful and considered attention if one is to bring Christianity, which is to say, the authority of scripture, and feminism together.[7]

In a vein of interpretive possibility similar to Fish's reader-response theory, the tradition of Jewish midrash as articulated by feminist and poet, Alicia Suskin Ostriker, offers a richly sophisticated understanding of scripture and interpretation: "The Bible, it should be evident to anyone who reads with open eyes, is an endlessly complex, provocative, layered, contradictory set of documents, as befits its composition over a period of millennia during which the very conception of God was changing" (xii). The revelation at Sinai, as rabbinic tradition teaches, contained all the possible interpretation of scripture that would ever be offered (xii); thus she advocates a central place to contemporary feminist readings of scripture:

> [M]any midrashists today are women; we should expect many more in the future. How could it be otherwise? The texts plainly beg and implore women to read them as freshly, energetically, passionately—and even playfully as they have been read by men. "Turn it and turn it," the rabbis say of Torah, "for everything is in it." Besides, they tell us, God has intended "all the meanings that He has made us capable of discovering." If so, the truths of women are present in this text, sacred comedy as well as sacred tragedy, but we will not see the truths until women do their own reading, perform their own acts of discovery. By the time the spiritual imagination of women has expressed itself as fully and variously as that of men, to be sure, whatever humanity means by God, religion, holiness, and truth will be completely transformed. (xii)

Her midrashist tradition of reading/interpreting scripture interfaces with Fish's theory to provide a strong foundation and ample room for feminist interpretations of scripture that challenge accepted patriarchal readings and theology.

One more point, germane to my situation as college professor in a Christian, liberal arts university, needs to be stated here. Many of the students with whom I work and for whom the issues of biblical authority and interpretation of scripture create serious challenges to their worldview are in truth only nascent readers of interpretive sophistication. This statement is not meant as a criticism only as a description of the stage in cognitive and experiential development at which most of these young women and men are during their undergraduate years. If I, as their teacher, am to help them develop their own understandings of and responses to the question of whether or not a Christian can be a feminist or a feminist can be a Christian, matters of biblical authority and interpretation of scripture are really central to the matter and must be acknowledged and addressed in as accessible and straightforward a way as possible. Further, it is easy to point to Old and New Testament passages, that even the staunchest literalist does not read, interpret, and in turn enact as the passages would literally admonish: for menstruating women to confine themselves during the course of their periods, for men to take multiple wives or for a father to offer his daughters as prostitutes, for slaves to obey their masters, and so on. What Fish offers in his reader-response theorizing as a "moral" I find a particularly helpful, honest, and humbling reminder in my efforts to bring feminism and Christianity together in my own life: "The moral is clear: the choice is never between objectivity and interpretation but between an interpretation that is *un*acknowledged as such and an interpretation that is at least aware of itself" (2084–2085 emphasis mine).

While I have always understood my identity to be Christian, I have not always understood my identity in terms of "named" (or claimed) feminism. The currents of feminism, however, though I certainly didn't call them that in my youth, ran in my life in no small measure because of the kind of girl I was. Being articulate brought me pleasure and the approval of most of the adults in my life; however, it also made me the butt end of much painful teasing and provoking by the young men with whom I went to a Christian high school, and some of whom I wanted to date. In addition, having strong opinions, though they were largely the opinions of my father, meant that I understood the world well and had the correct politics, but listening to my mother sometimes speak of herself, her intellect, routines, and modes of organization, as somehow inferior to those of my father set in motion a curious dislocation in my psyche. I am under no illusions that I have fully psychoanalyzed that aspect of my childhood relation to my parents or those high school boys. What I can say with some confidence is that I still remember the pain the teasing of my male peers caused me, and that I noticed and remembered my mother's narratives about her supposed inferiority. What I continue to wonder about is how deeply both compelled me to shape my identity in resistance to those influences that rendered women inferior to men and so dismissed them and any contribution they might have made.[8]

In my college years, though I did not call myself a feminist, I am fairly confident that my peers thought of me in that general light because I often asked questions and expressed frustrations about gendered differentiations and exclusions. More specifically, declaring a major course of study in my undergraduate education revealed an important intersection between my Christian and nascent feminist identity. I had entered college with a vision for my future that I had carried since about age 12: I was going to become a doctor and have my career and years of service as a medical missionary in Africa. In the summer between my freshman and sophomore years I made the very difficult decision that I was going to abandon a premed course of studies and declare a new major. This decision was truly an identity crisis for me since the premed part of my identity was attached to the medical missionary part; hence, if the premed part was slipping away, the missionary part was as well. It was absolutely crucial for me to preserve the missions aspect of my identity since I had felt certain of a "call" to the mission field at about age 12 and from which I had never wavered, until that moment. Consequently, I decided to become a pre-seminary major thinking that I would become a preacher and that preachers were needed as much on the mission field as were doctors. As a result of a series of conversations with my father and one of the school deans upon returning to my college in the fall, I settled on English Education rather than pre-seminary for a major. An English-Education major would provide me with a "marketable skill" (teaching) that my father, having earned a college education himself as a result of the GI bill following WWII, had taught me to value as a product of college education.

Prior to my college years, I never remember receiving any message from my parents other than the message that I could do anything I set my mind to doing and choosing a medical career was certainly acceptable since my father was a hospital administrator, but evidently, there was something about becoming a (woman) preacher that gave my father pause enough to parent me into a different major. From my perspective, teaching felt "missionary" enough that I didn't feel as if I was abandoning my "call" so I settled into my new major and new identity with a revised sense of what my future would look like. As I look back on these events of my undergraduate years now, I see them through a heightened feminist consciousness that views my father's (and likely my mother's tacit) perspectives and my own as shaped by the strong influences of patriarchy, a system that had little room for women in positions of church authority.

I have often heard it remarked of women who express strong feminist sentiments and/or commitments that there must have been something in their childhood experiences that "damaged" them and so turned them in a feminist direction. Perhaps some would want to make the same comment of my own history in the anecdote just related, but that judgment is less important to me than what my example illustrates of the subtle but profound influences of patriarchy and sexist oppression on an individual. What troubles me most about those influences is the lost potential and contribution of women throughout a history much broader and deeper than my own, simply because their callings, voices, and contributions have been discredited, redirected, or erased.

As many currents of contemporary feminist theorizing (black, postcolonial, lesbian, etc.) will show, women have always found ways to resist the oppressions of patriarchal forms, systems, and values. These currents in feminist theory are important for reminding us that women, though oppressed, need not be rendered essentially as victims; indeed, that many have found ways to make vital contributions in, around, and in spite of myriad forms of sexist oppression. As Virginia Woolf observes about uncovering and recovering women's literary history,

> Now and again an Emily Brontë . . . blazes out and proves its [genius'] presence. But certainly it never got itself on to paper. When, however, one reads of a witch being ducked, of a woman possessed by devils, of a wise woman selling herbs, or even of a very remarkable man who had a mother, then I think we are on the track of a lost novelist, a suppressed poet, of some mute and inglorious Jane Austen, some Emily Brontë who dashed her brains out on the moor or mopped and mowed about the highways crazed with the torture that her gift had put her to. (49)[9]

These currents of contemporary feminist theory are also important in reminding us that the nature and degree of sexist oppression perpetrated on women vary significantly, and it is vital to recognize these differences rather than to assume a totalizing notion of universal womanhood and/or sisterhood. Thus, my anecdote (even the whole of my autobiographical narrating and interpreting) itself must be taken as precisely situated historically, culturally, racially, socioeconomically, religiously, and so on—a description offered not as a flattening prescription for but as a possible suggestion to others.

The decision to marry brought whole new vistas of gendered differentiations and exclusions to consider, some of which were social and cultural, some religious and spiritual. My and my then fiancé's feelings about these had an important influence on the courtship and marriage ceremony we eventually designed. The request for life partnership did not come to me from a kneeling man nor was my father asked for "my hand in marriage." While both of these hallmarks of a so-called romantic courtship were familiar to us both, and held all the emotional and mythical appeal that fairy tales and screen romances imputed to them, we chose a different course of relating because we believed that choosing each other, as life partners, was a choice and a commitment best done with as clear a vision of reality (or as near as we could get to it without the experience of married life itself to teach us) as possible rather than under the dozy haze of "love will see us through." Instead we asked for my parents' blessing—to join with us in our joy at choosing one another.

In addition, since neither of us considered a woman to be the property of her husband, we could not accept the wording of the traditional Anglican wedding service, which we liked for its history and formality, but which asked my father to "give" me away in marriage. So, at the suggestion of our male and venerable minister, we replaced that wording with "presents." For the biblical texts read at our ceremony, we selected only those that spoke about the mutual responsibility of both woman and man to love and serve the other. In lighting our unity candle, we left the individual candles lit, rather than extinguished them, to symbolize our belief that our individual personalities as human beings would remain and not disappear just because we were choosing to work out our lives together rather than apart (marital life has more than confirmed this reality). At the close of the ceremony we were introduced as Mr. and Mrs. Keith and Bettina Pedersen. Such an introduction is more traditional than others we might have chosen, and that some do choose, but my feminist consciousness was still nascent at this time (as was my spouse's), and for us, then, this introduction was a significant statement of the kind of relationship we intended to announce and to form.

My feminism continued to emerge in the questions and frustrations that arose in the early years of my life as a married woman. Suddenly, in spite of all our efforts to shape our marriage ceremony and married identities, my identity was now profoundly understood and defined by my marital status—witness to the ubiquitous systemic power of patriarchy in contradistinction to the Enlightenment notion of the autonomous self bequeathed to me as a twentieth-century American citizen. Three examples will illustrate this reality well. First, the pastor of our Nazarene church, who happened to have been my youth pastor and so known me first and foremost as an unmarried individual, repeatedly sent messages to me through my spouse rather than approached me directly. Second, one of the elder men in our congregation addressed me as Keith's wife, after I had been an active and visible member in the congregation for several years. In response to this kind of a situation some would say his oversight meant nothing, or that it was no big deal, but I find such responses inadequate since it is virtually impossible for me to imagine anyone asking my husband to do something by calling him "Bettina's husband." Incidents like these irritated me, and reminded me that my position as a married woman took some kind of primacy over my skills, my education, or my individual contributions and identity. Third, now well on in married life and having completed a doctoral degree of my own, I continue to receive mail addressed to Dr. and Dr. Keith Pedersen, subsuming my personal as well as intellectual identity into my marital status, yet another witness to the systemic reality of patriarchal forms. Even computer databases participate in the solidifying of these forms.

My years and study in graduate school are what actually gave me the framework and language of feminism that have allowed me in great measure to theorize and articulate the dislocations, irritations, and pain of the gendered exclusions and differential treatment I had observed. Up to the point of graduate school I had understood and articulated my identity primarily as "Christian," though feminist currents were certainly present as well. My study of literature, in particular the literature written by women, revealed to me that the dislocations, irritations, and hurts I had experienced along with the feminist agitations of my youth in the 1970s were all too similar in theme and material reality to those written about by Western women in the eighteenth, nineteenth, and early twentieth centuries. Feminist literary theory and analysis opened up an awareness of oppression, oppression of women as well as of same-sex-desiring individuals, and of people of color. Further, it gave me a lens and a language for seeing and articulating these forms of oppression down through history, including the history of Christianity.

Crisis of Scriptural Authority and a Feminist Hermeneutic

Feminist theory also gave me a way of revisiting another key experience of my adolescence, an experience that may have been the most important but largely unacknowledged result of and reason for my awareness of gendered exclusions and erasures. The experience was the startling epiphany I had about gender exclusions set in motion by the logic of a Pauline passage in 1 Corinthians that I read during one of my daily devotions. Paul writes there:

> Now I want you to realize that the head of every man is Christ, and the head of the woman is man, and the head of Christ is God. Every man who prays or prophesies with his head covered dishonors his head. And every woman who prays or prophesies with her head uncovered dishonors her head—it is just as though her head were shaved. If a woman does not cover her head, she should have her hair cut off; and if it is a disgrace for a woman to have her hair cut or shaved off, she should cover her head. A man ought not to cover his head, since he is the image and glory of God; but the woman is the glory of man. For man did not come from woman, but woman from man; neither was man created for woman, but woman for man. For this reason, and because of the angels, the woman ought to have a sign of authority on her head. (1 Cor. 11:3–10 NIV).

The horrifying thought that arose in my mind, and I mean horrifying because it shook me to the very core, was this: does this passage mean that I am not created in the image of God, that somehow I was different in my fundamental relation to God simply because I was a woman and not a man? In fact, I think the possibility was so terrifying to me then that I simply buried it, but the disturbing resonance of the experience lingered and kept bubbling to the surface in the awareness and questions I had about the different ways in which women and men were identified, treated, and esteemed. I think it was the primary understanding of myself as a Christian, who believed that all people were created in the image of God, which compelled me to bury the experience.

I don't ever recall hearing any sermons grounded in solid biblical exegesis that expounded upon this text either to expose the situatedness of its sexism, or to shine the light of Jesus' example on gender relations, but I did hear one of my college professors preach a sermon in chapel on women and Jesus that provided a strong counterpoint to the gender exclusion I had inferred from the 1 Corinthians passages. His sermon was an early moment, from which others have followed, that opened up the possibility of a feminist understanding of and corrective to some Christian history, practice, and biblical interpretation. I don't think he used the term "feminism" in his sermon, but he brought feminism's posture and questions to bear on biblical accounts and demonstrated with incisive clarity the importance of what was at stake in biblical interpretation. In effect, the interpretive ground and content of his sermon demonstrated the theological praxis of using Jesus as the hermeneutic for interpreting biblical passages and Christian teachings that have rendered women inferior in myriad ways. This hermeneutical practice has been important in my feminist coming of age for three reasons. One, it resonated with my experience of and resistance to gendered differentiations, exclusions, and erasures that I've already mentioned; two, it helped me to see sexism for what it is, no matter where it appears; and three it gave me a language for articulating the ways in which feminism—its postures, questions, and consciousness— could act as a corrective to Christianity, to expose rather than sanitize or overlook the sexist practices historically recorded in the Bible, and to eradicate the sexism of Christian practice, including certain interpretations of biblical texts and deployments of their derived meanings.

Christian Feminist to Feminist Christian

My earlier exploring of the syntactic and semantic differences between a Christian feminist and a feminist Christian identity or praxis is perhaps easier to understand here. To accept a Christian feminist paradigm rather than a feminist Christian one may help us skirt the hard questions and realities of sexist oppression recorded in the Christian tradition itself, perpetuated in ongoing Christian practice, and ubiquitous in the wide world. It may, and I believe often does, dull our awareness that we have a moral responsibility, a spiritual calling if you will, to be about the business of converting ourselves, our Christian tradition and churches, and our world from our sins of sexist oppression to the abundant life in Christ's redemption of the world. In my life, feminism's theory and praxis has unquestionably sharpened my awareness of social injustice and oppression, both of which Wesleyan Christianity in its deepest commitments works against as a material expression of Christ's redemption of the world. Indeed, the causes and commitments of feminism have often enabled me to see, more than much I've observed and learned in church, the deep-seated practices of oppression and injustice within the institutions and members of communities, Christian or otherwise. For me, feminism has preserved the piercing vigilance characteristic of the radical person and practice of Jesus Christ. This vigilance keeps me hovering between despair and commitment, as my opening anecdotes illustrate: despair over the fact that social change affecting the lives of women can and does take so dreadfully long to achieve and commitment to the justice of work that keeps ever in view the full partnership of women and men in all human endeavors of spiritual, intellectual, emotional, and physical value and import.

What is most at stake for me in this argument and journey is not ultimately whether one calls oneself "Christian feminist" or "feminist Christian" but rather how conscious are we in claiming or eschewing our names and identities, why should we take up Christian or feminist names and identities, what do they really mean, and in what ways do they change our lives and help to bring about the full redemption of the world in Christ. In reality, the fact that I began my life journey in a Christian milieu is likely what causes me to see feminism as a helpful corrective. Someone else, having begun life in a feminist milieu, would perhaps see Christianity as the salutary corrective. Either way what must be seen and resisted is the oppression of sexism that both feminism and Christianity aim to eradicate. This is the commitment clearly stated in hooks's definition of feminism, offered, as she notes, in two of her books *Feminism is for Everybody* and *Feminist Theory: From Margin to Center.* "Feminism is a movement to end sexism, sexist exploitation, and oppression" (viii).

The critique and corrective of feminism expresses for me in large measure what living in/by faith means. I live in the hope of an unseen and barely imaginable world—a world in which a profound change of vision and heart, not just increased or equal access, but conversion will declare the full soul and body wholeness of woman everywhere and at all times, and this declaration will be expressed in every texture and terrain of that world. Mary Wollstonecraft expressed something of the same yearning over two hundred years ago, in her 1792 *A Vindication of the Rights of Woman.* In her "prayer" she clearly understands the failed logic and insupportable morality of the emerging separate spheres ideology of the eighteenth and nineteenth centuries (men "naturally" belonging in the public/career and women in the private/domestic spheres), a dominant form of sexist oppression in those eras and which we have inherited:

Gracious Creator of the whole human race! hast thou created such a being as woman, who can trace thy wisdom in thy works, and feel that thou alone art by thy nature exalted above her,—for no better purpose?—Can she believe that she was only made to submit to man, her equal, a being, who, like her, was sent into the world to acquire virtue?—Can she consent to be occupied merely to please him; merely to adorn the earth, when her soul is capable of rising to thee?—And can she rest supinely dependent on man for reason, when she ought to mount with him the arduous steeps of knowledge?—

Yet, if love be the supreme good, let women be only educated to inspire it, and let every charm be polished to intoxicate the senses; but, if they be moral beings, let them have a chance to become intelligent; and let love to man be only a part of that glowing flame of universal love, which, after encircling humanity, mounts in grateful incense to God. (67–68)

Wollstonecraft led a life that violated the Christian sensibility of her own century and the two that have followed, but my feminist Christianity/Christian feminism is sharpened by her words and witness.

Elizabeth Johnson, feminist theologian and author of *She Who Is: The Mystery of God in Feminist Theological Discourse*, writes about the persisting sexism of the Christian church today. Her "prayer," which expresses a longing and vision for conversion from sexism, also sharpens my feminist vision and commitment:

We can say, *Gloria Dei vivens mulier*: the glory of God is woman, all women, every woman everywhere, fully alive. Wherever women are violated, diminished, have their life drained away, God's glory is dimmed and put at historical risk: hence sexism is religiously unconscionable. Conversely, fragmentary experiences of women's flourishing anticipate that new heaven and new earth where the glory of God will be unfathomably justified. A community of justice and peace, including women's flourishing, and God's glory increase in direct and not inverse proportion. (15)

If sexism is "religiously unconscionable," then would it not follow that a Christian's apathetic, uncommitted, or resistant response to a feminist commitment is also "religiously unconscionable?" At the very least, a Christian partaking in the redemptive work of Christ, who resisted sin in all its forms of oppression, ought, it seems to me, engage the term— its ideologies and commitments—consciously, intelligently, prayerfully, and vigilantly.

Both Wollstonecraft and Johnson are writing about a world that did not and does not exist, but it is a world for which they express a vision, and it is a vision I share. That vision is an unfolding one the tenor of which is hope. Thinking about the implications of the terms I have been discussing—feminism, Christian feminism, feminist Christianity—keeps that unfolding vision invigorated and growing in my mind and heart. Using the term Christian feminism, which foregrounds the Christian part of the dialogue, helps me remember that forgiveness is a defining characteristic of what a Christian life is and that forgiveness has to include all of us who are guilty of the sin of sexism and who remain complicit with it because of the distancing maneuvers we employ in regards to the term and the praxis of feminism. In other words, I have to keep forgiving, not excusing, the perpetuators of sexism, and this is very hard spiritual work, at least it is for me. And if it is hard for me, I cannot begin to imagine what it must be for women who live at the risk of sexist-bound practices such as marital rape, genital mutilation, and honor mutilations or killings. Using the term feminist Christianity keeps me from too easily reifying Christianity—its historical tradition and praxis and/or my own personal experience/version of it—into an idol, and helps me not to retreat from the messy complexities of other Christian women and men whose lives demand that they confront questions of abortion, sexual orientation, abusive partners, and corrosive marriages. It also compels me to recognize that the church has never yet fully realized the "feminist" example of Jesus, who validated a choice other than/in addition to domestic Martha for women, a man who labored together with women in his work on earth, and who gave women the priestly task of bearing the resurrection news to the world.

To use the term feminist, about which that young man in my interview meetings helpfully tried to warn me, will help, even compel, those of us in a North American, Evangelical, Christian context to address directly such matters as the ways in which we engage our own local churches in conversation and action about sexist oppression; the forms of address we use for women as opposed to those we use for men; the values we place on female but not necessarily male chastity in the rituals and practices of dating and wedding ceremonies; the toys we see as suitable for our daughters but not for our sons, and vice versa; the importance we give to female beauty and marriage as "natural" and appropriate pursuits for women; the ultimate esteem we give to mothering as opposed to other endeavors or careers women may choose; the authority we do or do not accord to women called to the vocation of preaching; the language we privilege or censure as appropriate language about God; and the political issues we understand to be moral beyond abortion and gay/lesbian rights. A list like this one, incomplete as it is, illustrates some of the currents of feminist theorizing and activism that have much to compel Christian engagement and commitment. Taking up the term feminist and a feminist commitment helps us see that the redemptive work of God is not quarantined in Christian domains of discourse. Indeed it may even be the redemptive correction those very discourses require and may help us to see and to resist the sexist pattern of this world.

Notes

1. See Elizabeth Cady Stanton, *The Woman's Bible* (Boston: Northeastern University Press, 1993).
2. I am indebted to Adrienne Rich's essay "Compulsory Heterosexuality," *The Norton Anthology of Theory and Criticism*, ed. Vincent B. Leitch (New York and London: Norton, 2001) in pointing me to Barry's work.
3. *God of Nature and of Grace: Reading the World in a Wesleyan Way* (Nashville: Abingdon Press, 2003); *The Story of God: Wesleyan Theology and Biblical Narrative* (Kansas City: Beacon Hill Press, 1994).
4. Most contemporary literary critiques would be thoroughly unconvinced with such an interpretive stance as well.
5. The exceptions to this statement might be acts of reading that are so rudimentary and straight-forward as to be utterly obvious and uninteresting.
6. See especially Stanley Fish's essay "Interpreting the Variorum," *The Norton Anthology of Theory and Criticism*, ed. Vincent B. Leitch (New York and London: Norton, 2001), 2071–2089.
7. A useful and accessible study of just this sort is Don Williams's *The Apostle Paul and Women in the Church* (Glendale, CA: Regal Books, 1977) and is noteworthy in light of my discussion because Williams, who is situated in the Reformed Tradition, is working to show that the Pauline texts that create the most challenge to a feminist position are, in fact, compatible with a feminist commitment when appropriately and adequately interpreted.
8. Although I have taken some care to articulate some of the sites of resistance that I have come to understand and name as part of coming to a feminist consciousness, I want to make clear that my experience is as ambivalent and contradictory as is typically human. I was also involved in activities, such as cheerleading and viewing/participating in beauty pageants, which I have come to understand and eschew as practices that participate in and promulgate a sexist view of women that is harmful and debilitating.
9. The hunches and intuitions that Woolf describes in this passage seem similar to my own adolescent searching for remarkable women that expressed itself in the books I chose to read during high school (*Jane Eyre, Wuthering Heights, Anna Karenina*, etc.) in place of the then standard fare for Christian young women by Grace Livingston Hill that most of my girlfriends seemed to be reading.

Bibliography

Barry, K. (1979). *Female sexual slavery*. Englewood Cliffs, NJ: Prentice Hall, Inc.
——. (1984). Female *sexual slavery*. New York and London: New York University Press.
Brontë, C. (1847). *Jane Eyre*. Ed. M. Smith. (1998). Oxford World's Classics. Oxford; New York: Oxford University Press.
Fish, S. (2001). "Interpreting the variorum." *The Norton anthology of theory and criticism*. Ed. V. B. Leitch. New York and London: W. W. Norton & Company. 2071–2089.

hooks, bell. (2000). *Feminism is for everybody: Passionate politics.* Cambridge, MA: South End Press.

Johnson, E. (1992). *She who is: The mystery of God in feminist theological discourse.* New York: The Crossroad Publishing Company.

Kilbourne, J. (2000). *Killing us softly III.* Prod., Dir., Ed. S. Jhally. Video recording. Northampton, MA: Media Education Foundation.

Lodahl, M. (April 11, 2005). "Religious practices." Panel Lecture. Margaret Stevens Women's Studies Center and Wesleyan Center for Twentieth-Century Studies Joint Forum. Point Loma Nazarene University, San Diego.

The New Oxford Annotated Bible. New revised standard version. (2001). Ed. M. D. Coogan. 3rd ed. Oxford and New York: Oxford University Press.

Ostriker, A. S. (1994). *The nakedness of the fathers: Biblical visions and revisions.* New Brunswick, NJ: Rutgers University Press.

Rhys, J. (1966). *Wide Sargasso Sea.* Ed. J. L. Raiskin. (1999). A Norton critical edition. New York: W. W. Norton & Company.

Rich, A. (2001). "Compulsory heterosexuality and lesbian existence." *The Norton anthology of theory and criticism.* Ed. V. B. Leitch. New York and London: W. W. Norton & Company. 1762–1780.

Stanton, E. C. (1895). *The woman's Bible.* For. M. Fitzgerald. (1993). Boston: Northeastern University Press.

Storkey, E. and Hebblethwaite, M. (1999). *Conversations on Christian feminism: Speaking heart to heart.* London: Fount.

The Thompson chain-reference Bible. New international version. (1983). Ed. F. C. Thompson. Indianapolis, IN: B. B. Kirkbride Bible Co., Inc.; Grand Rapids, MI: Zondervan Bible Publishers.

Weems, L. H. Jr. (1991). *John Wesley's message today.* Nashville: Abingdon Press.

Wesley, J. (1958). *The works of John Wesley.* Volume XIV. Grand Rapids, MI: Zondervan Publishing House. Rpt. of the authorized edition published by the Wesleyan Conference Office in London, England, 1872.

Williams, D. (1977). *The Apostle Paul and women in the church.* Glendale, CA: Regal Books.

Woolf, V. (1929). *A room of one's own.* San Diego; New York; London: Harcourt.

Wollstonecraft, M. (1988). *A vindication of the rights of woman* [1792]. Ed. C. H. Poston. A Norton critical edition. 2nd ed. New York: W. W. Norton & Company.

"Women outnumber men among college graduates." (May 17, 2005). *Morning Edition.* National Public Radio. KPBS, San Diego.

CHAPTER TWO

Silence as Femininity?:
A Look at Performances of Gender in Theology College Classrooms

ALLYSON JULE

My work as an academic, among various administrative and teaching tasks, has been primarily concerned with the effect of gender on language use and effect of language on performances of gender in classrooms. That is to say, I am an applied feminist linguist-educationalist; I explore the patterns of girls and boys and women and men in various contexts, particularly educational contexts such as classrooms. However, what has recently become clearer and clearer to me is that my fascination in gender[1] began in my childhood, a childhood shaped and influenced by my being raised Catholic.

I grew up attending Catholic schools and attending weekly mass with my family. On Fridays we ate fish (usually tuna) or baked beans and both Lent and Advent were faithfully observed. My father was the head usher at our city's cathedral; my brother was a busy altar boy; and my mother was active in the Catholic Women's League (the CWL) and played the organ at weekly mass and at parish weddings and funerals. My sister and I took piano lessons from Sister Agnes at the associated convent. As a family, we were devout and involved. The parish priests often came for shared meals at our home, something I remember very fondly because of the warm conversations around the table—conversations that included everyone, regardless of age or gender or positions of authority. My mother and my sister and I contributed fully, and the assembly of the meal and its eventual cleaning up included my father and brother as well as the visiting priests. All in all, I grew up believing a religious life was meaningful, important, and vibrant. I was taught and believed that God was loving and just and liberating through Christ's sacrifice, liberating humanity from the darkness of sin; I believed this fully and without hesitation. Although I don't recall my brother or sister expressing any intention of taking holy orders, I distinctly remember wanting to be a nun and wanting a life of goodness in the service to others.

Leaving the Catholic Church was not due to some deep, thoughtful, or even thorough conversion to another set of compelling beliefs—not a bolt from beyond that turned my life around. The change was more subtle and perhaps a more common conversion because it was a gradual slide into another community, one that happened slowly over time. One dull summer day in 1973, my sister and I ventured over to the neighborhood Daily Vacation Bible School (DVBS) meeting held that year at the Pentecostal church. At eight years of age, I was intrigued with their child-centered service and felt drawn to the "personal relationship with God," which was promoted heavily. I was also curious about the well-advertised weekly Sunday School continuing throughout the year. As a result of my attendance at the DVBS, I attended Sunday School down the street for years, joining my open-minded family later for noon mass. This became my childhood routine: Protestant Sunday School at 10:00, Catholic mass at noon. I had a spiritual experience in the summer of 1973 at the Pentecostal DVBS, one that deeply touched me and secured my heart for godly things thereafter. My family rejoiced with me in "feeling" God in such a personal way and I took my Catholic first communion and confirmation of faith without incident and in due course. Even the parish priests and school religion teachers were encouraging of my explorations and asked regular questions about my Protestant Sunday School lessons. When I married an evangelical Baptist man, this news was also greeted with unquestionable delight because my family genuinely liked my choice of husband; the matter of difference of religion was seen as minor because it was felt that a Christian faith was a Christian faith, whether expressed inside a Catholic community or inside a Protestant one. It didn't matter to them and, perhaps as a result, it didn't matter to me. I now see that their view was highly unusual, though I didn't fully appreciate this at the time nor did I understand how my childhood curiosities would propel my work.

That I would find my life's vocational calling in feminist linguistics is perhaps surprising for a religious believer, however ecumenical and open-minded. People have asked me to explain. My feminist colleagues want to know whether I am "really a Christian"; and, equally, my Christian colleagues want to know whether I am "really a feminist." The short and honest answer is that I couldn't be one without the other: I couldn't be a feminist without my Christian faith and I couldn't be a Christian without being a feminist either. Why? For me, the liberation at the center of Christianity has allowed me and encouraged me to connect with the liberation I see as at the center of feminism. The scripture stating "In Christ there is . . . no male or female" (Gal. 3:28) seems self-explanatory: at the root of Christianity is equality and human dignity. This was and is pretty clear to me. In fact, I can't completely understand how anyone could be a Christian and not be a feminist: why not be committed to the equality of all people? However, I also couldn't imagine wading into radical feminist theory without my background in Christian thought to help moor me. Any antimale rhetoric inside feminism I discount as I do any antifemale rhetoric inside Christianity. The extremes in either camp are unhelpful and largely irrelevant to me.

To me, Christianity and feminism are connected because of an important guiding principle: a life not free is a life mired in bondage and oppression. I am fascinated in the human experience as it moves toward and wrestles with freedom, equality, and genuine wholeness, and I see both Christianity and feminism as similarly concerned with liberation. Yet, in spite of these views, I can admit that the varied and lived experience with Christianity is not necessarily liberating. Within Christianity, perhaps particularly in certain groups, is a strange paradox that calls for a personal relationship with God while at the same time requiring this personal relationship to look and be performed in particular, communal ways. I now think that my Catholic childhood may have equipped me to look for and recognize redemption as the sacred within the secular, a redemption I see as helped along by feminism. "Women's Lib" (as feminism was known in my childhood) was a movement assumed to be enlightened and reasonable in much the same way the Civil Rights Movement for blacks was understood in my community: that one's dignity and worth are not to be influenced by race, social class, or sex. Human rights are sacred. Such an understanding influences my position here.

As a feminist linguist-educationalist, who is also a Christian, I want to explore certain questions in a Christian community/classroom. What might gendered patterns in language use mean when they intersect with a religious identity? To explore a connection, I want to take feminist linguistic assumptions and methods to a Christian community.

Language and Gender

The particular relationship between language use and the female experience has been a source of much discussion and debate for feminist linguists (such as Lakoff, 1975; Spender, 1980; Cameron, 1992, 1995a, 1995b; Coates, 1993, 1996, 1998, among a host of other scholars). In 1975, Robin Lakoff published a book entitled *Language and Woman's Place*. In it, she argued that women have a different way of speaking from men—a way of speaking that reflects and produces a subordinate position in society. According to Lakoff, women's language is full of linguistic and paralinguistic devices that render women's speech tentative, powerless, and trivial. As such, Lakoff believed that women's use of language disqualified them from positions of power and authority. Their use of particular linguistic strategies, such as using rising intonation, hedges (such as "kind of" or "sort of"), intensifiers ("very," "so") or their use of more tag questions are examples of gendered linguistic tendencies. In this way, language serves as a tool of oppression, an oppression that women collude in by way of their using such strategies. Such patterns are learned as part of learning to be a woman, imposed on women by societal expectations, and used by women to rehearse themselves into supportive and submissive roles.

Lakoff's publication brought about a flurry of research and debate that developed into the field of feminist linguistics during 1970s' feminism. For many scholars at the time and many who have followed, the issue emerged into a search for empirical evidence to support Lakoff's claim. Her view that women and men talk differently propelled a central debate in the field of feminist linguistics, what became known as the Deficit/Dominance/Difference Debate that raged for 20 years or so. Those 1970s scholars who explained the difference as a woman's deficit (like Lakoff did) influenced others in the 1980s (like Dale Spender) to assert that women spoke in such submissive ways because they had been dominated and required by men to do so. Others in the 1990s (like Deborah Tannen) suggested that the differences are simply there and benign. No one is deficit and no one is dominant; the differences are a result of being raised in different *gender cultures*.

Regardless of the interpretation of the differences, linguistic patterns do appear to be systematically found and found to be largely used by one gender compared with the other. My own feminist linguistic scholarship has been focused on specific language structures found in classrooms, a prime location for the performance of gender. One of the themes running through the related work of Walkerdine (1990) is that classrooms are often sites of struggle—often passive struggles on the part of many girls and later teenage girls and women. Such struggles may be partly understood by exploring language use; that is, the struggles of girls and women may be partly witnessed by their words or by their silence.

Of particular concern in understanding silence of females in religious settings (like the theology classrooms I examine here) is what I call "linguistic space" (Jule, 2004a; 2004b). By focusing on linguistic space, I mean that I am focusing on the silence versus the speaking inside the classroom discourse: the words used. Classrooms are key locations for language use, in part because language is so closely associated with learning. Mahony (1985) found that it was "normal" for a teacher to ignore girls in classrooms for long periods of time, for boys to call out, and for boys to dominate classroom talk. I believe that evidence of gendered differences in classrooms may derive partly from an examination of the amount or proportion of talk-time, particularly during the formal teacher-led lessons. According to Corson (1993), many studies confirm that teachers are unaware of the fact that they treat boys differently from girls (allowing them a different access to linguistic space) and even disbelieve the evidence when confronted with it. Indeed it seems to be common for teachers of students of all ages to defend their practices with the sincere disclaimer that they "treat them all the same" (144).

Thornborrow's (2002) research highlights the ways that many teachers control classroom participation through their "teacher talk," seeing their speech as creating and maintaining asymmetrical power relationships through the amount of time they spend doing the talking. Teacher-led classroom talk is often organized around the teacher playing the role of authority figure and this is seen in how the teacher controls the group by controlling the dynamics of the language used, the discourse: "the teacher takes turns at will, allocates turns to others, determines topics, interrupts and reallocates turns judged to be irrelevant to these topics, and provides a running commentary on what is being said and meant" (176). It was argued by both Stanworth (1981) and Mahony (1985) that the implicit message to the students was that extra time given to male students suggests that boys are more interesting to the teacher. In light of the extra attention paid to boys (even if much of it may be corrective), there is the resulting issue of girls' relative silence in these same classrooms. Spender's (1980b) work contributes to an understanding of a girl's silent classroom participation. She says, "Both sexes bring to the classroom the understanding that it is males who should 'have the floor' and females who should be dutiful and attentive listeners. . . . Within educational institutions girls are quickly made aware that their talk is evaluated differently from boys" (149).

Other findings on gender and language do not seem to vary much concerning the amount of teacher talk, even as the participants and context of the interaction vary regarding age, social class, ethnicity, level of schooling, subject matter, and sex of the teacher. In Swann and Graddol's (1989) research, both female and male teachers paid less attention to girls than to boys at all ages, in various socioeconomic and ethnic groupings, and in all subjects. Also, girls received less behavioral criticism, fewer instructional contacts, fewer high-level questions and academic criticism, and slightly less praise than boys. There are also reports that teachers direct more open-ended questions at boys in the early years of schooling, and more yes/no questions at girls (in Swann and Graddol, 1989). It appears that boys tend to be "first in" to classroom discussions because of the teachers' own nonverbal cues, particularly their gaze-attention. This eye contact is important in systematically offering boys more opportunities for participation. I wanted to focus on such classroom habits in a religiously based group. As such, I use the guiding principles of Applied Linguistics to better understand gender performances, particularly the silence of those born female.

While silence in female speech was not identified in the early work of Lakoff (1975), it has become significant in her more recent ideas. Silence is the absence of speech and, therefore, it is potentially complicated to identify in transcription work. Silence is ambiguous and may only be understood by an interpretation of context. Lakoff (1995) admits that not all female silence is necessarily about power (teacher power or more male power), but she advises that researchers should consider this possibility. In addition, Gal (1991) sees a major difference between self-imposed silence and externally imposed silence, though such a distinction may be difficult to perceive from the outside. There is evidence to suggest that a sense of feeling silenced and of feeling unheard are painful and frustrating experiences for many girls and women in the role of student in classrooms today. That the women attending the theology classes I look at here are also very quiet supports ideas emerging from secular feminist linguistics.

Regardless of the Deficit/Dominance/Difference Debate, differences do seem to exist; there seems to be a connection between one's performance of gender and the use of language. Such a relationship fascinates me as a woman: how does the way and when I speak reflect my view of myself as a female? Do I perform a particular femininity through when I decide to speak? Would a man perform differently in the same classroom? If so, why or which men? Might associations with a religious identity, such as a Christian identity, impact on linguistic performances of gender?

Female Silence in a Theology Classroom

I believe that there are certain classroom teaching methods that legitimate and encourage verbal participation of some students while serving to maintain silence among others. Some students respond better to certain methods. An important question to an educator is: Who is talking? The nature of the female voice seems to me one that is burdened by expectations of female silence, whether it is young girls in primary education or women in other settings, such as at this Protestant/evangelical theology college.

The research concerned with gender in influencing classroom experiences points to the influence of a masculinist discourse that values what is male or masculine over what is female or feminine. Even current feminist linguistic research, while increasingly more concerned with specific events and situations rather than questions of difference, still cannot escape the tendency of males in classrooms to speak in certain circumstances when females in those same circumstances do not.

We know that teachers (including college professors) talk more to their male than to their female students (Swann and Graddol, 1989; Kelly, 1991). Sadker and Sadker (1990) suggest that female college students in particular are invisible members of the classroom. That women in theology colleges may be yet further silenced because of their belonging to a particular religious identity tells us something about the relationship of gender to other variables so that related "situations and events" create part of a larger tapestry of gendered experience (Bing and Bergvall, 1998). There are many forces at work in each situation so that the teasing out of gender or the focus on it inevitably intersects with other influences. I hope to suggest that one of the intersections includes a collision of religious identity with gender performances.

Lecturing as Teaching Method

Lecturing is a common teaching method at the college level: an expert prepares the lecture well in advance, allowing for considerable research, study, and rumination. University lectures are part of the participants' daily schedules; both lecturers and students are usually present for obligatory reasons. Lectures are meant to disseminate knowledge for the set purposes of fulfilling the requirements of a given course. Depending on the nature of the course or on whether the class/module/lecture is mandatory or optional, lectures may well constitute up to 30 hours of a given module in any one term—up to three hours per week for ten weeks of an undergraduate module or class in most institutions. Such lectures occur with such frequency (for a set period of time) that personal involvement of the participants may appear necessarily limited.

Barthes (1977) considered the university lecture in terms of belonging, and as a location to rehearse *performance discourse*. While the lecturer is lecturing, the students are often silently attending to the ideas and writing notes on specific new vocabulary or content pertaining to the lesson material. Much freedom is allowed concerning the lecturer's ideas, power/ego issues, and ability at discursive performance. As such, the lecturer has enormous control over the mood and the dynamics of the room. Lecturing as teaching method works by conveying information through summary and elaboration—and all at the discretion of the lecturer. It is often during a student question period that students have an opportunity to publicly interact with the lecturer, briefly taking on the role of performer themselves and signaling their investment, interest, and involvement by asking a question aloud.

However, some lecturers are better than others. Goffman's (1981) ideas on the lecture differentiate between *aloud reading*, which is often perceived as more scholarly, and what he calls *fresh talk*, which is perceived as more informal though not necessarily more engaging. *Aloud reading* is a scripted lecture, one in which the lecturer presents the material with a heavy reliance on prepared notes. *Fresh talk* lectures are those lectures in which the lecturer speaks more off the cuff, without the benefit of prepared notes. Lecturers may use a combination of both styles, while some may be more consistent in using one or the other. Barthes (1977), Goffman (1981), and Frank (1995) all recognize the lecture as a multilayered discourse performance. In spite of more and more collaborative seminar-style classes, the university lecture persists as a marker of scholastic participation; both attending lectures and performing lectures are part of the academic experience. Spoken delivery is usually understood as more candid and dynamic, more "real," than listening to a lecture on tape or reading the notes of a lecture silently at home. A valuable, charismatic academic lecturer is certainly one to be encountered if at all possible. As a result, the pedagogy of the lecturer is "intensely personal" (intensely masculine or feminine), even if it is appears impersonal (Frank, 1995, 30).

Lecturing as Power

A lecture is a mark of the lecturer's expertise and authority. It is the lecturer who holds the power—or at least this is the idea. However,

Lacan (1968), and specifically his work on *the other*, highlights the role of the performance as a specific role of power and status. There is in any community one who is performing the central lead role and there are many others who perform the roles of audience. The performer is *the subject* of significance, while in other ways the performer may also be *the object* of observation and significance: there are various ways to interpret speaking and listening. In any case, power and powerlessness are performed and are performed in understood ways. The university lecturer, however, may well be both *the subject* (the performer) as well as *the object* (the one who is observed by others). Lacan's ideas have influenced my own understanding of power relations in classrooms and propel these questions: Who is performing? Who is observing? Which action (performing or observing) signals and evokes power? Which evokes less power?

Feminist linguistics offers various responses to these questions but it may be fair to say, in the light of the vast feminist scholarship concerning pedagogy, that power largely lies in the lecturer's hands. Often male, the lecturer performs and observes, and both may signal [his] power. *Holding the floor* is the lecturer's prerogative and is something that demonstrates the classroom's point of reference; that is, power is revealed in and created through the language practices of the (often male) lecturer. The lecturer is perceived as the one knowing. The students are the ones seeking the knowledge. What is said in lectures implicitly and explicitly hints at the lecturer's views and opinions, including religious and moral ones. The students serve to support these views. The lecturer performs power, status, and significance, while the students perform attentive and supportive audience roles.

What about lectures in a Christian context? Does lecturing, followed by student question periods, as is the pattern in the college I focus on here, alienate some female students because of the oppositional feminine/masculine role tendencies in the classroom? Is gender constructed into oppositional feminine/masculine patterns of behavior that may also be further constructed by interaction with Christianity? The prevalence of lecturing done by mostly men positions it as a masculinist tool, one that may rehearse female students into feminine positions of silence while rehearsing male students into masculine speech and one uniquely connected with seminary students' future roles of leadership in the church. If so, then the use of lectures as a teaching method works to reinforce and support a kind of hegemonic masculinity (Connell, 1995)—a masculinity that insists on feminine subservience and feminine reverent awe (Gilligan, 1982). Because of the transference of information or knowledge that lecturing presupposes, the silence of some students during question-answer time (a time in which they could speak) may affirm the possibility that those consistently silent are performing a specific and understood role that the silence signifies. Men in religiously based classrooms are set up to talk because of the prevalent and shared views that support their voice, while perhaps women are quiet in such settings because the particular community values their silence.

Gendered Performances: Good Girls are Quiet Girls?

In Gilligan's (1982) *In a Different Voice*, she explores various themes of gendered language patterns, including gendered patterns of expressing morality. To Gilligan, morality appears closely if not entirely connected with one's sense of obligation and one's view of personal sacrifice. She goes on to suggest that masculine morality is concerned with the public world of social performance and influence, while feminine morality is concerned with the private and personal realm. As a result, the moral judgments and moral behaviors of women tend to differ from those of men. In light of Gilligan's ideas, it may be possible to suggest that students within an evangelical subculture are encouraged to perform gender so that masculine behavior is connected to public displays of influence and so that feminine behavior is connected with intimate, more private displays. Men are rehearsed into the role of performer; women are rehearsed into the role of silent audience member—all for apparently moral reasons. Women's silence demonstrates to others and to the women themselves their devoutness to God, seen in their ability to be supportive. A woman's silence is her way of being good.

Worth mentioning here is that in Canada 46 percent of the population is Catholic, while in the United States there are substantially fewer Catholics: 28 percent (Nation Master, 2005, online). The particular expression of American-style evangelical Protestantism is a growing influence. *The New York Times* (Goldstein, 2004) reported that religion, in the last 20 years in particular, has edged its way into the forefront of American life. As a result, there are now 70 million evangelical Christians living in the United States, making it the most popular religious subgroup in the entire Western world. It is now considered "a normal thing" to discuss religion within American society (Goodstein, 2004, 2), and perhaps as "normal" in the Canadian, more Catholic, context.

Paglia (1992) discusses the power and significance of American-style Protestant Christianity in her essay, "The Joy of Presbyterian Sex," saying there are particular looks, manners, and values central in American society. Because of Canada's proximity to the United States and because of the vast influence America currently wields in Canada and around the world, my personal experiences with Christianity that have been both Catholic and Protestant are not that unusual. In Canada there may be more Catholics in the general population but the dynamic appeal of individual-based American evangelicalism is strong. That there are particular cultural manners inside Christianity in general, however, is where I enter more specifically now as a feminist linguist-educationalist: I want to better understand how gender is made evident in language patterns inside various Christian groups. This study is one introductory sample; there is more research necessary to make any larger claims. As such, I offer this small glimpse and no major claims on the matter of gendered language use inside Christian communities. This is one story among many.

My Study

I am investigating here the ways Christian men and women may appear to perform gender roles, drawing on my notion of linguistic space in particular because it is a concept that I believe allows for a focus on community participants and on those who participate and gain status by speaking aloud in a public context. In my search for an understanding of gendered linguistic performances, I can't help but link religious identity and religious heritage to the female voice or, in this case, religious affiliation to the lack of a female voice, something I see as possibly unique in religious groups, a view partially influenced by my Christian heritage. In this way, I am using ethnography: exploring a group by making the strange familiar (even to me) and making the familiar strange (even to me) (Hammersley, 1998).

I locate this sample of what I mean by gendered linguistic space inside a Canadian-American graduate theology college. Such a location allows for my understanding of a Christian, religious identity as lived practice. The currently experienced American-Christian manners and values are understood here as heavily influencing Canadian Christianity as well (Stackhouse, 2002).

Though women inside Catholicism may have other women's issues and feminist concerns from those inside Protestant expressions of Christianity, one of the most observable influences of feminism on Christianity in the last 20 years is the increase of women in Protestant theological education and in greater positions of leadership within the church (Mutch, 2003). However, their presence in coeducational lectures while they are in training for positions in church leadership may reveal traditional power discrepancies as deeply embedded in religious identity. I wonder if being male may include speaking in public as specifically demonstrative of masculinity or if being female may include the avoidance of speaking in public as specifically demonstrative of femininity. Because theology has long been the domain of men, women in today's theological education may experience a particular set of patriarchal conditions in comparison with those in mainstream university education where women's place and equality are perhaps more solidly assumed. But such a claim would need much more research to support it.

Some women enter theological training en route to ordination—that is, en route to becoming ministers or pastors as leaders in churches. However, many of today's American and Canadian Christians see ordination as something still reserved for men, with women better suited to more supportive roles in church life. While debates within Christianity concerning the ordination of women are vigorous and dynamic (Grenz and Kjesbo, 1995; Scanzoni, 1996; Ruether, 1998; Storkey, 2001; Porter, 2002), it is interesting to see that, regardless of the controversy, more and more women pursue theological graduate degrees. In spite of the range of views on women's roles in the church, increasing numbers of women today enroll in and graduate from theological education, and then some go on to careers of leadership in many churches (Grenz and Kjesbo, 1995; Busse, 1998; Hancock, 2003; Mutch, 2003). Indeed there is growing feminist thought within modern evangelicalism itself, in spite of strong antifeminist lobby groups on the American religious right, such as *Focus on the Family* or *Concerned Women for America* (Coontz, 2003).

One would think that the current presence of women in theological education, the simultaneous rise of feminist theology, and the increase of female ordination would have significantly changed the nature of such theological education. However, recent research into the lives of evangelical women in particular who chose theological education indicates that the lived experiences of such women are often painful and confusing (Gallagher, 2003; Ingersoll, 2003; Mutch, 2003). With various other religious experiences possible (including none at all), some women appear to remain and invest further and further in an evangelical subculture because they experience something meaningful and worthwhile that compels them to stay. And yet women who study theology say they are often dismissed as feminists for pursuing theology and are often marginalized as a result of this label (Mutch, 2003). Canadian women in theological education report that being a woman in ministry requires "commitment of conviction" that is carried out within a constant "context of challenge" (Busse, 1998). Most cite both loneliness and stress as parts of their career choice and as major issues in their theological education experiences. Nevertheless, some women continue to pursue graduate training in theology.

This Theology College

For one year, I worked on a research project at a postgraduate theology college. That project was to focus on the views of feminism among devout Christians living in the area. The results of that interview study are discussed elsewhere (Jule, 2004c, 2004d). However, as one trained in ethnographic methods and feminist linguistics, the year took on a slightly different focus for me personally, one that worked alongside the interview study. As a visiting scholar, I was able to sit in on any class of interest, either as a regular attendee or as a drop-in/on-off visitor. The college was very hospitable to me and welcoming of my questions and comments. I was affirmed and encouraged by the faculty and students alike and am grateful for the year in powerful ways. It is not often that a feminist linguist-educationalist has such an opportunity. What emerged for me was a meaningful ethnographic experience, one where I became a connected participant–observer, seeking the patterns of belonging in this community of which, for a time, I also belonged.

The particular theology college I explored is located in Canada. The college markets itself as "an international graduate school of Christian studies" (school website). It also advertises itself as a "transdenominational graduate school," not affiliated with any specific Christian denomination, though it articulates Protestant evangelical Christian ideas, such as "to live and work as servant leaders in vocations within the home, the marketplace, and the church."

Forty percent of the student population is Canadian with an equal number (40 percent) from the United States; the remaining 20 percent are from other areas including Britain and Australia as well as several who travel from parts of Asia, Africa, and Latin America. There are 350 full-time students and approximately 350 part-time students. Because the college is for graduate students, most are over the age of 25 and all have one degree behind them. Their first degree need not be theology; students come from a variety of fields, including education, medicine, law, arts, sciences and so on. There are roughly 60 percent male to 40 percent female students a nearly exact inverse of the composition of undergraduate populations in the United States.

Students choose from a variety of Master's programs, including a Masters of Divinity, the degree needed for ordination in many Protestant denominations, though not all students invest in graduate classes for the purposes of ordination: many participate for personal growth and to enrich their education more generally. The college is a well-respected one internationally. Some students go on to pursue a qualification as Doctor of Theology at larger theology colleges, such as Oxford, Harvard, Yale, or Princeton. As such, this college is a way for men and women who are called to ministry to train for their careers in church leadership.

The college employs 19 full-time faculty members: 17 are male, 2 are female. This imbalance of male to female faculty members, particularly in light of the male: female ratio represented in the student body may be relevant in understanding the gender roles in this community, though more research would be needed to make larger claims. The lecture-style classes at the college happened to be taught by male faculty; the classes taught by the two women happened to be smaller grouped classes. Perhaps if women's presence in theology is a controversy, then maybe it takes a certain kind of woman to reach the levels of scholastic achievement needed to teach at this level.

Methodology

The study used ethnographic methods alongside the quantitative method of measuring of linguistic space. That is to say, I was a participant- observer over the year; I was welcomed to sit in on many offered classes, acting as both a student and a researcher; I also kept a detailed observation diary and discussed my observations with several interested colleagues. I selected two classes in particular to focus on because these two shared the male: female ratio that existed in the college at large: 60 : 40. If I was attempting to measure in some quantitative way the breakdown of linguistic space in these lectures, then I needed similar sample groups in terms of the male : female distribution as well as in terms of the class size. Both classes were compulsory; both filled the lecture hall with 200 students. I also had semi-structured-interviews with both lecturers; their brief comments are recorded here. In addition, I spoke with five women who were in both classes, asking them (for the purposes of my study) why they had participated the way they did during the question sessions in these lectures. Their comments are also included in the findings.

The Two Theology Classes

Both classes were held once a week during the fall term in 2003. Both classes ran for three hours with one or two breaks. Both lecturers were male. The male lecturers were known as senior scholars in their fields; both were well published and well-known in evangelical circles. The lectures were held in the same lecture hall and were taped onto audio-cassettes and sold in the college bookstore. As such, validation of the findings is assured.

It was clear that both lecturers, Dr. MacKay and Dr. Jones,[2] had lectured on their material before, perhaps for years. Dr. MacKay was well over 50 years old; Dr. Jones was in his late forties. Both lectured from prepared outlines previously given to students. Both were well-liked by the student body, and both were open to my research questions and my attendance in their classes.

Findings

The Male Lecturers

Dr. MacKay began each class with approximately five minutes of announcements, such as where to collect marked assignments, before beginning his lecture. Dr. MacKay had three tutorial assistants who marked weekly essay submissions. Sometimes one of the tutorial assistants would speak to these details before Dr. MacKay would ascend the podium. A microphone was usually clipped onto the lapel of his suit by a sound technician so as to record the lecture as well as to allow the entire lecture hall to hear adequately. The lecture would then begin with a two or three minute prayer by Dr. MacKay. He would lecture without visible notes, though students followed along in the student packs where each lecture was provided in outline form—something purchased at the beginning of term. Most students appeared to use the lecture outlines to follow along and to write steady notes throughout, filling relevant sections of the page. Dr. MacKay spoke in a clear, steady voice; he rarely used humor or personal anecdotes and demonstrated more "aloud reading" style of performance discourse. At the end of the three hour class (including the one half-hour break), 20 minutes would be given over to questions from the students. For the 12 weeks of lectures in Dr. MacKay's class, not one woman asked a question. Three to five male students would ask suitable questions, all higher order questions spoken into standing microphones. Each week, different male students would ask questions that would last between one and five minutes. Dr. MacKay's responses would follow suit, generally running from four to eight minutes. No female students spoke publicly during the entire term.

Dr. Jones's class appeared less formal than Dr. MacKay's. Dr. Jones wore more casual clothes and often arrived a bit late. Dr. Jones also had the aid of three tutorial assistants who often started the class on time for him with announcements of assignments or sometimes reminders of college activities (such as the Christmas banquet ticket sales). Dr. Jones usually began his lectures with a joke or humorous anecdote from his family life. Eventually an opening quick 30-second prayer was said, and Dr. Jones would begin his lecture. Dr. Jones used PowerPoint images that would include particular Bible passages under examination in the lecture or photographs of biblical sites or maps. Dr. Jones used more *fresh talk* as part of his performance discourse. Students took copious notes; the class outline indicated the general lecture topic per week. Dr. Jones gave a one-hour break at the half-way point. During the hour, Dr. Jones would retreat to his office; the students ate their lunches or went to the library. Dr. Jones also planned time for questions, sometimes ten minutes but averaging seven minutes most weeks. In the 12 weeks spent sitting in on Dr. Jones's lectures, one woman asked a question. It was brief and answered quickly, and it stood out to me as perhaps an indication of some accessibility for women in the less formal, more *fresh talk* lecture, but this is conjecture.

In my opinion, Dr. Jones seemed to be the more engaging of the two lecturers, though in casual conversations with students, they noted very little difference and expressed similar respect for both. The content of each class seemed of more significance to the students than the personality or delivery style of the professors; all students were aware of the distinguished academics in their midst and affirmed this to me when casually asked more about their lecturers. When I asked both lecturers whether they noticed that only men seemed to ask questions during question-answer times, Dr. MacKay said he had not noticed this and Dr. Jones said he had also noticed this "years ago." Dr. Jones also said, "Women don't like to ask questions in public."

The Female Students

Five female students attended the lectures of both Dr. MacKay and Dr. Jones. As such, I asked them through email correspondence why they had remained silent in both classes throughout the full term. One of the respondents, Ruthie, was the one woman who asked a question to Dr. Jones. Her response as to why she did so is recorded here first.

Ruthie: I was actually really nervous when I got up to ask Dr. Jones that question but I really wanted to know and he didn't seem to be getting close to saying it. I have noticed though that most lecturers at . . . respond to people who are most like themselves so I think the guys asked the questions all the time because they respond better to the men as professors. I ask questions all the time in the classes I take lead by women. I think this is because I relate to them better.

Bethany: Dr. MacKay is fairly aggressive and if you don't sound intelligent he makes no excuses for you. It's his pedagogy, not his personality as such. He is just very masculine and old-school. I don't know why I didn't ask a question in Dr. Jones's class. Maybe I did feeler weaker—I am weaker! They are the experts.

Judith: I didn't feel that I had a firm enough grasp of the subject matter to even phrase a question. I'm just learning.

Lydia: I never ask questions in such a large space. I'd have to get up and stand by the mic and I'd never do that. Besides, I didn't know what I would have asked. It was all new to me. I would rather someone else asked for me than doing it myself. I usually wait it out and usually my question gets answered without my having to ask it.

Joy: I noticed the way they both leapt to answer the questions and I didn't want to defend my question—though I can't remember having one I wanted to ask. I also think that the men knew what they were talking about and so I was in learning mode, not speaking mode.

Discussion

Both Dr. MacKay and Dr. Jones clearly use most of the available linguistic space during their respective lectures. This is not surprising, considering the method of instruction. However, of the remaining linguistic space, men used disproportionately more; the women hardly spoke at all. For the entire term, the women attended and listened inside their classrooms, but they did not say anything. Why was this? Perhaps the responses given by the women themselves offer some possible reasons as to why they remained silent.

Only Ruthie said anything in either class: she asked the one brief question. It was the male students in both classes who talked during the question-answer period. As such, they seemed to perform their masculinity by posing questions during this time, while the female students seemed to perform differently—they performed a femininity where they were silent throughout. Clearly not all the male students asked questions; some of them also remained silent during the times they could have spoken. However, all of the female students, all of the time, were silent; they never spoke at all (the only exception being Ruthie). Instead, the women appeared as consistently supportive listeners—not speakers. When the women responded to my observation that they had not asked questions during the term they spent with Dr. MacKay and with Dr. Jones, in general they seemed not to see themselves as equipped or ready (as seen in the comments made by Bethany and Judith) or not able to perform in such a circumstance (such as expressed by Lydia and Joy).

Is the silence of the women here a bad thing? There are various ways to interpret the meaning of silence, as explored to a great extent by Jaworski (1993). And in light of Lacan's (1968) ideas, the silence could signal the role of the observer and a certain kind of power. There are multiple interpretations of what the silence may mean. However, regardless of the interpretations of the silence or the value attached to the speaking role or to the silent role, the linguistic space is occupied by the men in the room and not by the women. If who speaks signals who is significant or who has the right to speak or who was the status of performer, then the men's roles here may position them into power.

Given the prominence of Christian voices in current American and Canadian life, it is not surprising there are now differing connections made with gender and language use within religious communities. Many other researchers have undertaken studies on the relationship of faith and femininity and masculinity, most recently and rigorously Gallagher (2003) and Ingersoll (2003). Both of these scholars offer robust research on gender and the evangelical subculture, and both suggest that evangelicalism appears a salient religious experience to many, even with or perhaps because of the necessary adherence to traditional Christian teachings concerning gender roles. Evangelicalism's ability to thrive in the midst of larger secularism and current religious pluralism may in part be because it is a subculture that accommodates cultural engagement while preserving conservative theological orthodoxy (Gallagher, 2003). Perhaps Christian women participate in Christian groups by being quiet because this performance of femininity is one at ease in their particular religious communities.

The current American-Christian "right" has also begun to assert political pressure on issues concerning the family in direct opposition to feminist causes. Today's evangelicals in particular often articulate a view of society that rejects liberalism and equality in favor of certainty and moral conservatism. The views seems to emerge from a belief that men lead as benign but clear patriarchs who can and must insulate their families from the complexity of secular life, while women serve to support these efforts (Gallagher, 2003). As a result, both Christian men and women may be further rehearsed into stereotypically masculine and feminine performances with men to lead and women to submit to male leadership and significance.

It may well be that women choose evangelicalism in particular and precisely as a way to find meaningful communities and to reduce navigation of more complex gender roles within society (Busse, 1998). Gallagher (2003) suggests that women remain in evangelicalism precisely because of the set roles for women, not in spite of them. Such women find the clarity "empowering" (11). These set roles for women may encourage silence. The rhetoric of a strong masculine Christianity may also appeal. Even organizations within evangelicalism that support and promote female ordination do so within the set dogma, offering differing interpretations of key scriptures concerning the role of women but not differing interpretations of gendered behavior. Men are to be strong and rational, and women are to be supportive of male "headship," even if the women are ordained or in the positions of leadership.

These realities within some Christian circles, specifically Protestantism in which one could be a female and an ordained minister and still remain committed to submission as a key moral and gendered behavior, suggest that some Christian women manage the contradictions around them. Some women have proceeded to pursue theological education not for reasons of liberation or female emancipation from male domination in the church, but as a way to serve the church with their gifts of service and support. Though some women may have difficulty in such a context, most appear to remain and further invest themselves precisely because of a sense of calling. They remain in their "context of challenge" because of their "commitment of conviction" (Busse, 1998). They work out their gender roles within a specific framework of male leadership and domination around them. Even if ordained, these women see their roles as supportive and not leadership-driven and their language use reflects this.

That lecturing and question-answer periods are used in such a way in this theology college suggests a clash between conservative/spiritual masculinity with pro-feminist/social justice masculinity seen within the larger

university experience (Clatterbaugh, 1990; Skelton, 2001). Such a domination of linguistic space is what Skelton calls "the school and machismo":
that the ways males experience or exploit educational opportunities are
"skills" that males in society "learn to develop" (2001, 93). From an early
age, those born male are rehearsed into speaking roles, and those born
female are rehearsed into listening roles. Christian boys and men may also
be rehearsed into public, voiced leadership, and Christian girls and women
may be rehearsed to be silent, to listen and to support male leadership.

Conclusion

Paglia (1992) says that there are distinctively Christian "looks, manners, and
values." I suggest that these include codes of silence for women and public
voice for men. That women choose to belong to and to support a subculture
that views stereotypically gendered roles as desirable might explain their
silence in these theology classrooms. In any resulting claim, the questions
this study raises are many. The women remained silent all term. Are
these specific manners and values part of their being seen and understood as
devout inside their Christian community? If so, how could we know this,
and what would it mean to us if we did make such a claim?

Women's roles may be supportive roles, even if the women appear to
reach for the top levels of church governance by enrolling in Masters of
Divinity programs. But these supportive roles are not necessarily less
valuable than the performances of masculinity on the part of the men in
the classrooms. Any value-judgment would depend on the viewpoint.
Christian "looks, manners, and values" seem to include feminine silence,
but silence does not necessarily mean lack of importance. Though the
Christian world has competing debates within it concerning the role of
women, it appears to be the case at this college that female presence in
traditionally male contexts has not meant a challenge to traditional
gender roles.

The masculine style of speaking in this group seems linked to public
influence and participation as a way to be a man; men play the part of
knowing, of belonging to, and of participating in power, while women
play the part of consistent and supportive audience members. These patterns are so commonly seen in other pedagogical and feminist linguistic
research that the findings are not surprising, even if Christianity at its
purest would seek equality of worth and significance for all people.
Religious-identity issues that have perhaps appeared to some feminists as
patriarchal oppression also reveal women consciously or subconsciously

colluding in their circumstances. Women choose to be quiet. Have they been conditioned to expect or even want the men to dominate? Has masculinist discourse positioned the women to participate through silence? Such questions and a host of others can only be answered with yet more research, and it is my hope that this study invites further applied linguistic exploration.

Many women participate fully in Christianity; and some women within it appear to participate by being silent. Lecturing is a pedagogical tool and a popular teaching method in universities today. What are all the connections? It seems to me that many girls and women continue to serve as audience members in their own educational experiences. Based on my participation and observations over the year at the evangelical theology college, my view is that both men and women who belong to various expressions of Christianity are rehearsed or constructed into certain linguistic patterns. The popularity of evangelical Christianity in particular requires more feminist linguistic scholarship in the search for understanding the experiences in religious communities.

I grew up Catholic and, as such, my work as a feminist linguist is influenced by my own Christian heritage. Yes, I think we perform gender roles for a host of reasons, including a belief that such roles may be viewed well by our communities. Yes, I think feminism offers an important interruption to assumed male privilege, but why are women in Christian communities (as well as other communities/classrooms) so often quiet? If Christianity is to liberate, then Christian communities could reveal such liberation in the performances surrounding gender. But they do not. Both Christianity and feminism, in their purest forms, support a quest for becoming fully human. As such, I think their working alongside each other is a necessary responsibility of both.

Why is the silence of the would-be female clerics of significance to me or to others who are not or do not want to be in positions of leadership in the church? My own thoughts on the matter settle on gender roles we put on like costumes. Do we perform our gender in certain ways because we think certain styles are closely related to being godly or good? Perhaps. Do Christian women in various church-related contexts rehearse themselves into voicelessness? Perhaps. Are we limiting ourselves and each other by such gendered performances? If so, how? The questions and implications may be endless. If we are Christ-followers in a largely and traditionally patriarchal world, finding and using our voices (actually speaking) may be a key to liberation.

Protestant denominations seem to offer greater freedom for women, such as ordination. However, it seems to me that the liberation specifically advertised in evangelicalism (like in the child-centered DVBS in the summer of 1973) contradicts some of the lived experiences of women in such circles. Did growing up Catholic, in a liberal-education-based Catholic home, lead me to this view? Perhaps. Perhaps the less demanding day-to-day expression of Christianity found in my childhood where my faith was private allowed me to develop a voice and, as a result, invited me to use it. Such a journey toward gaining voice is both a professionally and personally compelling issue, and one I hope others join in on with full volume.

Notes

1. By using the word "gender" I mean the social behaviors developed and understood as masculine or feminine as distinct from "sex" and the physiology of maleness or femaleness.
2. The names have been changed to protect the identity of the participants.

Bibliography

Barthes, R. (1977). "Writers, intellectuals, teachers." *Image-Music-Text*. Trans. and ed. S. Heath. New York: Hill. 190–215.

Bing, J. and Bergvall, V. (1998). "The question of questions: Beyond binary thinking." *Language and gender: A reader*. Ed. J. Coates. Oxford: Blackwell. 495–510.

Busse, C. (1998). Evangelical women in the 1990s: Examining internal dynamics. MA thesis. Briercrest Bible Seminary, Caronport, Saskatchewan.

Cameron, D. (1992). *Feminism and linguistic theory*, 2nd ed. London: Routledge.

——. (1995a). *Verbal hygiene*. London: Routledge.

——. (1995b). "Rethinking language and gender studies: Some issues for the 1990s." *Language and gender: Interdisciplinary studies*. Ed. S. Mills. London: Sage. 31–44.

Clatterbaugh, K. (1990). *Contemporary perspectives on masculinity: Men, women and politics in modern society*. Washington, DC: Westview Press.

Coates, J. (1993). *Women, men, and language: A sociolinguistic account of gender differences in language*, 2nd ed. London: Longman.

——. (1996). *Women talk: Conversations between women friends*. Oxford: Blackwell.

——. (1998). "Introduction." *Language and gender: A reader*. 2nd ed. Ed. J. Coates. London: Routledge. 295–322.

Connell, R. (1995). *Masculinities*. Cambridge: Polity Press.

Coontz, S. (2003). *The way we never were: American families and the nostalgia trap*. New York: Basic Books.

Corson, D. (1993). *Language, minority education and gender: linking social justice and power*. Clevedon, UK: Multilingual Matters.

Frank, A. W. (1995). "Lecturing and transference: The undercover work of pedagogy." *Pedagogy: The question of impersonation*. Ed. J. Gallop. Bloomington, IN: Indiana University Press.

Gal, S. (1991). "Between speech and silence: The problematics of research on language and gender." *Papers in pragmatics*. 3.1: 1–38.

Gallagher, S. K. (2003). *Evangelical identity and gendered family life*. London: Rutgers University Press.

Gilligan, C. (1982/1993). *In a different voice*. Cambridge, MA: Harvard University Press.

Goffman, E. (1981). *Forms of talk*. Philadelphia: University of Pennsylvania Press.

Goodstein, L. (July 4, 2004). "Politicians talk more about religion, and people expect them to." *The New York Times*. Weekend, 2.

Grenz, S. and Kjesbo, D. M. (1995). *Women in the church*. Downers Grove, IL: Intervarsity Press.

Hancock, M., ed. (2003). *Christian perspectives on gender, sexuality, and community*. Vancouver, BC: Regent College Publishing.

Hammersley, M. (1998). *Reading ethnographic research: A critical guide*. 2nd ed. Essex: Addison Wesley Longman.

Ingersoll, J. (2003). *Evangelical Christian women: War stories in the gender battles*. New York: New York University Press.

Jaworski, A. (1993). *The power of silence*. London: Sage.

Jule, A. (2004a). *Gender, participation and silence in the language classroom: Sh-shushing the girls*. Basingstoke, UK: Palgrave Macmillan.

———. (2004b). "Speaking in silence: A case study of a Canadian Punjabi girl." *Gender and English language learners*. Ed. B. Norton and A. Pavlenko. Virginia: TESOL Press. 69–78.

———. (2004c). Gender and religion: Christian feminism. Paper presented at the Western Regional Conference on Christianity and Literature, Point Loma University, San Diego, California (March 23–26).

———. (2004d). God's daughters? Evangelical women speak for themselves on feminism. Poster presented at IGALA3, Cornell University, Ithaca, NY (June 5–7).

Lacan, J. (1968). *The language of the self: The function of language in psychoanalysis*. Trans. A. Wilden. Baltimore, MD: Johns Hopkins University Press.

Lakoff, R. (1975). *Language and woman's place*. New York: Harper and Row.

———. (1995). "Cries and whispers: The shattering of the silence." *Gender articulated: Language and the socially constructed self*. Ed. K. Hall and M. Bucholtz. London: Routledge. 25

Mahony, P. (1985). *Schools for the boys?: Co-education reassessed*. London: Hutchinson.

Mutch, B. H. (2003). "Women in the church: A North American perspective." *Christian perspectives on gender, sexuality, and community*. Ed. M. Hancock. Vancouver, BC: Regent College Press. 181–193.

Nation Master (2005). http://www.nationmaster.com

Paglia, C. (1992). *Sex, art, and American culture: Essays*. New York: Vintage Books.

Porter, F. (2002). *Changing women, changing worlds: Evangelical women in church, community and politics*. Belfast, UK: The Blackstaff Press.

Ruether, R. R. (1998). *Introducing redemption in Christian feminism*. Sheffield, UK: Sheffield Academic Press.

Sadker, M. and Sadker, D. (1990). "Confronting sexism in the college classroom." *Gender in the classroom: Power and pedagogy*. Ed. S. Gabriel and I. Smithson. Chicago: University of Illinois Press. 176–187.

Scanzoni, L. D. (1996). "Women's place: Silence or service?" *Eternity*. 17 (February): 14–16.

Skelton, C. (2001). *Schooling the boys: Masculinities and primary education*. Buckingham, UK: Open University Press.

Spender, D. (1980a). *Man made language*. London: Routledge Kegan Paul

———. (1980b). "Talking in the class." *Learning to lose: Sexism and education*. Ed. D. Spender and E. Sarah. London: The Women's Press. 148–154.

———. (1982). *Invisible women: The schooling scandal*. London: Writers and Readers Publishing.

Spender, D. and Sarah, E., eds. (1980). *Learning to lose: Sexism and education*. London: The Women's Press.

Stackhouse, J. G. (2002). *Evangelical landscapes*. Grand Rapids, MI: Baker Book House Company.

Stanworth, M. (1981). *Gender and schooling: A study of sexual divisions in the classroom*. London: Women's Research and Resources Centre.

Storkey, E. (2001). *Origins of difference: The gender debate revisited*. Grand Rapids, MI: Baker Book House Company.

Swann, J. (1998). "Talk control: An illustration from the classroom of problems in analyzing male dominance of conversation." *Language and gender: A reader*. Ed. J. Coates. Oxford: Blackwell. 185–196.

Swann, J. and Graddol, D. (1989). "Gender inequalities in classroom talk." *English in education*. 22 (1): 48–65.

Thornborrow, J. (2002). *Power talk*. London: Longman.

CHAPTER THREE

Blessed Mother or Material Mom: Which Madonna Am I?

LINDA BEAIL

I clear my throat nervously, gripping the lectern for support as I look out across the congregation on this bright Sunday morning. It's Mother's Day, and I've been asked to say a few words at the beginning of the service to commemorate the occasion, a task that I both welcome and fear. On the one hand, it is a happy day: I am holding my beautiful two-year-old daughter in my arms, and I welcome the chance to share my joy in mothering with the wider world. I appreciate the opportunity to celebrate the often invisible, undervalued care-giving work that mothers do. On the other hand, I desperately want to avoid the sappy clichés and romanticized versions of motherhood that often mark this day. I want to choose my words carefully, so as not to conflate womanhood with motherhood, or to reify yet again childbearing as the ultimate destiny and duty of a Christian woman. As I gaze across the room, I see a diverse audience of worshippers. There is a mother with a baby only a few weeks old cradled in her arms and several serene-looking grandmothers with white hair and sweet smiles. But I also see friends whose stories are more complicated, whose children have come to them via adoption from places far across the globe; a childless, middle-aged couple who are vital pillars of our church community; other families whose children have brought them deep heartache and tragedy, not just moments of joy; and people full of hurt and uneasiness this morning, remembering the imperfect and inadequate ways their own mothers loved them. Sitting in front of me are even some of my students at the university, young women already struggling with questions about their future careers and families, wondering whether they will ever truly feel fulfilled unless they marry and have children, yet fearful that Prince Charming might not ever come their way. What can I say to all of them about the meaning of motherhood? What does mothering have to teach all of us, in all of our variety of life experiences, about Christ's relationship with us and our identities within the community of faith?

Competing Madonnas: Narratives of Female Identity

This is not the first time I've struggled with the meaning of maternal identity. It feels like a question I've wrestled with for much of my life. As a little girl, I loved to play with dolls. Before I had any inkling of other career ambitions, I would proudly announce that when I grew up, I wanted to be a mommy. And all of my life, I was surrounded by Madonna narratives, stories of motherhood that mapped the way. Of course there was the Virgin Mary, the ultimate archetype of Christian mothering. Her message seemed to be one of deep sacrifice and selfless love. She gives up what seems to be a happily normal life and decent reputation, accepting a mysteriously holy pregnancy that turns her life upside down. She is separated from family and friends for years, giving birth in a barn and then fleeing to Egypt—but instead of complaining, she simply "ponders these things in her heart" (Luke 2:19). She is some- times rebuffed by her growing son, as he stays behind in the Temple or when she makes a request at the wedding in Cana, so the gospels can make the point of his divinity and devotion to God rather than empha- size earthly ties. She endures watching her firstborn die a torturous, humiliating death, unimaginably faithful to the end.

In the Christian tradition, few images are more powerful and moving than the Pieta. We see the sacrifice necessary for our salvation in the crucified Christ; but we also see the limitless love and sorrow of Mary as she cradles her lifeless son in her arms. It is her sacrifice too. The image makes real the violence of sin, so evil that it requires the severing of normal, appropriate maternal protection and care. Yet Mary remains, loving, selfless, persever- ing, her entire life defined not on its own terms, but by her relationship to her child. Growing up in an evangelical church, I was very familiar with the idea that this was the model of Christian womanhood one should seek to emulate: quiet, submissive to the will of God, and self-sacrificing.

I was also surrounded by another Madonna narrative, definitely a more contemporary version. With her empowered sexuality and sense of irony, pop culture icon and "Material Girl" Madonna Ciccone seemed a lot more relevant to millennial womanhood. Pop singer and actress Madonna embodied qualities that spoke to a more modern, feminist sensibility: women inventing (and reinventing) themselves, not being afraid to exercise power, and enjoying sexual pleasure. In the 1980s, her music and videos mocked traditional femininity as much as it celebrated it. In "Material Girl" she evoked the breathy sexuality of Marilyn Monroe, paying homage to women's ability to get rich by using men; yet her alter ego in the video is more attracted to a guy who simply brings her daisies and drives her off in a pickup truck. It was both celebration and critique of consumerism, in a particularly gendered way.

Following both the wane of 1950s-style June Cleaver iconography and the early 1980s advice for "superwomen" to dress like men in navy power suits if they wanted to succeed, Madonna offered a version of empowerment that let women use traditional female wiles to gain power and use it on their own terms. Another early hit song, "Like a Virgin," played with notions of feminine sexuality. Writhing around in a wedding dress, Madonna unapologetically claimed sexual experience—"a bad girl"—but reclaimed the virtues of romance and virginity in a special sexual relationship marked by "true love" and not just lust. In this music video, traditional divide between virgin and whore was transformed, as women were depicted as both simultaneously. In Western culture, which has long divided women as virgins versus whores, or Mother Mary versus Temptress Eve, Madonna stakes a claim for womanhood that transcends these boundaries. Far from limiting women as selfless, silent, and defined by their relationships to men and children, Madonna claims the kind of identity normally only allowed men: independent, powerful, autonomous, sexual, and self-interested.

As her career continued, Madonna reveled in being one of the richest and most powerful women in the entertainment industry. She became well known for continually changing her look and persona, recreating her image, and boldly addressing taboo issues like sadomasochism or religion. Quite unlike the original Madonna, this Madonna played with shifting, fragmented notions of identity to encourage women to achieve self-actualization, power, and pleasure. Even her decision to become a mother seemed more like a quest for self-fulfillment than maternal self-sacrifice: she made very public her desire for a child, then became pregnant by her personal trainer and chose not to marry, making clear this was "her" child to raise on her own. Nicknamed the "Material Mom" by the press, it did seem that becoming a mother might be just another lifestyle choice for Madonna, a personal experience that would lead to even greater self-actualization. (Interestingly, in recent years Madonna has restyled herself into a more traditional version of maternity. She married the father of her second child in a fairy-tale wedding in a Scottish castle, sometimes refers to herself publicly as "Mrs. Ritchie," has devoted her time to writing several children's books, and was recently photographed for *Vogue* in demure tweeds and sweater sets with her family on the grounds of her British estate.) For this Madonna, being a mother is only one facet of a multidimensional and sometimes controversial identity, in which creativity, freedom, pleasure, and self-expression are priorities.

The Impossibility of Motherhood

These two different Madonna stories are a bit simplistic, but reflect the common images of women often seen in our culture. Most narratives offer women an either/or choice: one can be an independent, self-interested, "equal" person in her own right, or one can be a nurturing, sacrificial "good mother." There is no middle ground. In Western culture, we have typically categorized reality into mutually exclusive dichotomies—such as mind versus body, reason versus emotion, public versus private, civilization/technology versus nature—and valued the first term while discounting the second. Women have commonly been identified with the latter, lesser term of these dichotomies. Seen as weaker and morally inferior, women have had a difficult time arguing for the status of full *personhood*, as opposed to more traditional notions regarding them as deficient or deformed male (truly) human beings. Women face an impossible choice. They can be feminine, expressing ideal maternal virtues of emotion, tenderness, generosity, and selflessness. This femininity may win them admiration, but limits them to a passive and dependent role. Or they can demand to be treated as persons, with the freedom to make their own decisions and take responsibility for them. But if a woman approaches life "like a man"—as tough, assertive, logical, and strong, seeking to maximize her own self-interest—then society begins to see her as unnatural and unfeminine, and definitely not capable of being maternal. Indeed, this is precisely why the Material Mom has been so successful—and so controversial. She has aggressively pursued her own desires, insisted on being in control of her image and career, made no secret of her ambition and used her sexuality boldly rather than cloaking it in feminine, romanticized ideals. She has been rewarded by fame and wealth—markers of status and power in our culture. Yet there is something "not quite womanly" about all this, something that brings scorn and approbation as well as a celebrity status.

This clash of narratives is confusing for women in the twenty-first century. After all, few of us envision ourselves as silent Blessed Mothers, defined solely through our identities as someone's wife or someone's mother. We have eagerly embraced the opportunities that 150 years of feminism have brought. We want to be educated; to play sports and have strong, healthy bodies; to be given respect and equal pay for the work that we do; to find what we are passionate about and pursue our dreams; to have a variety of choices about our lives, instead of all being forced into one singular female role. The Material Mom story has empowered us to be creative, to demand freedom, respect, and pleasure *as women*. Yet if the cost of that autonomy and personhood is to give up all the traditional maternal joys of love, connection, and nurturance— we worry that perhaps the price is too high.

In her 1899 novel *The Awakening*, Kate Chopin illustrates this dilemma. Her heroine, Edna Pontellier, is a young New Orleans society matron. In many ways she is quite ordinary. Yet as she begins to "awaken" to her own artistic and sensual appetites, she feels trapped by her society's rigid, Victorian norms and expectations. Her husband and friends cannot even understand, much less fulfill, her longing for greater self-knowledge and intellectual and emotional stimulation. Many have read the novel as a tale of sexual awakening; indeed, Edna does have affairs, and the novel makes a strong claim that women are entitled to emotional love and sexual pleasure, not just a respectable marriage and financial security. But ultimately it is motherhood that serves as the crux of Edna's dilemma. Edna's friend Adele, the perfect "mother-woman" who immerses herself completely and happily in her large brood of children, symbolizes the Blessed Mother archetype that Edna finds so limiting and suffocating. Edna loves her two small boys, Raoul and Etienne, deeply but erratically. Like many mothers, she finds them delicious but draining. She loves to feel their little arms clasping her and soothes them to sleep with caresses, tender names, and bedtime stories; yet she finds them wearying and feels "a sort of relief" when they leave her to spend part of the summer with their grandmother (Chopin, 1976, 42, 46, 20).

The Material Mom alternatives—a creative but solitary artistic career like the spinster pianist Mme. Reisz, or relationships with a series of lovers—do not satisfy Edna either. As the sterility of pure artistic ambition is flatly rejected, so is the illusion of sexual freedom for women. During her tryst with Robert, Edna is summoned to Adele's side for a terrifying glimpse of childbirth—the inevitable result of women's passion. As she witnesses this "scene of torture," she realizes that "pleasure and pain, conception and delivery, are inextricably intertwined" (Chopin, 1976, 120; Seyersted, 1994, 146, 159). Sexual desire is merely an illusion, nature's way of "securing mothers for the race," the doctor assures Edna conversationally. She witnesses Adele's delivery "with inward agony, with a flaming, outspoken revolt against the ways of Nature" that imprison her in a female body (Chopin, 1976, 119). When it is over, she remains haunted by Adele's warning: "Think of the children, Edna. Oh think of the children! Remember them!" (Chopin, 1976, 119–120).

Edna does think of her children. She realizes that she may be able to escape the roles others thrust upon her—"mother-woman," artist, wife, lover—but she can never sever the bond of motherhood established with her sons. Edna declares to Dr. Mandelet that no one has any right to force her into doing things; yet she falters and adds, "except children, perhaps—and even then, it seems to me—or it did seem—" (Chopin, 1976, 119–120). Awakened to her autonomous individuality, she vehemently asserts, "I don't want anything but my own way." But she has also been awakened to her complicated relationship with her sons and immediately amends, "Still, I shouldn't want to trample upon the little lives" (Chopin, 1976, 120).

Leonce Pontellier, Alcee Arobin, Robert Lebrun, her artistic career—all of these are "unessentials" Edna easily gives up. The children, "antagonists who had overpowered and sought to drag her into the soul's slavery for the rest of her days," are the ones she cannot elude or escape. Raoul and Etienne alone have a right she cannot deny: to claim her time, energies, and love. They are a part of her very being. As she takes her final swim, Edna thinks of them and admits that "they were a part of her life," acknowledging her immutable attachment to them even as she rejects their attempt to "possess her, body and soul" (Chopin, 1976, 125). She loves them beyond anything she has ever known—and she hates them for limiting her within her body and within her society. At her death, she fully understands what she told Adele the summer before:

> "I would give up the unessential; I would give my money, I would give my life for my children; but I wouldn't give myself."
>
> "I don't know what you would call the essential, or what you mean by the unessential," said Madame Ratignolle, cheerfully; "but a woman who would give her life for her children could do no more than that."
>
> "Oh, yes you could!" laughed Edna. (Chopin, 1976, 51)

She does give up her life—literally—when she drowns herself at the end of the novel. But unlike the "mother-women," who bury their own opinions and desires in deference to their families, she never does give up her hard-won sense of "self." Perhaps, like many contemporary women, she feels that she would be cheating not only herself but also her children if she settled for less. Through Edna, Chopin affirms the difficulty of the dream of selfhood in a society that defines women as selfless. Even more importantly, she reveals the limits of this definition of selfhood as an ego only and always in control, always a subject but never subjected to responsibilities and relations to others, as women inevitably are. Edna's suicide is depicted as bittersweet. Edna does achieve some measure of selfhood that women normally are denied, and yet she is a woman who also acts selflessly in giving up her life:

> In Edna's triumph Chopin suggests the hope of a self that is also selfless, one not wholly defined by others or wholly careless of the responsibility of others, neither wholly object or subject of desire. In that ambivalent triumph, then, lies a revolutionary image of the dream of female selfhood. (Ewell, 1992, 165)

Patrice DiQuinzio echoes this sentiment in the title of her book, *The Impossibility of Motherhood*. Being a "mother" and a "person" are incompatible identities in our current social and political context, dominated by an ideology of individualism. She argues that individualism conceptualizes human subjectivity as "a set of capacities, primarily reason, consciousness, or rational autonomy, which enable rational, independent self-determination and action" for which the body is merely instrumental (DiQuinzio, 1999, 7). This fundamentally disembodied subjectivity is also coherent, stable, and singular; political agency and entitlement are a function of possessing this subjectivity.

This is in stark contrast to what she calls the ideology of "essential motherhood," which conflates motherhood with womanhood, making it inevitable and natural, and requiring women's "exclusive and selfless attention to and care of children based on women's psychological and emotional capacities for empathy, awareness of the needs of others, and self-sacrifice" (DiQuinzio, 1999, xiii). Personhood, or subjectivity, is understood in terms of a unified, self-interested rational actor; motherhood, beginning with the blurred boundaries contained in the pregnant body, is neither wholly singular nor allowing room to consider only oneself. Thus motherhood and subjectivity are inherently at odds with one another in our current cultural conceptualizations—as the title of one essay so aptly puts it, "Are Mothers Persons?" (Bordo, 1993).

DiQuinzio goes on to argue for a rejection of this dichotomy in a "paradoxical politics of motherhood" that takes on the project of theorizing embodied subjectivity. This might include taking seriously the ways that the mind and the body mutually constitute one another, rather than seeing them as opposites in competition with each other for superiority; understanding subjectivity as partial, fragmented, and sometimes contradictory; and recognizing the ways that subjectivity is continually being redefined or renegotiated within a set of reciprocal social relationships. In this way, "maternal embodied subjectivity" represents

> [not] a deviant or failed subjectivity, but a paradigmatically human subjectivity, [with] pregnancy as a crucially important instance of the embodied processes of subject constitution in which all subjects continually participate . . . and represents the mother-child relationship, in which a mutual, reciprocal, and ongoing constitution of subjectivity occurs, as a paradigmatically human relationship. (DiQuinzio, 1999, 245)

This not only helps women by removing the false, forced choice between personhood/subjectivity/political agency and being a mother, but in fact highlights the value of women's experience, and feminist theorizing, for all persons. It creates a conceptualization of subjectivity that, particularly in light of postmodern critiques of modern individualism, is perhaps more useful and realistic.

A Feminist Critique of Perfect Motherhood

Feminists have long critiqued this unfair choice for women between personhood or motherhood, Material Mom or Blessed Mother. Though often portrayed in the media as anti-motherhood, many feminists have long demanded a more realistic view of motherhood and more concrete valuing of the work mothers do. In 1976, Adrienne Rich's classic *Of Woman Born* distinguished between motherhood as *institution* and motherhood as *experience*. In Western culture, the institution of motherhood can be disheartening and demeaning for women. Mothers are supposed to be happy and fulfilled all the time, totally fascinated by and devoted to their children, without any needs of their own. If they do not feel this way, they must be "bad mothers." Yet they mother in a culture that does not recognize them as full human beings, and takes for granted the hard work that goes into raising children. Under patriarchy, Rich argues, motherhood is more difficult for women than it has to be. Women mother in isolation, without emotional support or physical help, and often in conditions of poverty or violence. The countless hours of cooking meals, rocking crying infants, wiping runny noses, driving carpool, washing clothes, and helping with homework are made invisible. Women become exhausted and depressed, feeling worn out and worthless—even questioning their sanity.

Mothering as an experience can be quite different, Rich posits. In their individual relationships with their children, mothers find a rich and varied experience of emotions. She speaks of the incomparable joy and delight she finds in her own sons, as well as moments of anger and frustration. Women can find a sense of power and competence in mothering, as they learn the skills necessary to help children thrive. Nurturing a child as it grows and develops can be a source of tremendous satisfaction and pride. The feminist project, as she envisions it, is to move contemporary motherhood from an institution that dehumanizes and devalues women, to an experience that is defined by mothers themselves, centered around the knowledge and feelings of women as they mother.

As Sharon Hays points out in *The Cultural Contradictions of Motherhood* (1996), an ideology of "intensive motherhood" has evolved as a foil to our reifying the competitive pursuit of self-interest in public and professional settings. She argues that we have raised the societal standards of motherhood to unrealistic levels. Thus we hold individual mothers primarily responsible for child-rearing practices that are increasingly child-centered, expert-guided, emotionally absorbing, labor-intensive, and financially expensive. She writes that our cultural ambivalence about competition and self-interest have led to overidealization of motherhood as the opposite. This has the consequence that working mothers— expected to be ambitious and competitive in the workplace but nurturing and selfless at home—face an impossible double-bind: how to be Material Mom in the office, but Blessed Mother at home?

Feminists have pointed out the unfair division of labor within the household, and argued for more participation by men in taking care of families, as well as greater opportunities for women outside the domestic sphere. This critique is not just about the personal dissatisfaction of bored housewives, or women whining for more power and excitement. The idealization of motherhood has real, material consequences for both mothers and children—and thus, for society as a whole. As Ann Crittenden explains, "Motherhood is the single biggest risk factor for

poverty in old age" (2001, 6). Women pay a tremendously high financial
price for mothering. They forego wages if they take time—whether
years, or just a few brief months—out of paid careers to be home taking
care of their children. They will probably not be promoted as fast, or as
far, as men or women without children who are not trying to balance
family and work. They may end up in less lucrative jobs or career fields
because of the demands of mothering, or may work part-time and for-
feit costly benefits. They will earn smaller pensions and less Social
Security. The "mommy tax" of lost income over a lifetime will be over
$1 million for the average college-educated American woman
(Crittenden, 2001, 5, 89). While Crittenden left her own career to be a
mother at home for several years—and feels it was well worth it—she
declares the following:

> It isn't fair to demand that the nurturing of human capabilities, the
> national service primarily rendered by women, be valued . . . less. It
> isn't fair that mothers' life-sustaining work forces women to be soci-
> ety's involuntary philanthropists. It isn't fair to expect mothers to
> make sacrifices that no one else is asked to make, or have virtues that
> no one else possesses, such as dignified subordination of their per-
> sonal agenda and reliance on altruism for life's meaning. (2001, 9)

Rather than penalizing women for giving of themselves to raise children,
we should recognize that rearing the next generation of workers and
citizens is a public good to be supported and rewarded.

Thus feminism offers not just a critique of overidealizing motherhood, but a response. Feminist activists have made the personal circumstances of mothering political; they want changes in public policy to
better support mothering. For example, MOTHERS (an acronym for
Mothers Ought to Have Equal Rights), an advocacy group founded by
Crittenden and Naomi Wolf, lobbies for Social Security credits for
homemakers, to help alleviate women's poverty in old age. The
Mothers Movement Online and Playground Revolution urge
government and private workplaces to offer families more options for
balancing work and parenting, such as "good" part-time work with benefits and decent pay for professionals, paid family leave, and on-site child-
care (Peskowitz, 2005, 228–232). Rather than fueling the "Mommy
Wars" by judging one another as "good" or "bad" mothers, or setting up
more idealized standards of mother perfection, mothers are coming
together to support each others' similar needs and different choices
(Peskowitz, 2005).

Feminist stories of mothering—from Anne Lamott's irreverent and honest *Operating Instructions* to Andi Buchanan's poignant and hilarious *Mother Shock*—provide new narratives for a saner, kinder image of motherhood. These mothers do not seek to resist or retreat from motherhood, but to embrace it—without losing their sense of self. They fight the old assumption, from others and even from themselves, that

> a mom is not quite a person, that a mom is someone who can think only about playgroups and poopy diapers, who lives vicariously through her kids, who doesn't have a real job, who totes around a giant purse containing everything from wipes and crushed Goldfish crackers to sippy cups and slobbery teething rings, running from here to there to make it to soccer and music on time and still be home with enough time to slap a nutritious dinner on the table. (Buchanan, 2003, 67)

Feminist mothering has taught me that motherhood should not be impossible. The ambivalence is real: "I worry about having enough energy, enough patience, enough compassion, enough love. I worry about losing myself," writes Andi Buchanan (2003, 91). Like Buchanan, I want neither to be swallowed up by motherhood, nor to escape its precious, painful bonds of love and connection. I want to give of myself to my child—but I must have a self of my own from which to freely give.

A Christian Response to Perfect Motherhood

It is my Christian faith, as well as feminism, that lead me to reject this all-or-nothing paradigm of maternal identity. Church tradition may sometimes seem to urge women to fulfill their spiritual calling via wifehood and motherhood. In truth, faith calls us to reject what Carla Barnhill (2004) calls "the myth of the perfect mother." If the Blessed Mother archetype demands the loss of one's very self in service to her family, Christianity calls women to full and responsible personhood— not for our own self-fulfillment, but in relationship to our Creator and for the sake of the Body of Christ.

In fact, it was my faith that caused me to embrace feminism, for everything I knew and experienced of God affirmed that I was not inferior or subordinate as a woman, but equally loved, called, and saved. When I read scripture, I saw more than just temptresses like Eve or silent icons of virginal holiness. I discovered strong, courageous leaders like

Deborah the Judge. The gospels presented a portrait of Jesus treating women in radical, countercultural ways: speaking with a lowly Samaritan woman, encouraging disciples like Mary to be educated by his teaching, appearing to announce his resurrection first to a woman, creating the first woman evangelist by exhorting her to go and tell his other followers the good news. Paul acknowledged women as benefactors and coworkers with him in the early church, and the Holy Spirit is poured out on believing men and women at Pentecost, so that both "your sons and daughters will prophesy" (Acts 2:17). I took seriously the declaration in the third chapter of Galatians that "in Christ, there is now neither male nor female" but all new creations, with former systems of caste and oppression transformed into the freedom of the body of Christ.

My church heritage gave me many feminist role models, from Susannah Wesley to Phoebe Palmer. My heroines growing up were not from fairy tales or superheroes, but extraordinary women missionaries like Fairy Chism and Louise Robinson Chapman in Africa and Esther Carson Winans in the Andes—women who seemed brave, adventurous and daring in breaking normal feminine taboos in service to God. I learned that the first wave of American feminism, begun in 1848 at the Wesley Chapel in Seneca Falls, New York, was founded and fueled by devout Quaker women like Lucretia Mott and Susan B. Anthony. Their faith caused them first to protest slavery; out of their abolitionist activities grew a recognition of injustices against women as well, that led to the suffrage movement, marital property reform, and other activism on behalf of women's equality.

My faith has given me a deep sense of self. Because I am created in the very image of God, my personhood is sacred, wondrous, and holy. Losing one's self in motherhood can be dangerous and destructive, as Toni Morrison (1987) illustrates in her Nobel-Prize-winning novel, *Beloved*. A lyrical and chilling account of the legacy of slavery in America, *Beloved* tells the story of a runaway slave mother, Sethe, who kills her infant daughter rather than let her be recaptured into the horrors of that peculiar institution. The child's murder (based on a true historical event) is horrific, demonstrating the incomprehensible evil of slavery as it calls into question the notion of "mother love." Is Sethe a monster for killing her child, or a mother protecting her young from even worse terrors? Morrison makes it clear that Sethe's actions are motivated by powerful love. As Sethe describes the murder of her daughter, "She had to be safe and I put her where she would be. But my love was tough . . . if I hadn't killed her she would have died and that is something I could not bear to happen to her" (Morrison, 1987, 200). Yet Morrison does not evade the difficult issue of the possessive, even obsessive nature of motherhood. She shows how Sethe's love for her daughter may be "too thick"—how the overwhelming, engulfing nature of motherhood may become too powerful to maintain one's own subjectivity (Morrison, 1987, 164).

The real horror story begins when the dead child, Beloved, returns to haunt the family. Sethe, in a mixture of guilt, loss, and longing, welcomes the ghost, who wreaks greedy childlike destruction on the family. Beloved demands everything from her mother—time, attention, food, her mother's lover, and finally her sanity. The explanations Sethe offers as to why she spilled her baby's blood, declarations of true love, do not satisfy Beloved; she seems to be sucking the lifeblood out of Sethe in return. Identities have become so merged that the one feeds off of the other; there is an element of cannibalism at work.

> The bigger Beloved got, the smaller Sethe became; the brighter Beloved's eyes, the more those eyes that used never to look away became slits of sleeplessness. Sethe no longer combed her hair or splashed her face with water. She sat in the chair licking her lips like a chastised child while Beloved ate up her life, took it, swelled up with it, grew taller on it. And the older woman yielded it up without a murmur. (Morrison, 1987, 250)

Sethe allows Beloved to consume her, even invites it. Her greatest fear is not being destroyed by her ravenous daughter, but the exact opposite: that Beloved might leave her (Morrison, 1987, 251). Indeed, though Beloved nearly destroys Sethe before being exorcised, the mother still insists that "she was my best thing." Sethe's companion Paul D refutes this assertion. "*You* your best thing, Sethe. *You* are" (Morrison, 1987, 272–273, italics added). Sethe's incredulous response—"Me? Me?"—reveals the continuing difficulty for women of asserting a genuine maternal self.

Theologian Diane Leclerc (2001) notes a similar temptation for women. She posits that our understanding of "sin" may itself be gendered. While many preachers have emphasized pride and self-sufficiency as the roots of sinfulness and rejection of God, this "idolatry of the self" may be more typical of masculine behavior in our culture. Historically and culturally, women have had less opportunity for self-aggrandizement, and may have even been praised for their spiritual virtues of meekness, self-denial, and sacrifice on behalf of others. But if God is wrongfully

displaced by love of self in many men, many women may fall short of the
"singleness of heart" required for true holiness by loving children and
husbands more than their Redeemer. Leclerc cautions women to avoid
this idolatry of relationships by devoting themselves to God: not com-
mitting the sin of self-obliteration, but cultivating both a sense of self and
the joyous freedom of that self in service and relationship to her Creator.
The gospel calls us not to the "cult of family" (Barnhill, 2004) so prevalent in contemporary Christian rhetoric, but to the ultimate Lordship of
Jesus Christ.

The call of the gospel is not one that turns us inward, to simply love
and care for those within our own four walls, but outward to serve "the
least of these" as Christ himself. To parent as a Christian is to have a
"dual vocation," both to care within the home and to seek Kingdom
values of peace and justice beyond it (Rubio, 2003, 98–99). Julie
Hanlon Rubio argues, "One cannot fully realize the demands of
discipleship to Jesus of Nazareth unless one also has a public vocation"
(2003, 99). Just as Christ called his disciples to leave father and mother
to follow him, so too the Christian parent must obey a call to more than
family life. God encourages us to practice hospitality not just to our relatives, but to a hurting world. God asks us to find our primary identity
as brothers and sisters in Christ, not as spouses or parents. Women are
called to significant work and service—a connection to the wider world
and God's work in it—not to be subsumed by motherhood alone
(Rubio, 2003, 100, 105).

Finding My Place

As Christian and feminist, then, which Madonna am I? Neither narrative—
of selfless Blessed Mother or self-interested Material Mom—seems to fit. I
have learned to appreciate the ambivalence of motherhood—the desire to
nurture and sacrifice for my child, while at the same time trying to hang on
to some sense of self and not be swallowed up completely in motherhood. I
reject both the totalizing selflessness of the Blessed Mother, and the self-
centered focus of the Material Mom, searching for a way to be that self-in-
relation that is more healthful and human. Instead of those archetypes, I seek
a maternal subjectivity that is both responsive and responsible. This self-in-
relation is a person who can speak and act for herself, without being engulfed
by the agency of others; yet who can move beyond the boundaries of the
solitary self to feel and act in ways that take others' needs into account. What is

needed is a self who knows her place: neither at the center of the universe, nor erased from it.

Caring for children is a great lesson in humility. Once my daughter was born, I discovered that my plans and schedule were no longer my own. Even now, long after the jolting awake for middle-of-the-night feedings has passed, I find life is often more unpredictable than orderly. Just as I think we are ready to head out the door on time, my toddler dissolves into tears because I didn't let her put on her shoes all by herself. Playing chase down the hall interrupts the carefully calculated hours I need to finish grading papers. Whether unexpectedly mopping up messes, kissing skinned knees, or discovering ladybugs in the garden, I have learned that time ebbs and flows differently now that I'm a mother. I'm no longer in control. And yet I'm not abandoned to total chaos; part of mothering is the responsibility to set the pace, to order the days, if somewhat imperfectly. Our time needs a rhythm, of snacks and fresh air and naps and cuddling for stories. So I muster my best judgment and chart the day's course, knowing at any moment I may have to pause, to change directions, to provide safe harbor in a sudden squall. This is the sense of place that mothering has taught me: I belong in the tug and flow of these waves, morally responsible, free to act, yet always connected to others, always responding to the growth and change in those I care for. I am truly my own self, yet I am not isolated. Mothering as both a feminist and a Christian has taught me where I belong. I no longer try to usurp the place of the Ruler of the Universe, controlling everything in my own freedom and power. I am human, finite; yet valuable, cherished, made to love, and to be loved.

Mothering as Relationship

Motherhood—like spiritual life—is paradoxically both relationship and practice. The emphasis on self-in-relationship, rather than fixed and oppositional individual identities, begins with pregnancy. The pregnant woman is not merely one, but not yet two. Her gestating body challenges all the ideas of bodily autonomy and integrity underlying our notion of singular personhood. Through pregnancy, childbirth, and lactating, women "know" from experience that rigid physical boundaries can easily blur, and that bodily interdependence is not necessarily weakness to be feared, but can be a source of strength and even pleasure (Chodorow and

Rich, in Hartsock, 1983, 225). As feminist theologian Elizabeth Johnson (1997) points out, God is also "always already" relational. In the Trinity, God is three-in-one. Father, Son, and Holy Spirit are fully themselves, while simultaneously wholly in communion with one another. The idea of a connected subjectivity—as opposed to separation, individuation, and autonomy—is deeply feminist and profoundly Christian.

In most instances, the mother–child relationship is powerful, beautiful, and mysterious. When I was pregnant, I was intrigued and bemused by the way so many people would tell me, "Just wait. When you become a parent, everything changes." Much to my relief, my own unique personality and sense of humor seem to have survived childbirth intact, and my world did not pop from black and white into glorious Technicolor when my daughter appeared. But they were right about the overwhelming emotion that washed over me the moment Caroline was born, changing something about my basic identity and loyalties forever. Instantly and inexplicably, I became her mother—with all of the love, protectiveness, anxiety, and wonder that one human being can feel for another. It was as though I stepped through a doorway, and I can never return; I can never go back to not knowing the burden of this awesome responsibility. My self was transformed in that moment in ways I can barely understand but will spend the rest of my life coming to terms with. Like the moment of salvation, when one is transformed from outcast sinner to redeemed child of God, I do not fully understand the change; but I know it to be true and unshakeable. I am a different person.

Just as I was marked in baptism as Christ's own, so when I gave birth I was marked forever as Caroline's mother. But as surely as I became her mother in that instant, I have had to *become* her mother in the days and years since. Caring for children is hard work—and relentless. It is often not exciting, but routine and tedious and difficult. It is work that literally creates us. Feminist philosopher Nancy Hartsock (1983) reminds us that material life structures understanding—in other words, that what we do with our bodies shapes who we are and how we think. Our reality, our consciousness, is created from our tangible life experiences. Thus it matters that women typically have done very different kinds of work than men have done. Women's productive labor is structured by repetition (tasks that have to be done over and over again, like cooking and cleaning) and its products are consumed, leaving one little sense "transcendence" or of tangible accomplishment.

Women do not only participate in different modes of production than men do; they also engage in the work of reproduction, Hartsock notes that the work of reproducing other human beings creates a very unique consciousness for women. Pregnancy and lactation challenge the boundaries between two discrete bodies, encouraging us to think in terms of connection rather than strict separation. Physically and emotionally nurturing a child unites mental and manual labor, often juxtaposed for men. Women develop a "connected" consciousness, rather than an individuated and oppositional consciousness. Because of the kinds of work they do and the experiences they have, women are more likely to value "concrete, everyday life" and feel a "sense of connectedness and continuities both with other persons and with the natural world," which makes dichotomies (like the conflicting Madonna narratives) "foreign" (Hartsock, 1983, 229).

Sara Ruddick elaborates on the importance of mothering "practices" for women's epistemologies. She is careful to note that mothering is not exclusively or instinctively a female duty. Motherhood is not the "essence" of womanhood, and men can—and should—develop qualities of "maternal thinking" when they do more care-giving work. It is not the identity of mother, but the everyday practices involved in caring for children, that shape a person (Ruddick, 1980, 587). The three distinctive values that maternal practices encourage are preservation (of the child's life), growth, and acceptability (raising the child to fit in to society) (Ruddick, 1980, 589). These lead mothers to develop several important traits, such as a humble sense of the limits of one's actions. Humility is necessary, for a mother can never totally protect her child from illness, death, or natural disasters; the world is an unpredictable place, and the child itself is unpredictable. A mother has the paradoxical job of helping the child she loves to become his or her own separate self, who may act in ways quite different from what the mother might choose or expect (Ruddick, 1980, 590). "Kind, resilient good humor" is another trait helpful to develop in the face of this growth and unpredictability; so is respect for persons and time-consuming, attentive love (Ruddick, 590–592, 595). "Love, the love of children at any rate, is not only the most intense of attachments; it is also a detachment, a giving up, a letting grow. To love a child without seizing or using it, to see *the child's* reality with the patient, loving eye of attention—such loving and attending might well describe the separation of mother and child from the mother's point of view" (Ruddick, 1980, 596). Mothering can teach empathy without demanding sameness, and teaches one to live in an attitude of responsiveness, not control. But these qualities and values are not adopted as an ideology; they are learned through the hundreds of times a mother wakes to feed a crying a baby, or answers "But why is the sky blue?," or comforts a brokenhearted eight-year-old not invited to a classmate's birthday party. What we do turns us into the mothers we need to be.

Being a mother brought me more fully into the world of everyday, physical reality. Before I had my daughter, I lived more in my mind than in my body. I read, lectured, wrote. If I had a deadline, I worked late into the night until I finished, and caught up on as much sleep as I wanted when the project was over. I had something to show for my efforts at the end of the project, and moved on to something new and different. Now I live a very embodied, and repetitive, life. I know the bone-deep weariness of waking up with a child throughout the night. I cannot take a break or call in sick when I am busy or tired; mind-bogglingly, Caroline needs clean diapers and breakfast *every single day*. I have had mornings where I want to put my head down on the kitchen table and weep with exhaustion and frustration. Cheerios? Again? Didn't I just feed her these, and pick them up from every corner of the kitchen floor, yesterday and the day before that and the day before that? Some days I just don't think I can read *The Very Hungry Caterpillar* for the 47th time.

Like the Christian life itself, motherhood is work. Christianity is not just about beliefs, emotions, and transcendent moments. It is about the daily practices and disciplines that make us followers of Christ, and make those moments of grace possible. As Christians, we do things that reorient our minds and bodies to the arc of the gospel. We read the Bible, we pray, we fast, we practice generosity and hospitality through our tithes and sharing what we have with those in need. Over time, these practices literally change my mind and my heart. One of the greatest gifts mother-hood has given me is the grace of daily obligation. I don't want to be at the breakfast table every morning. I'd rather sleep in, and fast forward to the "Kodak moments" of my daughter's life. But what I've come to realize is that these *are* the important, grace-filled moments. In listening to her babble every morning over Cheerios, I began to hear real words and know her thoughts. Without attempting to read *The Very Hungry Caterpillar* for the 48th time, I would not have discovered that she had a new favorite story. Only through these endless routines of care taking have I come to know her moods and to sense what she needs before she does. In just being with her, even when it's mind-numbingly dull or exhausting, I am learning about her and how to be her mother. The practice of mothering has made me more present to my life—both with my daughter and with God.

Mothering Points Me to the Wider World

Motherhood has given me a little more of a glimpse into the heart of God, and the love God has for our world. One of the temptations of early motherhood has been to retreat back into myself. At first I couldn't watch the news or read the paper, because all of the evil was just too overwhelming. All I felt was desperate fear, and the need to protect this tiny new life at any cost. My feelings shocked me. I have always cared deeply about poverty and injustice, about bringing peace and redemption to the dark places in our world. But now, especially in the aftermath of 9/11 and the vulnerability to terror many of us feel, the problems seemed utterly unsolvable. All I wanted to do was to make sure my own child was safe and well fed. I found myself building a high wall around my heart, unable to care about the violence and evil threatening others all about me.

One day when my daughter was just a few weeks old, I was sitting on the floor babbling to her and playing with some toys she had been given. "Look, Caroline," I said. "Look at the pretty colors on this rattle. Do you hear its sound? Feel how soft this bunny is. You are such a lucky little girl, to have all these toys, and friends who care for us so much to send you these things. A lot of people love you. And Mommy loves you, so very much . . . All mommies love their babies like I love you, but not all of them can take care of their babies the way they want to." I suddenly began to cry. "Not all of those mommies can keep their babies safe, or give them enough to eat, or keep them well."

Tears, unbidden, streamed down my face as I held my girl close, my heart broken by the knowledge that mothers in Afghanistan, and Sudan, and even in other neighborhoods in my own city, felt this same overwhelming love for their babies but were helplessly watching them starve to death, get caught in the crossfire of bombs and violence, become AIDS orphans, or other horrors. I knew that I was blessed—but that I had done nothing to deserve my privilege. My faith felt shaken by the stark reality of evil, and I wondered again how an all-loving God could tolerate such suffering.

But something in me broke open that day as I held my daughter and wept for those other mothers. I ached for them in some small way as God must ache for his beloved children who suffer. I felt a solidarity and sisterhood with those women, that their fate could so easily be mine. A deep responsibility to share my abundance and to help end their grief grew within me. And while participating in merciful solutions to the world's enormous problems is indeed important, what I have learned more from mothering is how to share another's sorrow, even if it means risking my own fears and doubt. I resist the urge to hide behind flimsy walls of self-protection, and ask God for the courage to mourn with those who mourn. As a feminist and Christian, I stand in unity with suffering women around the globe, with tears and fear and yet defiant hope.

Mothering Points Me to God

Being a mother has helped me glimpse not just God's heart of compassion, but the true nature of God's own self. Although Christians are most familiar with images of God as Father—beginning with our most common liturgy, the Lord's Prayer—a fuller understanding of the nature of God transcends gender. The point is not to substitute an image of Mother-God for Father-God; all anthropomorphic language for God is bound to fall short of the fullness and magnificence of the one who created and exceeds us, limiting and distorting our understanding of the Divine (Elizabeth Johnson, 1997). Yet there are good reasons to draw attention to the feminine, maternal qualities of God described in scripture. When we see God as a mother giving birth (Deut. 32:18), teaching her children to walk and feeding them (Hosea 11:3–4), and giving comfort to her child (Isa. 66:13), we are explicitly reminded that God is not exclusively male. Thus men are not, in their masculinity, created closer to the image of God than women; men do not conform more closely to Christ or his priestly duties merely because of their sex. Rather, the equal value and worth of women is affirmed. Likewise, when we see God groaning in labor (Isa. 66:9), an angry mother robbed of her cubs (Hosea 13:8), or a mother hen who would gather Jerusalem like chicks under her wing (Matt. 23:37, Luke 13:34), we see the importance of nurturing work. Care-giving cannot be devalued as menial or mere "women's work" when modeled by the omnipotent and sovereign God of the universe.

Conclusion

So this is what I told my fellow worshippers that bright Mother's Day morning: that mothering is neither our "destiny" nor the sentimental-ized ideal in a greeting card, but real, joyous, difficult work. Feminists have done much to show us how unrealistic common caricatures of motherhood are, to claim respect and support for this demanding work, and to point out the unique knowledge and perspective that mothering can provide. Mothering is not just an experience for individual women to embrace or struggle with; motherhood is given by God to all of us, as a sign of how Christ is present and at work among us. As in spiritual life, in motherhood God shows us the paradox of a defining, transforming identity that is also a set of practices that daily shape us into becoming who we are. Parenting demonstrates yet again the humility of not being the self that is in control, but instead asks us to share the heart of God, aching with compassion for mothers and children that suffer. Mothering and being mothered gives us a glimpse of one facet of the nature of our Creator and Redeemer. So I continue to delight and wrestle daily with the challenges of being a feminist, Christian mother: neither Blessed Mother nor Material Mom, but an embodied witness of love and grace in the world.

Bibliography

Barnhill, C. (2004). *The myth of the perfect mother: Rethinking the spirituality of women.* Grand Rapids, MI: Baker Books.

Bordo, S. (1993). *Unbearable weight: Feminism, western culture, and the body.* Berkeley: University of California Press.

Buchanan, A. (2003). *Mother shock: Loving every (other) minute of it.* New York: Seal Press.

Chopin, K. (1976). *The awakening and selected stories.* Ed. B. H. Solomon. New York: Signet.

Crittenden, A. (2001). *The price of motherhood: Why the most important job in the world is still the least valued.* New York: Henry Holt.

DiQuinzio, P. (1999). *The impossibility of motherhood: Feminism, individualism, and the problem of mothering.* New York: Routledge.

Ewell, B. C. (1992). "Chopin and the dream of female selfhood." *Kate Chopin reconsidered: Beyond the bayou.* Ed. L. S. Boren and S. deSaussure Davis. Baton Rouge: Louisiana State University Press.

Hartsock, N. C. M. (1983). "The feminist standpoint: Developing the ground for a specifically feminist historical materialism." Reprinted in *The second wave: A reader in feminist theory.* Ed. L. Nicholson. New York: Routledge.

Hays, S. (1996). *The cultural contradictions of motherhood.* New Haven, CT: Yale University Press.

Holy Bible, New International Version. (1973, 1978, 1984). Grand Rapids, MI: Zondervan.

Johnson, E. (1997). *She who is: The mystery of God in feminist theological discourse.* New York: Crossroad Publishing.

Leclerc, D. (2001). *Singleness of heart: Gender, sin and holiness in historical perspective.* Lanham, MD: Rowman and Littlefield.

Morrison, T. (1987). *Beloved.* New York: Plume.

Peskowitz, M. (2005). *The truth behind the mommy wars.* Emeryville, CA: Seal Press.

Rich, A. (1976). *Of woman born: Motherhood as experience and institution.* New York: W. W. Norton & Company.

Rubio, J. H. (2003). *A Christian theology of marriage and family*. New York: Paulist Press.

Ruddick, S. (1980). "Maternal thinking," *Feminist studies* 6.2; reprinted in *Feminist social thought: A reader*. Ed. D. T. Meyers, New York: Routledge, 1997.

Seyersted, P. (1994). "Kate Chopin and the American realists." *Kate Chopin: The awakening*. Ed. M. Culley. New York: W. W. Norton & Company.

CHAPTER FOUR

In Search of Bodily Perspective: A Study of Simone de Beauvoir and Luce Irigaray

ELIZABETH POWELL

To be a feminist today is to be part of a contentious and creative legacy. As feminist thinkers and writers, it is important that we recognize the women who have gone before us, who have enabled our work and practice. To understand them will be, to a great extent, to understand ourselves. Simone de Beauvoir and Luce Irigaray are two French feminist theorists who have deeply shaped my feminist questioning and living even though I am half-a-world away geographically and perhaps even further removed culturally and in matters of faith. What is more, the two are themselves often understood as representing philosophical and political perspectives that are opposite one another. Despite this, my common affection for both is neither accident nor contradiction, for all three of us share passionate concern for one matter in particular: the establishment of woman's subjectivity.

Beauvoir first expresses the problem involved in this process in her introduction to *The Second Sex*. She writes,

In the midst of an abstract discussion it is vexing to hear a man say: "You think thus and so because you are a woman"; but I know that my only defense is to reply: "I think thus and so because it is true," thereby removing my subjective self from the argument. It would be out of the question to retort: "And you think the contrary because you are a man," for it is understood that the fact of being a man is no peculiarity. (xxi)

The problem here is how women may hold on to their embodied subjective self and still be accorded speaking status in a world where the masculine defines what it is to be a subjective self. In other words, how might women speak as subjects in themselves, rather than only as the Other to man? These questions lead me to the more specific question of whether and/or how women may accord significance to their sexed embodiment in relation to their struggle to attain recognition as human beings. This question forms a crucial topic of feminist theory: how are we to best think about the body as it relates to the feminist concern for the flourishing of women's subjectivity? The question is a contentious one for feminist theory because it has so often been on the basis of the body that women's exploitation has been justified (Grosz, *Volatile* 14). Despite the tension, this question will be my central concern as I engage with the work of Beauvoir and Irigaray, for I believe it elucidates feminist struggles to establish and support women's subjectivities.

Typically, Anglo-American feminism has offered two options for thinking through this question of sexed embodiment and its political significance, namely, gender-construction and essentialism. In the former, the body (sex) is raw material on which socially constructed mores (gender) inscribe themselves. Social change is achieved through challenging patriarchal determinations of women's femininity. In essentialism, however, it is contended that the female body carries meaning in and of itself, which is the ground for women's identity and also potentially for women's solidarity as a group. This position typically results in a separatist politics in which women find liberation through identification with a female culture that is distinct from and independent of male culture. Beauvoir has often been identified as representative of the gender-construction position and Irigaray as emblematic of the essentialist position. However, it is important for us to reconsider Beauvoirian and Irigarayan perspectives on the body in terms other than those set by these categories and their surrounding debates. The insights uncovered offer alternatives for conceiving the relation of the body and woman's subjectivity beyond those prominent in Anglo-American feminism, and may also provide more nuanced and politically effective strategies. As such, they are invaluable resources of the feminist legacy from which we may learn as we develop our own bodily perspectives.

I first describe in more detail the interpretations of Beauvoir and Irigaray that have been used to construct or support gender-construction and essentialism as opposing feminist positions concerning the body. The main purpose of this description will be to point out the difficulties and problems inherent in each position. Then I turn to explore readings of Beauvoir and Irigaray that challenge these more accepted interpretations in hopes that our engagement with them will expand and enrich our thinking about the significance of all humans' sexed embodiment. Finally, I explore bodily perspective through my own reflections as a Christian woman.

Beauvoir and Gender-Construction

Beauvoir's[1] most recognized contribution to thinking about the body as it relates to the feminist concern for the flourishing of women's subjectivity is her powerful articulation of the sex-gender distinction, stemming from her poignant statement that "one is not born, but rather one becomes, a woman" (301). The distinction is yielded against a biological essentialism or determinism that is used to justify women's position as no more than man's Other. Woman as Other signifies that the masculine is the Absolute, standing for both the positive and the neutral of humankind, and against which woman is understood and defined. "The Other is posed as such by the One in defining himself as the One" (Beauvoir xxiv), and so she is excluded from a genuine subject position. According to Beauvoir, this state of oppression is justified and perpetuated by reference to an anatomical or social reality that supposedly determines woman's position as, for example, merely the helpmate of man, or worse his inferior. Beauvoir's decisive critique of these naturalistic explanations is that they are merely cultural creations and, as such, changeable. In comparing women's oppression with that of African Americans, she writes,

> In both cases, the dominant class bases its argument on a state of affairs that it has itself created. As George Bernard Shaw puts it, in substance, "The American white relegates the black to the rank of shoeshine boy; and he concludes from this that the black is good for nothing but shining shoes." This vicious circle is met with in all analogous circumstances; when an individual (or a group of individuals) is kept in a situation of inferiority, the fact is that he *is* inferior. (xxx)

Beauvoir challenges this naturalism by interrogating the meaning of the verb "is" as "to have become" rather than as "to be." Thus, her dictum that "one is not born, but rather becomes, a woman" means that there is nothing innate about woman that determines her to be Other, but that her position is a result of cultural processes. This analysis incited women to work for "equality in the belief that sex did not determine their destinies, gender did—and since gender was a social construct, it was also capable of change" (Chanter 32). In this paradigm, then, "the difference between women as biologically sexed and women as acculturated social beings" is emphasized and used as a politically strategic mode to break a cycle of justifications for the oppression of women (Chanter 49).

Beauvoir does not use the terminology "sex-gender distinction" to express these ideas in *The Second Sex*, but rather employs the existentialist vocabulary of transcendence and immanence. Her battle against essentialism was fueled primarily by her commitment to the existentialist belief that existence precedes essence, that is, that meanings are not written on the surface of the world (including bodies) but must be given meaning by human consciousness. Transcendence signifies this meaning-giving activity, which is the inescapable responsibility of every human being. In Beauvoir's words, "Every individual concerned to justify his existence feels that his existence involves an undefined need to transcend himself, to engage in freely chosen projects" (xxx). Immanence, on the other hand, is the natural, given, static world of objects to which humans accord meaning. As Beauvoir declares,

> There is no justification for present existence other than its expansion into an indefinitely open future. Every time transcendence falls back into immanence, stagnation, there is a degradation of existence into the "*en-soi*"—the brutish life of subjection to given conditions—and of liberty into constraint and contingence. (xxxv)

This falling "back into immanence" has moral connotations: "This downfall represents a moral fault if the subject consents to it; if it is inflicted upon him, it spells frustration and oppression. In both cases it is an absolute evil" (xxxv).

Beauvoir applies this existential ethic of freedom to formulate the argument that women's oppression consists in society's refusal to allow them to establish their subjectivity through the free exercise of their transcendence. They have instead been confined to the immanent spheres, primarily represented for her by confinement to the home or to the role of motherhood. The predicament of women in patriarchal cultures is that they nonetheless cannot renounce the need to justify their existence (as this need is common to all human beings). Beauvoir gives many examples of women's efforts to justify their existence under these conditions. She describes women who alienate themselves in a narcissistic love of self, believing they can find meaning through an emphasis on physical beauty or charm. Other women may seek justification for their lives through their attachments to others, whether, husband, lover, child, or even God. In these relationships, the other's acts of transcendence are the means for the woman's attainment of freedom through the alienation of herself in the other. These efforts however are always insufficient, for they necessitate a reduction of subjectivity to the sphere of immanence and preclude woman's individual responsibility to create meaningful projects in the world.

The purported immoral situation of femininity must be overcome because it denies women genuine subjectivity and the concomitant possibility of transforming society. For Beauvoir, women will establish authentic subjectivity only through the free exercise of their transcendence. As she writes,

> When at last it will be possible for every human being to set his pride beyond the sexual differentiation, in the difficult glory of his free existence, then only will woman be able to identify her history, her problems, her doubts, her hopes, with those of humanity; then only will she be able to seek in her life and her works to reveal the whole of reality and not merely her personal self. As long as she still has to struggle to become a human being, she cannot become a creator. (714)

By taking responsibility for her self and for the world by engaging in freely chosen projects, woman will be liberated and become part of the "real" world of transcendence.

The gains women have made toward establishing their subjectivity through the use of the sex-gender distinction can hardly be overestimated. However, there is a need for an evaluation of the distinction according to how well it conceives of women's embodied subjectivity. From this perspective, the body itself is understood to be ahistorical and fixed while gender is cultural, historical, and changeable; all attention is thus focused on changing cultural constructions of gender. This focus makes the body itself irrelevant to political transformation. Elizabeth Grosz explains:

> The mind is regarded as a social, cultural, and historical object, a product of ideology, while the body remains naturalistic and

precultural; bodies provide the base, the raw materials for the
inculcation of and interpellation into ideology but are merely
media of communication rather than the object of focus of ideological production/reproduction. Political struggles are thus
directed toward neutralization of the sexually specific body. . . . So
while male and female bodies remain untouched by and irrelevant
to such programs, the associated gender traits of masculinity and
femininity would, ideally, be transformed and equalized through a
transformation in ideology. (*Volatile* 17)

There are several significant weaknesses with this "naturalistic and precultural" configuration of the body. First, the sex/gender dichotomy is too
simplistic an account of human subjectivity, relying as it does on
mind/body dualism. One may ask whether the body is as fixed as this
theory proposes. Are not interactions between the body and the mind
much more complex, deep, and nuanced? Does the body's role in subjectivity not exceed that of a *tabula rasa*, or blank slate, on which things
may be written and then erased again? (*Volatile* 18) To embrace this fundamental dichotomy is to risk embracing a pronouncement of patriarchal
discourse that fosters alienation between mind and body and privileges
the mind as that which controls the body. This is especially dangerous
given that patriarchy has traditionally aligned woman (and/or the feminine) with the body and man (and/or masculinity) with the mind.

The sex-gender distinction is also insufficient as it does not move us
beyond the frustration Beauvoir touched on when recounting her
"vexing" theoretical discussions with a man. Recall that she writes of a
situation in which her voice is dismissed on the grounds of her sex, and she
can only gain respect for her voice by claiming an objective, de-sexed
stance. Her sexed embodiment must be made irrelevant to her speaking
status. Yet surely our bodies are a crucial part of what it means to be
a subject. According to the above interpretation, Beauvoir does not provide women any way out of this conundrum. Instead, the need to overcome patriarchy's negative uses of the female body forms a position that
idealizes an embodied subjectivity in which sexed differences are of no
significance. Women are to aspire to a neutral subject position, and so
may not accord significance to their sexed embodiment in their struggle
to attain recognition as human beings.

Beauvoir's own definition of patriarchal man as the Absolute Subject
controlling both the positive and neutral poles of what counts as being
human, however, ought to raise concern about this admonition for
women to achieve a neutral subject position. Women might too hastily

adopt an illusory neutral position that is, in fact, masculine. In this case, women are to not only overcome their femininity, but are to become like men. Thus, women's emancipation would not necessarily result in a transformation of patriarchal values, but may merely be the adoption of them by women. Another negative outcome of women's equality based only on their sameness to men is that it is likely to be a weak platform for representation of women's specific needs. It becomes very difficult, for example, for the significance of women's sexed differences to be represented in the public sphere of law on such issues as surrogate rights or maternity leave.[2]

These weaknesses are paralleled and amplified in Beauvoir's discussion of transcendence and immanence. According to this reading of Beauvoir, women are not to reject or confuse the metaphysical opposi- tions of patriarchal philosophy (i.e., transcendence/immanence), but are to take up a position in relation to the positive term (i.e., transcendence) (Hollywood 134). Left in place is an equation of subjectivity with transcendence, while immanence is that which is to be overcome and left behind in women's emancipation. Not only does this denigrate the body, it also does not take into account the possibility that it is often an individual's bodily potential or communal situatedness that enables tran- scendence or through which transcendence is genuinely experienced. Instead, women's biological specificity is only a limiting factor for the achievement of freedom, which means that liberation efforts are focused on finding ways to help reduce "bodily interference," such as through use of birth control (Grosz, *Volatile* 15–16). While such scientific advancements have proved revolutionary for women, they provide only superficial answers to those who are seeking perspectives that may transform their relation to their body rather than deny or ignore it.

Irigaray and Essentialism

If the body is downplayed in this reading of Beauvoir's philosophy, it is made to carry all the weight of women's subjectivity according to many interpretations in the Anglo-American feminist theory of Luce Irigaray. These interpretations of Irigaray were first formed during the early stages of the translation of her work into English during the 1980s. Significantly, at this time, the Anglo-American scene was dominated by the essence/anti-essence debates, fueled by reaction against a strong cur- rent of feminism that had formed during the 1960s and 1970s. Glorifying the feminine and seeking women's separatism from male-dominated society, this strand of feminism was itself a reaction to the strong current of anti-essentialism and gender-construction formed during the 1940s and 1950s and largely influenced by Beauvoir's *The Second Sex*. Irigaray's work in this context was identified as representative of essentialist feminists, who sought to distance themselves from their predecessors because they believed that it required women to aspire to a masculine ideal in order to be liberated (Chanter 32–34).

Essence is a philosophical term meaning that by virtue of which a thing is what it is, in contrast to an attribute, which is a contingent characteristic of an object. Irigaray is an essentialist in that she claims there is an unchanging and universal substance without which women would not exist as women. Though it has gone unrecognized and repressed by society, this essence may be located in the body of women. Thus, "the potential existence of woman . . . depends on the discovery of her essence, which lies in the specificity of her body" (Schor, "Previous Engagements" 6). Until the bodily essence of woman is recognized in society, women will continue to be defined only in relation to the male model of subjectivity. Whether identical, opposite, or complement to man, it is man who determines the position of woman (Grosz, *Sexual* 105). There is no room for woman to define herself autonomously. As we saw in Beauvoir's astute analyses of oppression, in a society where the masculine defines human subjectivity, a woman has only two choices: to be either masculine identified, or to subordinate herself to man and allow her subjectivity to be mediated through him.

Elizabeth Grosz explains the problem of women's lack of autonomous identity through use of an example from the philosophical discourse, namely, the law of the logic of identity. The logic of identity states that A is not B. A defines B only in terms of itself, such that B is more accurately represented as $-A$ (not A). There is one term, A, and the other term is its negative $(-A)$. Rather than representing a reciprocal relation between two autonomous, different things (represented by A and B), the relation does not actually allow difference because one term controls the other (*Sexual* 106). This logic is also present in the binary oppositions that structure much of Western thinking, such as day/night; rational/irrational; man/woman. These relations are better stated as day/not day; man/not man, and so on. Thus we see how "a phallic economy [is] based on sameness, oneness or identity with the masculine subject—an 'a priori' of the same' " (106). A "law of the one" structures patriarchal culture.

Irigaray gives this culture ruled by "law of the one" a name: phallocentrism. "Phallocentrism is the use of one model of subjectivity, the male, by which all others are positively or negatively defined" (Grosz, *Sexual* 105). The term connects the male sexed body to patriarchal culture. "Phallus" signifies the male organ, the penis, and phallocentrism signifies a culture or discourse that takes the phallus as its defining term; the phallus is then the basis for a male culture, analyzed by Irigaray as privileging singularity, unity or oneness, rationality, and the visible or specularisable. According to this reading then, Irigaray differs from Beauvoir by establishing a necessary connection between (male) body and (patriarchal) culture.

In phallocentric culture, women's sexuality can only be defined in its relation to the male body. Freud, for example, produced a description of girls and women as only either lacking a penis or having a little penis (the clitoris) (Grosz, *Sexual* 104–105). Irigaray opposes this representation of women's sexuality by asserting that women's subjectivity must be established on the basis of female bodies, rather than on male bodies. She posits an alternative description of women's sexuality as "two lips": "Woman 'touches herself' all the time, and moreover no one can forbid her to do so, for her genitals are formed of two lips in continuous contact. Thus, within herself, she is already two—but not divisible into one(s)—that caress each other" (*This Sex* 24). Irigaray reverses the negative statement that woman is not one (or phallic) to mean that she is therefore more than one. Consequently, women's two lips present many truths about women's subjectivity that distinguish her from men's. Unlike male subjectivity that privileges oneness or unity, the visible, and the specularisable (according to the model of the phallus), woman privileges multiplicity, ambiguity, fluidity, and the touch (according to the model of the two lips). Irigaray also writes of women's speech as fluid as opposed to the solidity and rationality of male discourse: "And yet that woman-thing speaks. But not 'like,' not 'the *same*', not 'identical with itself' nor to any x, etc. . . . It speaks 'fluid' " (*This Sex* 111). Woman's speech as fluid is drawn from the "fluidity" characterizing her anatomy, such as amniotic fluids of the womb. Irigaray's own poetic style is exemplary of this kind of speaking as woman.

Irigaray uses the female body to form a feminism that forcefully combats misogyny by establishing women's autonomous subjectivity:

Speak, all the same. It's our good fortune that your language isn't formed of a single thread, a single strand or pattern. It comes from everywhere at once. You touch me all over at the same time. In all senses. Why only one song, one speech, one text at a time? To seduce, to satisfy, to fill one of my "holes"? With you, I don't have any. We are not lack, voids awaiting sustenance, plenitude, fulfillment from the other. By our lips we are women. (*This Sex* 209–210)

Women's sexual body has two lips, and thus exceeds the oneness of the phallus—instead of the law of the one there is the law of the two.

The essentialist position relating the body and women's subjectivity has served to consolidate women's solidarity and thus helped gain strength for the women's movement; it provides ground for women's commonality and their specific identity apart from those identities prescribed for them within a patriarchal culture. However, the position's weaknesses outweigh these strengths in that they ultimately inhibit more than they further the establishment of women's subjectivity. There are many critiques of essentialism (Schor, "This Essentialism" 60–62); I will outline the two most relevant here.

The most prominent reason for rejecting essentialism comes from the gender-constructionist camp outlined in the previous discussion of Beauvoir. For constructionists, femininity is a cultural construct and liberation is achieved through breaking down cultural definitions of femininity that justify and perpetuate women's oppression. Essentialists do no more than reinstate these misogynist constructions.

By promoting an essential difference of woman grounded in the body . . . essentialism plays straight into the hands of the patriarchal order, which has traditionally invoked anatomical and physiological differences to legitimate the sociopolitical disempowerment of women. (Schor, "This Essentialism" 60)

By endorsing these differences as essential rather than as social constructs that are to be dismantled, essentialists become "the brakes on the wheel of progress" (Schor, "The Essentialism" 61).

Another strong critique is the feminist concern for the representation of the differences among women. In the 1980s, feminists were strongly critiqued by women who found themselves excluded by the women's movement, particularly black, Hispanic, poor, and lesbian women. Their voices and actions caused feminism to take stock of its own biases and exclusionary acts. The need for feminism to find ways to allow recognition of the multiple and significant differences among women has thus become tantamount to the feminist struggle. Essentialism is negative because it erases and covers over these differences by the all-encompassing concept Woman: "By its majestic singularity Woman conspires in the denial of the very real lived differences—sexual, ethnic, racial, national, cultural, economic, generational—that divide women from each other and from themselves" (Schor, "This Essentialism" 62). Essentialism is a dangerous form of universalism that sustains blindness to alterity and threatens to silence the voices and bodies of women who are only beginning to be heard.

These two interpretations of Beauvoir and Irigaray, aligning with the Anglo-American options of constructivism or essentialism, have come up short in a number of respects as paradigms for thinking about the significance of sexed embodiment in women's liberatory struggles. The sex-gender distinction, as the grid used to interpret Beauvoir's work on transcendence and immanence, is based on a fundamental indifference to the body that ultimately results in the denigration of women's sexed embodiment. The essentialist camp, in bringing the body back into feminist discussions, reifies it and so becomes a naive and ultimately destructive universalism. The dominant responses to our question, how might we best think about the body as it relates to the feminist concern for the flourishing of women's subjectivity, are insufficient as they answer either with indifference to or the reification of the body.

Hope for a way out of this impasse can be drawn from alternative readings of these same two thinkers, Simone de Beauvoir and Luce Irigaray. As our horizon of Anglo-American feminism has changed, so too have we come to engage with the French feminist horizon differently. The meeting of these two horizons throughout the last few decades has continued to produce multiple and, in some cases, better understandings of these French feminists. The alternative interpretations of Beauvoir and Irigaray, which I will outline below, are examples of these new productions that bring us closer to an adequate engagement with the significance of our sexed embodiment.[3]

Beauvoir Reinterpreted

As critiques of the sex-gender distinction came to gain more and more weight, many theorists rejected Simone de Beauvoir's work as a place to begin thinking through feminist concerns of the body. Others, however, were motivated to take a second look at *The Second Sex*. A revival of Beauvoir scholarship began in the 1990s with a focus on her philosophical influences.[4] Hitherto, she had solely been read as applying Sartrean existentialism to an analysis of women's oppression.[5] New work questions this assumption of the Sartre-Beauvoir relationship and has uncovered a

much richer and more nuanced account of the originality of her thinking and of the many philosophers from which she drew. On the basis of
these new resources for interpreting Beauvoir, I summarize a different
understanding of the body in relation to women's emancipation in *The
Second Sex.*

The crucial problem with past appropriations of Beauvoir is that they
relied too heavily on the discourse of the sex-gender distinction. Reading
Beauvoir through the lens of this distinction conceals her commitment to
the phenomenological concept of the lived body. This occurs because the
sex-gender distinction organizes the relation of the mind and body
according to a subject/object dichotomy that is exactly what Beauvoir's
notion of the lived body intends to transgress. As described above, the
sex-gender distinction leaves the body (sex) in the position of the object,
that is, as fixed, stable, and unchangeable. Humans work in the realm of
culture to change society's gender coding of sexed bodies; the split
between culture and body, however, remains in place where culture
alone is the sphere of human activity. The concept of the lived body,
though, challenges this Cartesian dualism and thereby offers many new
insights for thinking the body. Unpacking this concept will require
definition of a few crucial terms of Beauvoir's philosophy.

First is Beauvoir's definition of situation. Typically, we use the word
"situation" to signify that which we subjects find ourselves in (namely,
the world or the realm of objects). Beauvoir's usage is more complex.
Her notion of situation overcomes this implicit subject/object
dichotomy by defining a structural relationship between the two (Moi 65).
For Beauvoir, situation is

> comprised of both my surroundings *and* my freedom or projects. . . .
> If I want to climb a crag, my situation is my project as it exists in the
> encounter with the brute facticity of the crag. In this view, the crag
> alone is not a situation. My situation is not *outside* me, it does not
> relate to me as an object to a subject; it is a synthesis of facticity and
> freedom. If your project is to climb, and my project is to enjoy the
> mountain views, then the very same crag would present itself to you
> as being easy or difficult to scale, and to me as "imposing" or "unre-
> markable." Faced with the same crag, our situations would be differ-
> ent because our projects are different. We are always in a situation,
> but the situation is always part of us. (Moi 63, 65)

Seen this way, facts gain their meaning from me and thus will gain
different meanings according to the different projects I intend; on the

other hand, these facts similarly shape my projects and possibilities for action in the world.

When Beauvoir considers the body with the help of this understanding of situation, she finds that the body is not only *in* a situation, but is itself a situation: "The body is not a thing, it is a *situation*: it is our grasp on the world and a sketch of our projects" (Beauvoir 34). To say that the body is *in* a situation signifies the familiar idea that social and cultural contexts give the body meaning. While Beauvoir agrees with this statement, her declaration that the body is a situation pushes conceptually beyond this. First, it acknowledges biology itself as being intimately bound up with human existence. Each person's body is unique, and these differences may invite each person to experience the world differently. A person's size, age, ethnicity, ability, and so on may significantly shape his or her being-in-the-world in subtle or not so subtle ways. For example, males are able to father many children without doing themselves physical harm; a female, however, risks much bodily wellness if she gives birth to even ten children (Moi 62). Beauvoir asserts that

> these biological considerations are extremely important. In the history of woman they play a part of the first rank and constitute an essential element in her situation. . . . For, the body being the instrument of our grasp upon the world, the world is bound to seem a very different thing when apprehended in one manner or another. (Beauvoir 32)

We are body-subjects—the body is not a separate reality but the horizon of all our activities. The objective shape and functioning of our body is integrally connected then with who we are and what we do.

On the other hand, body as situation means that these biological facts cannot alone provide meaning for human existence. She writes, "It has been said that the human species is antinatural, a statement that is hardly exact, since man cannot deny facts; but he establishes their truth by the way in which he deals with them" (Beauvoir 34–35). And again, "it is not the body-object described by biologists that actually exists, but the body as lived in and by the subject. . . . It is not nature that defines woman; it is she who defines herself by dealing with nature on her own account in her emotional life" (Beauvoir 38). Therefore, a woman's biology or anatomy is an essential factor comprising woman's situation, though it is not her destiny. There is a myriad of ways a woman may live her bodily potential, depending on her projects, lived experience, and other economic and social situations (Moi 66). By conceiving of the body as not only in a situation, but also as a situation, Beauvoir is able to find a way of thinking the body that avoids biological essentialism and indifference to the sexed body.[6]

Another important term for fleshing out the meaning of the lived body is lived experience. One's past, present, and projected future are integrally related in one's lived experience. Lived experience may be gathered up, or sedimented, in one's body in a way that accords a kind of body-knowledge, a process of sedimentation in which "each of us develops a habitual way of patterning existence . . . and the character of this patterning depends on the social and institutional setting in which our embodiment, and hence our world, is constituted" (Diprose 91). The sedimentation of lived experience forms our "carnal style," and so becomes a part of one's bodily situation (Moi 63). Individuals may have different "bodily tolerances" to certain situations. Women who have experienced sexual abuse in their past history, for example, may experience involuntary somatic flashbacks when placed in similar situations. The idea of sedimentation thus accounts for a kind of "body-knowledge" rooted in one's lived experience.

Understanding Beauvoir's concept of the lived body allows us to hear a different voice relating the transcendent and immanent spheres of human existence in her analysis of women's oppression. Human subjectivity is ambiguous in that it is both transcendent *and* immanent; transcendence only exists *through* immanence, while our immanence shapes, whether enabling or limiting, our transcendence (Cataldi 89). Beauvoir describes the "bad faith" of patriarchal man as forgetting that "man too is the plaything of his hormones" (Beauvoir 728). By man's failure to recognize his own bodily immanence, woman becomes figured as "the repository" for them (Hollywood 139). In Beauvoir's words,

> Now what peculiarly signalizes the situation of woman is that she—
> a free and autonomous being like all human creatures—nevertheless
> finds herself living in a world where men compel her to assume the
> status of the Other. They propose to stabilize her as object and
> to doom her to immanence since her transcendence is to be
> overshadowed and forever transcended by another ego (conscience)
> which is essential and sovereign. (Beauvoir xxxv)

Much of the remainder of *The Second Sex* consists of Beauvoir's descriptions of women's lived experience within this situation of repressed transcendence. These descriptions are accounts of women who have taken up in their bodily existence the limitations and prejudices of patriarchal society. Internalized and sedimented beliefs are recounted as distortions of women's ambiguous existence in which they need to recover the transcendent aspect of their bodily being (Cataldi 105). Beauvoir, however, imagines a society in which both male and female are able to live the ambiguity of their existence, a society where it is recognized that "man also is flesh for woman; and woman is not merely a carnal object; and the flesh is clothed in special significance for each person and in each experience" (Beauvoir 255).

Irigaray Reinterpreted

Beauvoir is an existentialist philosopher, and so she is very focused on the individual, albeit the individual in situation. She also focuses on humans as beings of action, so that the transformation of the world and the shaping of the self are effected primarily through the human activity of taking up meaning-giving projects. Irigaray's unique contribution to our question of how are we to best think the body stems from her concern with humans as fundamentally linguistic beings. She helps us to see how our experience of the body is formed by language, and how language about the body influences discourses as abstract as philosophy. Because of the intimacy of language in the formation of our subjectivities, Irigaray hopes to effect an opening up of phallocentric discourses through the creation of new "body languages" wherein new subjectivities will be established. How might I accord significance to my body in my struggle to attain subjectivity? Irigaray will answer: by creating a symbolic home for ourselves that does not depend on the denigration or invisibility of the female body. In political terms, Irigaray thinks that creating greater equal opportunity for the sexes is not enough on its own for the establishment of women's subjectivity; it must be accompanied by transformations in the linguistic sphere.[7]

We must be able to move beyond the essentialist reading given in the first interpretation of Irigaray if we are to hear this other "bodily perspective." As mentioned before, the timing of Irigaray's reception was significant for the Anglo-American reading of her. Arguably, the timing was also unfortunate in that identifying Irigaray with essentialism meant her reception was really more of a rejection, for Anglo-American academia has historically been "anti-essentialist." In the later 1980s, however, several seminal secondary sources on Irigaray were published by scholars that challenged the appropriation of Irigaray in terms of the essence/anti-essence debate.[8] These readings take a closer look at Irigaray's philosophical and cultural context and reveal that her work cannot be fitted so easily into the categories of essentialism. At the same time, our context was also changing. The essence/anti-essence debates were ending not with one side as victor over the other, but with a questioning of the dichotomy itself; this changing context, in conjunction with the new interpretations of her work, is redefining our engagement with Irigaray (Chanter 31–39).[9]

Of primary importance is to distinguish Irigaray's definition of sexual difference from an essentialist definition of sexual difference. The latter, explained previously, reifies notions of femininity that have been used to keep women oppressed for ages; it valorizes femininity and effects a reversal of the hierarchy of oppression. In contrast, Irigaray, at her best, argues not for a respect for an identifiable essence of sexual difference, but a respect for the *possibility* of sexual difference (Deutscher 17). That is, her concern is not to define the content of sexual difference, but to point out that the possibility that men and women may have genuinely different subjectivities has never been allowed in Western discourse.[10] The disavowal of this possibility is termed "sexual indifference," meaning "a lack of interest in potential differentiation among men and women. Sexual indifference supposes from the outset the sexual neutrality of subjects with regard to language, habits, needs, responsibilities, embodiment, or experiences" (Deutscher 26). This sexual indifference is supported by the structure of Western discourse as a logic of the one. Without the disruption of this logic, women's accession to subjectivity is dependent on their likeness or sameness to men. Consequently, Irigaray is concerned with the possibility of a "logic of the two" that is behind her emphasis on sexual difference.

The genuine difference creating the logic of the two means the existence of two subject positions in which one pole is not reduced to the image of the other, whether as opposite, complement or same (Grosz, *Sexual* 344).[11] In the words of Margaret Whitford, "We still need woman, but that woman has not yet arrived. Essence is not a given, behind us, but a collective creation, ahead of us, a horizon" (139). In other words, Irigaray does not ask us to begin with the belief that there are certain, essential differences between men and women, but asks us to engage with her in the question of whether something is wrong with the reluctance to consider the question of sexual difference at all. While leaving open the question of the content of sexual difference, her questioning points to the often unnoticed or invisible cultural limits that shape our horizons (Deutscher 51). It is intended to incite women (and men) to work toward developing new possibilities for images and symbols that allow for genuine difference between human beings.

A concern with sexual difference raises a focus on embodiment as sexed, which is often the cause of alarm in feminist theory. Irigaray, however, has made a strong argument for the importance of bringing the sexed body back into feminist work before too quickly assuming we have surpassed its significance, and she is able to bring the sexed body back into play without essentializing it (Chanter 46).

Of primary importance for hearing Irigaray's writing on the body anew is to understand the connection she makes between bodies and language. Irigaray is poststructuralist in her understanding of language. She does not believe humans have access to reality outside of the medium of language; there is no prediscursive reality for human consciousness.[12] Our experience of things is always already mediated through our language. Language becomes highly significant for human existence in this view, for words do not merely re-present objects outside of us. Rather, words constitute the world for us.

The tie between language and the body for Irigaray is also explainable in Lacanian terms. For Lacan as for Irigaray, human subjectivity is formed by the symbolic order (Grosz, *Sexual* 104), which is "the network of signifying systems in which we live—most crucially language, but also human practices and social institutions in so far as they carry meaning" (Hollywood 157). For Irigaray, the symbolic order is shaped, at least in part, by the imaginary order. Briefly stated, the concept of the imaginary order suggests that one's understanding of one's body is not objective, but always involves a degree of imagination that is influenced by one's identification with images beyond one's self. This includes "identifications with oneself in an anticipated future which has not yet been realized"; it also recognizes that these images are not produced apart from culture, but are informed by culture and language (i.e., the symbolic order) (Whitford 90). A person's body image is culturally influenced, while body images likewise shape culture.

Irigaray critiques Western culture and discourses for assuming a male imaginary, and for assuming that it is unchangeable. She then disrupts this imaginary by showing it is not necessary and seeks to unsettle it by bringing to the surface a feminine imaginary that the masculine imaginary excludes or represses. Therefore, Irigaray is not referring to a direct and unmediated relation to the body, but to an imaginary and symbolic representation of the body (Whitford 70). Thus, the concept of the imaginary allows Irigaray to recognize a relationship between bodies and language without having to posit a necessary tie between them. Sex (body) is not irrelevant to the formation of gender, or culture and language, but their relationship is also not static or essential (Whitford 62–70).

When Irigaray "writes" or "speaks" the body, she is offering new and surprising descriptions of the female body in the hopes that this will effect a change in women's embodied experience. In phallocentric cultures, the body is written along these lines:

> Whether male or female, the human body is . . . already coded, placed in a social network, and given meaning in and by culture, the male being constituted as virile or phallic, the female as passive or castrated. These are not the result of biology, but of the *social and psychical meaning of the body*. (Grosz, *Sexual* 111)

Irigaray's work is not solely in the realm of the natural or anatomical, but always in the realm of the social, which is also always lingual. The term morphology is thus more appropriate than anatomy for describing Irigaray's site of concern for sexed embodiment. She is seeking to provide an alternative feminine morphology in order to open up the current symbolic order. This new symbolic order will hopefully be able to "house" women's subjectivities and support their flourishing.

Irigaray's recognition of the significance of the female body is based on this complex and insightful understanding of the dynamic interplay between bodies and language or culture. Her creative work proceeds to uncover and construct images that displace patriarchal circumscriptions of female identity. However, she recognizes that a change in the symbolic order cannot be effected by fiat (Whitford 70). Irigaray also recognizes that one can never step entirely outside of that which one wishes to critique, so she adopts strategic movements that always work from within the discourses she is seeking to unsettle. She adopts ways of reading texts in which the explicit assumptions of a text are challenged through use of the text's own " 'repressed' or disavowed or subtext" (Grosz, "The Hetero" 337).

One powerful and controversial strategy Irigaray often adopts for breaking open phallocentric texts is mimicry.[13] She writes that "women have always been good mimics," that is, they have often been put in the position of parroting patriarchal discourse—fine examples are Beauvoir's descriptions of women's lived experience in *The Second Sex*. As a feminist, Irigaray does not choose to abandon her feminine position as mimic in order to move beyond it. Rather, she adopts mimicry in her own way in order to expose and subvert the negative views she parrots. The key to Irigaray's parroting of traditional feminine positions and imagery is that she parrots unfaithfully.

This strategy is part of the process for creating new symbolic orders, not the end goal. Irigaray herself explains:

There is, in an initial phase, perhaps only one "path," the one historically assigned to the feminine: that of *mimicry*. One must assume the feminine role deliberately. Which means already to convert a form of subordination into an affirmation, and thus to begin to thwart it. . . . To play with mimesis is thus, for a woman, to try to recover the place of her exploitation by discourse, without allowing herself to be simply reduced to it. (*This Sex* 76)

One way this path of mimicry works is by placing positive value on a feminine trait to such an extent as to render it exorbitant—a kind of defiance through excess (Deutscher 49). Elizabeth Grosz illustrates this defiance toward cultural expectations through a more serious example of the bodies of women who are anorexic. According to some understandings of anorexia, a girl takes on the cultural admonitions to be thin to such an extreme degree that it renders the cultural expectation of "thinness" exorbitant. This act, however, may be a form of resistance rather than acquiescence because the effect is to "comply to such a degree that the end result is the opposite of compliance: it unsettles the system by throwing back to it what it cannot accept about its own operations" (Grosz, *Sexual* 135). While anorexia can be understood as mimicry, it is most certainly a destructive form of it. Irigaray's mimicry is conscious and meant to transform these acts of self-destructive mimicry. She does not merely abandon the feminine as coded in patriarchy and mimicked in women's bodies, but instead uses it as a tool for undoing its patriarchal coding. In a revolutionary move, she seeks a transvaluation of the feminine, rather than its abandonment.

Irigaray's startlingly different depictions of the female body are not chosen ad hoc, but are productions from these strategic readings of specific texts. Further, they must be understood as analogies and so limited in their usefulness. She does not intend for them to be taken up as new master terms with an "absolute claim for their ontological status" (Burke 44). Irigaray herself states thus:

In other words, the issue is not one of elaborating a new theory of which woman would be the *subject* or the *object*, but of jamming the theoretical machinery itself, of suspending its pretension to the production of a truth and of meaning that are excessively univocal. (*This Sex* 77)

The new analogy created cannot take up a better, higher, or truer position than that which it deconstructs, for this would be to duplicate the same logic of the system which she is intending to critique, namely Western metaphysics as "a logic of meaning as an unequivocal structure of mastery" (Weed 83). Rather, these terms are intended to undo phallocentric discourses that define women only as man's other and also to create a space for women to speak in autonomous terms (Grosz, *Sexual* 109). The hoped-for symbolic order will then be a place where women may live with bodily, psychic, sexual, and emotional integrity.

A rather radical example of Irigaray's mimicry as a tool for interrogating the limits of our cultural horizons is found in her discussion of sexed rights in her *je, tu, nous: Toward a Culture of Difference.* Irigaray puts forth a seemingly absurd proposal for the basis of a new bill of rights that recognizes sexed differences: she proposes women's virginity as the basis of sexed rights. Women's virginity, however, is redefined as women's bodily or moral integrity. Traditionally, virginity is a sign of a woman's cleanliness, of whether she is a "used" commodity exchanged among men or a pure one. For Irigaray, virginity signifies women's inviolability, that is, their security from violation and profanation (Deutscher 50). This involves the spiritual, not just physical, sphere: "There's no doubt we are born virgins. But we also have to become virgins, to relieve our bodies and souls of cultural fetters. For me, becoming a virgin is synonymous with a woman's conquest of the spiritual" (Irigaray, *je, tu* 117). This meaning of virginity, created by a transvaluation of the feminine, is given status as the basis for women's right to human identity. Women, in other words, must have the right to protect their moral, spiritual, and physical inviolability, an autonomous identity status that will help protect against the use of female bodies as "cash-convertible" objects (e.g., commercial use of female images), for "girls need a positive identity to refer to as individual and social civil persons" (87).

Penelope Deutscher, in *The Politics of Impossible Difference,* helps explain the different effects this mimicry of women's virginity is intended to have (50–55). First, she argues that Irigaray's positive mimicry of virginity as the basis of sexed rights is intended to push the readers to raise the question of why a bill of rights based on a supposed neutral human subject is more valid than one based on sexed differences. Is it best that certain groups of people merely appropriate a bill of rights that they did not have any part in shaping? Will the assumed standard of equality be sufficient to embrace and represent the subjectivities of people who did not have a say in the process of defining the standard of equality? Further, is there "sufficient room for poetic reinvention and the construction of new imaginaries" in these processes of reform (Deutscher 51)? Irigaray asks us to question whether equality on the basis of difference might assure better representation of women's and other group's rights and needs specific to them. At least, she claims, efforts to gain equality ought to be accompanied by an interrogation of the assumed standard of equality.

Irigaray's mimicry of virginity has the hoped-for effect of reinscribing the meaning and value of women's bodies through a questioning of their representations in our cultural imaginary. In sum,

> many readers will find Irigaray's attempt to laud women's virginity regressive. But she asks what new meanings virginity could acquire. *Shouldn't the project of transforming, rather than reiterating, its meaning be our task?* Is it impossible for virginity to be refigured so that it no longer connotes the commodification of women for exchange between men? Is our culture premised on the exclusion of alternative connotations for women and femininity? (51)

This strategic interrogation of cultural limits is a potentially powerful one for the establishment and flourishing of women's subjectivities: it encourages women to imagine new ways of representing their femininity and their bodies; it hopes to enable women to love themselves as women, rather than merely as "like man"; and it also gives women a place to begin this reinvention of the cultural imaginary—from within their present cultures rather than from some impossible position outside. One of her most powerful admonitions to women is the following:

> It is crucial that we keep our bodies even as we bring them out of silence and servitude. Historically we are the guardians of the flesh. We should not give up that role, but identify it as our own, by inviting men not to make us into body for their benefit, not to make us into guarantees that their body exists. (*Sexes* 19)

Rather than try to leave behind alienating images of ourselves by reverting to the denial of our bodies' significance, we need to creatively reclaim what it means to be "guardians of the flesh."

Through this exploration of alternative interpretations of Beauvoir and Irigaray, a significant number of rich insights have been produced for helping us deal with the question of how to best think about embodiment in relation to the feminist concern for the flourishing of women's subjectivities. Our alternatives need not be restricted to essentialism or gender-construction, in which sexed embodiment is either reified or irrelevant.

Beauvoir's concept of body as situation and as in-situation takes into account the significance of women's sexed differences without making them determinants of women's subjectivity. Irigaray's concern for the imaginary and symbolic spheres of society teaches us to question more deeply culture's limited encoding of women's bodies in ways that often go unnoticed. She presents new strategies for working within the cultural imaginary in hopes of creating new symbolic orders in which women may speak legitimately *as women*.

Toward Christian Embodiments of Feminist Theory

There are many types of bodily suffering in human history. Chronic illness, poverty and lack of nourishment, and the violence of racism are some of these. In the human experience of bodily suffering, a common response is the search to separate one's self from the body. The body becomes identified with the disease or pain and the self often strives to amend a sense of integrity through a denial of the body as part of one's subjectivity. There is experienced at the core of the self an alienation from that which is most intimately one's own. The critiques of patriarchal ideology coming from feminist theory are responses to a specific, though often interrelated, kind of suffering in the female self. It is the kind of suffering produced when culture and community inform a woman that her self is less valuable in female form, that her body is more open to abuse and denigration because she is female. This suffering, whether experienced through physical violence or less explicit objectification, manipulation or exclusion, is a bodily suffering. As we have seen in this recounting of the recent history of feminist theory, the path toward an adequate response to these experiences is not an easy one to forge and we often reproduce that which we seek to change. However, there is a faithful resistance in feminist theory's ongoing search for bodily perspective. This resistance occurs in the very act of not giving up the fight for the bodied self, of continuing along in the journey with the conviction that we will find bodily integrity and wholeness as women. The power of this discourse resides for me in the discovery of the possibility of hope and renewal as stemming from the very places where so many have experienced the most intense suffering.

This search for bodily perspective that forms a crucial theme of the feminist legacy is one properly belonging to my Christian tradition as well. It is a Christian project to reclaim and set free this value as fundamental to the faith, namely, that women's whole selves reflect the image of God and that by working in cooperation with the healing and transforming power of Christ and the Spirit, women may become wholly human as a historical reality. From this perspective, the Christian feminist search for bodily integrity is not peripheral to the life of faith, but is central to the sanctifying work of the Spirit along the road of discipleship. There is not only a unity of concerns between feminist and Christian voices in this journey, but also a persistent and fruitful tension between them. Sustaining a dynamic dialogue between Christianity and feminism occurs when unique and distinct voices are not collapsed into one another. Preserving distinction when appropriate allows us to walk alongside those with whom we disagree, and it is this type of relation that the possibility of hearing a corrective voice or new word occurs. Often this means allowing the light of truth in feminist theory to perform the demanding work of chipping away at patriarchal traditions Christianity often inherits and generates. Equally important, it implies continually asking what light the revelation of God's self in scripture, tradition, and experience may bring to feminist theory. It means continually returning to the Voice of the One in Three as the source of sustenance and transformation through the power of grace.

In the context of this dynamic dialogue between theory and faith, the interpretations of Beauvoir and Irigaray that affirm embodiment as fundamental to all selves and female selves as valuable in their own right extend their fruitfulness when contextualized in the Christian faith. First, they help us to continue the hard work of identifying negative corporeal attitudes that are perpetuated in Christian theology and praxis. For example, the thinking that dichotomizes the natural and cultural spheres shapes many theological accounts of salvation history in which the stories of God's redeeming interventions in the world are limited to the cultural sphere, while the natural sphere is left outside the scope of discussion as irrelevant. This divide has often produced theologies that tend toward Gnosticism or asceticism, as care of the earth and of the body is not valued as relevant to the furthering of God's kingdom. Similarly, the body/spirit dichotomy shapes a theological language that focuses solely on the saving of souls and a spirituality that requires renunciation of this world and of the flesh in order to prepare for the afterlife in the heavens above. In this context, the body belongs to the fallen world and causes the human spirit to continually be tempted back into sin. Women have historically paid a heavy price for the inculcation of these antibody structures as female selves are aligned with the devalued body while male selves are freer to inhabit the spiritual world. Implications for women have been, for example, carrying the responsibility and shame for men's struggles with lust, or suppressing their rich variety of gifts within the circumscription of patriarchal definitions of the maternal role.

In the face of the multitude of women who bear the scars and muscles of their struggle for bodily integrity, the church is called to respond not only with critical introspection but also with constructive body theologies. This project is crucial to the life of faith as we learn to not confuse God's voice with the failings of culture and community to love our bodies as innately good and inviolable. It is not only women's experiences, but the self-revelation of God that calls us onward in this project. Here, in the biblical tradition, we find that that far from the body being identified as the locus of "sin" that is to be left behind in sanctification, it speaks of humanity as created persons that cannot be divided up into parts. It is as material and holistic beings that we are made and valued in the image of God. This embodied reality is deemed good by a transcendent God who promises to breathe life into hollow bones, who delights to walk in the earthly habitat of green gardens, and who Himself became formed in the sinuous textures of the womb. Irigaray's words capture the need for both these transcendent and immanent elements of our theology:

> And in this we still resemble plants. We climb toward God and remain in Him, without killing the mother earth where our roots lie, without denying the sky either. Rooted in the earth, fed by rain and spring waters, we grow and flourish in the air, thanks to the light from the sky, the warmth of the sun. (*Sexes* 69)

And in all this, our greatest gift will be to learn that it is God who climbs toward us and remains with us. It is here we may meet God anew as Creator, Suffering One, Empowering One. Our Father in whom we delight and seek justice.

Revaluing the body in the Christian tradition has the potential to restore many good things to the life of faith. To understand and embrace the body as the horizon of all our activities, as Beauvoir says, is to begin to help heal the rift between self and body caused by suffering. Rather than practices that denigrate the body, there would be many expressions of care as we tend not only to the many gardens of the earth, but to our own bodies' needs for nourishment, sleep, and touch. If it is through our bodies that we experience much pain, it will be in the care, respect, and love extended through and to our bodily selves that healing and wholeness will begin.

Irigaray's concern for sexed embodiment reminds us however that to be embodied is to be male or female, so discussions of embodiment in general are inadequate reflections of human reality. Further, we have seen how pretensions to neutral embodiment almost always implicitly take male embodiment as normative. scripture sheds light on this aspect of the search for bodily perspectives as well. Genesis 1:27 testifies that humanity is created male and female in the image of God. Humankind is not made first and foremost male, and woman formed as his complement, opposite, or same. Rather, we find "the original unity that is at the same time the original differentiation," enabling recognition of "distinction within harmony" (Trible 18). This significant theme for ethics concerning sexual differentiation is visited anew in Galatians 3:28: "There is neither Jew nor Greek, slave nor free, male nor female, for you are all one in Christ Jesus." This passage proclaims that distinctions of race, sex, or money do not give any group or person status or privilege at the table of God. In relation to sexed difference, this means that while many continue to "express the equality of Christian women with men only as 'manliness' or as abandonment of her own sexual nature, Galatians 3:28 does not extol maleness but the oneness of the body Christ" (Schüssler Fiorenza 218). As a founding vision of the early church, this does not mean that distinctions are denied, as though all the diversity of human bodies could or always should dissipate. Rather, the church's vision of unity is an egalitarian vision that welcomes difference since through faith in Christ Jesus, we "are no longer slaves, but God's children; and since [we] are his children, he has made [us] also heirs" (Gal. 4:7).

This creation and redemption theology carries many implications for the life of faith in the journey toward embodiment. First, "in terms of ministry within the worshiping community, the Holy Spirit was apparently indiscriminate, inspiring women and men alike, since in Christ Jesus such distinctions no longer have religious value in God's new eschatological kingdom" (Fee 885). In light of this, Christian feminists have long toiled to see women's ordination an unchallenged practice in the church. However, these efforts are continually being thwarted and undermined. Irigaray's point that equality does not mean sameness may help us to expand our energy to address the more subtle reasons why this occurs. For example, how a woman inhabits the position of minister is often measured by or limited to the way men have done it in the past. We need to open up the question of from where our standards defining the contours of pastoral ministry have come, and whether there is sufficient room for expressions of the Spirit's work to be as unique and diverse as are the people of God.

Recognizing the full humanity of women in the body of Christ will also be a communal process that requires a transformation of relationships between women. Often pitted against one another in a society where we are taught to judge and compete against each other, we need to forge relationships that enable us to appreciate one another as individuals and as companions from whom we may learn. Irigaray's concern for relationships among women reminds us that we must continue to learn to love ourselves on our way toward fulfilling the command to love others as ourselves. These creative collaborations may strengthen the whole body of Christ as they participate in the restoration of wholeness to our individual bodies.

Affirming "distinction in harmony" may also transform the battleground of the fight for equal rights into a fertile soil producing fecund relationships between the sexes. The Song of Songs stands as a persistent reminder in the biblical canon that there is hope and promise of transformation in this world, including even the space of the erotic. Far from abandoning embodiment and the erotic, this story of redemption secures them as central to it. Rather than the vulnerability of flesh as a threat to the self, it is embraced as the avenue by which, "for the one and the other, love would be the revelation of self by the gift of self and enrichment of the world" (Beauvoir 667). Each lover is respected as an embodied subject, neither mere bodies nor mere souls, and it is this holism that enables the genuinely erotic dynamics between them. This biblical text then is a story of redemption and is testimony to the goodness of creation, claiming embodied Eros as a site of hope and transformation as the lovers' delight in one another "becomes worship in the context of grace" (Trible 161).

These reflections are only the beginnings of possible directions the Christian feminist journey toward embodiment may take. There are many feminists and Christians who are rethinking inherited beliefs that disable the experience of wholeness in embodied subjectivity. Together with them, we are pushing toward new horizons in search of bodily perspectives. From Beauvoir we may find encouragement to embrace our bodies as the "horizon of all activities" as well as a challenge to expand our horizons through the ceaseless engagement of projects in a world for which we are responsible. Irigaray's discursive strategies, on the other hand, provide us with new tools for the creation of these projects. She reveals new paths for building a "symbolic home," and her style of writing the body may infuse us with a love and passion for our own and others' embodied subjectivities *as women*. While these horizons call us toward an open future, we have seen their lining may also be traced in the ancient, yet alive, biblical texts. Through the Spirit's moving, may we as Christian feminists continue to be awakened by images of a transcendent God who delights in molding earthly clay to bring forth dancing "earth creatures"; to images of lovers who together recreate the garden of delight through their embodied engagement and recognition; and, finally, to images of women announcing the beginning of what will some day be for all of us, a bodily resurrection.

Notes

1. I will be spending a significant amount of space on this interpretation of Beauvoir because it has had so much influence on Anglo-American feminism, to such an extent, in fact, that it has nearly excluded the possibility of other kinds of feminism. See T. Chanter, *Ethics of Eros: Irigaray's Rewriting of the Philosophers* (New York: Routledge, 1995), 21–44.
2. See Rosalyn Diprose, *The Bodies of Women: Ethics, Embodiment and Sexual Difference* (London and New York: Routledge, 1994) for longer discussion of this.
3. This is not to dismiss the readings outlined above. I have intentionally explained them in a manner that accords them authority and as deserving serious reading. This is because I do not desire to dismiss them as simply "bad" and mistaken readings, for I think each may point to certain weaknesses in Beauvoir and Irigaray that ought to be heard.
4. Some significant seminal works are Nancy Bauer, *Simone de Beauvoir, Philosophy & Feminism* (New York: Columbia University Press, 2001); Debra Bergoffen, *The Philosophy of Simone de Beauvoir: Gendered Phenomenologies, Erotic Generosities* (Albany: State University of New York); Claudia Card, ed., *The Cambridge Companion to Simone de Beauvoir* (Cambridge University Press, 2003); Sonia Kruks, *Situation and Human Existence: Freedom, Subjectivity and Society* (London: Unwin Hyman Ltd., 1990); Toril Moi, *What Is a Woman? and Other Essays* (Oxford University Press, 1999); Wendy O'Brien and Lester Embree, eds., *The Existential Phenomenology of Simone de Beauvoir* (Dordrecht, The Netherlands: Kluwer Academic Publishers, 2001); Margaret A. Simons, *Beauvoir and the Second Sex: Feminism, Race, and the Origins of Existentialism* (Lanham, MD: Rowman & Littlefield Publishers, Inc., 1999).
5. Beauvoir herself often endorses this.
6. The grammatical construction of the phrase "thinking the body" is intentional for it avoids the implicit subject/object dichotomy in the phrase "thinking *about/of* the body."
7. See Luce Irigaray, *je, tu, nous: Toward a Culture of Difference*, trans. A. Martin. (New York: Routledge, 1993), 9–14 for Irigaray's own comments regarding her philosophical and feminist position vis-à-vis Beauvoir.
8. Most notably Margaret Whitford's *Luce Irigaray: Philosophy in the Feminine* (London: Routledge, 1991). Other important works are Carolyn Burke, Naomi Schor, and Margaret Whitford, eds., *Engaging with Irigaray: Feminist Philosophy and Modern European Thought* (New York: Columbia University Press, 1994); Chanter, *Ethics of Eros*; Diana Fuss, *Essentially Speaking: Feminism, Nature, and Difference* (New York: Routledge, 1989); Jane Gallop, *Thinking Through the Body* (New York: Columbia University Press, 1988); Elizabeth Grosz, *Sexual Subversions: Three French Feminists* (New South Wales, Australia: Allen & Unwin, 1989).
9. For more detail regarding this history of essentialism in the Anglo-American scene, see Chanter, *Ethics of Eros*, 31–39.
10. The openness of the term "sexual difference" in Irigaray's earlier work is possibly compromised by more static definitions in her later works, such as *I Love to You* (New York: Routledge, 1996) and *To Be Two* (New York: Routledge, 2001). See P. Deutscher, *A Politics of Impossible Difference: The Later Work of Luce Irigaray* (Ithaca, New York: Cornell University Press, 2002), ch. 8 and 9.

11. For ethics between the sexes, this also means that relations between the sexes will not be governed by principles of universality or sameness (what each one has in common), but by a wonder and respect for the difference of the other.

12. Note that this doesn't mean Irigaray will deny it exists, nor that humans long for it to exist, but that human reality is structured such that we don't have pure access to things-in themselves. In Lacanian terms, there is no access to the signified, only the multitude of signifiers that slide along the chain of meaning.

13. This strategy has many similarities to Derridean deconstruction. For more on this relationship between Irigaray and Derrida, see Chanter, *Ethics of Eros*, 321–254; Whitford, *Luce Irigaray*, 124–139; and Elizabeth Weed's "The Question of Style," *Engaging with Irigaray: Feminist Philosophy and Modern European Thought*, ed. C. Burke, N. Schor, and M. Whitford (New York: Columbia University Press, 1994), 79–109.

Bibliography

Bauer, N. (2001). *Simone de Beauvoir, philosophy, and feminism*. New York: Columbia University Press.

Beauvoir, S. de. (1952). *The second sex*. Trans. H. M. Parsley. New York: Vintage.

Bergoffen, D. (1997). *The philosophy of Simone de Beauvoir: Gendered phenomenologies, erotic generosities*. Albany, NY: State University of New York.

Burke, C. (1994). "Irigaray through the looking glass." *Engaging with Irigaray: Feminist philosophy and modern European thought*. Ed. C. Burke, N. Schor, and M. Whitford. New York: Columbia University Press. 3–14

Burke, C., Schor, N., and Whitford, M., eds. (1994). *Engaging with Irigaray: Feminist philosophy and modern European thought*. New York: Columbia University Press.

Card, C., ed. (2003). *The Cambridge companion to Simone de Beauvoir*. New York: Cambridge University Press.

Cataldi, S. L. (2001). "Body as a basis for being: Simone de Beauvoir and Maurice Merleau-Ponty." *The existential phenomenology of Simone de Beauvoir*. Ed. W. O'Brien and L. Embree. Dordrecht, Netherlands: Kluwer Academic. 85–106.

Chanter, T. (1995). *Ethics of Eros: Irigaray's rewriting of the philosophers*. New York: Routledge.

Deutscher, P. (2002). *A politics of impossible difference: The later work of Luce Irigaray*. Ithaca, NY: Cornell University Press.

Diprose, R. (1994). *The bodies of women: Ethics, embodiment and sexual difference*. London and New York: Routledge.

———. (2002). *Corporeal generosity: On giving with Nietzsche, Merleau-Ponty, and Levinas*. Albany, NY: State University of New York.

Fee, G. D. (1994). *God's empowering presence: The Holy Spirit in the letters of Paul*. Peabody, MA: Hendrickson Publishers, Inc.

Fuss, D. (1989). *Essentially speaking: Feminism, nature, and difference*. New York: Routledge.

Gallop, J. (1988). *Thinking through the body*. New York: Columbia University Press.

Grosz, E. (1989). *Sexual subversions: Three French feminists*. New South Wales, Australia: Allen & Unwin. New York: Cornell University Press.

Irigaray, L. (1993). *Je, tu, nous: Toward a culture of difference*. Trans. A. Martin. New York: Routledge.

———. (1993). *Sexes and genealogies*. Trans. G. C. Gill. New York: Columbia University Press.

———. (1996). *I love to you: Sketch of a possible felicity in history*. Trans. A. Martin. New York: Routledge.

———. (2001). *To be two.* Trans. M. M. Rhodes and M. F. Cocito-Monoc. New York: Routledge.

Kruks, S. (1990). *Situation and human existence: Freedom, subjectivity, and society.* London: Unwin Hyman.

Moi, T. (1999). *What is a woman? And other essays.* Oxford University Press.

O'Brien, W. and Embree, L., eds. (2001). *The existential phenomenology of Simone de Beauvoir.* Dordrecht, Netherlands: Kluwer Academic.

Schor, N. (1994). "Previous engagements: The receptions of Irigaray." *Engaging with Irigaray: Feminist philosophy and modern European thought.* Ed. C. Burke, N. Schor, and M. Whitford. New York: Columbia University Press. 3–14.

———. (1994). "This essentialism which is not one." *Engaging with Irigaray: Feminist philosophy and modern European thought.* Ed. C. Burke, N. Schor, and M. Whitford. New York: Columbia University Press. 57–78.

Schüssler Fiorenza, E. (2002). *In memory of her: A feminist theological reconstruction of Christian origins.* 10th anniversary edition. New York: Crossroad Publishing Company.

Simons, M. A. (1999). *Beauvoir and the second sex: Feminism, race, and the origins of existentialism.* Lanham, MD: Rowman & Littlefield.

Trible, P. (1978). *God and the rhetoric of sexuality.* Philadelphia: Fortress Press.

Weed, E. (1994). "The question of style." *Engaging with Irigaray: Feminist philosophy and modern European thought.* Ed. C. Burke, N. Schor, and M. Whitford. New York: Columbia University Press. 79–109.

Whitford, M. (1991). *Luce Irigaray: Philosophy in the feminine.* London: Routledge.

CHAPTER FIVE

Two Women Speaking "Woman": The Strategic Essentialism of Luce Irigaray and Phoebe Palmer

DIANE LECLERC

In order to become, it is essential to have a gender or an essence (consequently a sexuate essence) as horizon. Otherwise, becoming remains partial and subject to the subject. When we become parts or multiples without a future of our own this means simply that we are leaving it up to the other . . . to put us together. To become means fulfilling the wholeness of what we are capable of being.

—Luce Irigaray[1]

In an article first printed in 1960, Valerie Saiving asserted that while "it would be ridiculous to deny that there is a structure of experience common to both men and women, so that we may legitimately speak of the 'human situation,' without reference to sexual identity," she goes on to ask rhetorically "whether we have described the human situation correctly by taking account of the experiences of both sexes."[2] Saiving's question helped ignite the fire of feminist theology for years to come. However, while Saiving's thesis—that theology has been dominated by men for centuries and thus represents an incomplete, if not inadequate perspective—has been embraced by most feminist theologians who themselves have challenged the "orthodox" paradigm, to speak, as Saiving has, of a "basic feminine character structure" is no longer "orthodox" among more recent feminist theorists. Indeed, such an "essentialist" construction has become a rather "heretical" view. In sum, the debate over essentialism focuses on the fact that affirming a "natural" female essence potentially reinstates and reinforces the very abuses feminism intends to fight, and actually makes women collaborators of patriarchy. Thus there have been those determined to eradicate the evils of essentialism from feminist theory; for them any notion of an *ontological* foundation that affirms a "female" nature, and anyone who might hold to such a position, has been relegated to the realm of the contemptible.[3] The philosophical underpinnings of Saiving's theory have been increasingly called into question over the course of the last 30 years. Even those who want to maintain the value of naming a female "essence" for the purpose of "suiting the situation,"[4] do so from a very different place. And that different place is the place where difference, not essence, is the new and dominant charter.[5] Metanarratives have been replaced by "microresistances."[6] The category of "femaleness" has become tenuous. The "characteristic" distinctions between "men" and "women" are now seen as culturally constructed. Even the casual differentiation between sex (as a biological reality) and gender (as a social construct) is now being questioned by some theorists; sex has itself been identified as a cultural construction.[7]

However, if gender can no longer be identified with certainty, if the differences and diversity among "women" are now the points of emphasis, and if there is nothing that is "essentially" female, where, many are asking, is the commonality that once fueled the political fires of the feminist movement?[8] Does "feminism" itself stand at the cliff of a theoretical paradox that elicits political despondency? Is it at the brink of a linguistic nonexistence? Can there *be* such a thing as a postmodern, poststructuralist, anti-essentialist feminism?[9] Feminism seems to be looking for a "courage to be" in the face of such anxiety over ontology.[10] The conundrum of the oxymoron "anti-essentialist feminism" has some advocating the "risk of essentialism" (i.e., a "strategic" essentialism) as a workable solution and as, it could be argued, a means of moderation and mediation in the whole debate. In the search for such a workable solution the work of Luce Irigaray beckons. Irigaray represents a different approach to woman's place as Other (than man) through her attempts to deconstruct misogynistic labeling and to open occasions for a very distinct signification as well as a different *reality* for women. Luce Irigaray's "essentialism" strategically enables her to extricate woman from her placement as the "not-male," and to give her another place in the world.

Luce Irigaray's Voice in the Matter

Luce Irigaray has purposely avoided much revelation about her personal life.[11] What is most known about Irigaray is her thought, which is thoroughly feminist; her feminism arises from her artful mimicry of (Freudian and Lacanian) psychoanalytic theory.[12] Crucial to this present study is Irigaray's understanding of female subjectivity as an immanent, bodily, and vocal subjectivity. Beneath the layers of linguistic play, philosophical restructuring, and iconoclastic unveiling in Irigaray's oeuvre, one can begin to infer a process of subjectification for women that has both internal and social consequences. Particularly in her more recent works, Irigaray implies that hope in the future depends on humanity's (men *and* women's) willingness to strive for true subjectivity; ironically, a recognition of *difference* between subjectivities is the very means of overcoming the linguistic and psychic patterns that maintain alienation and a destructive alterity. She warns, "It is vital that a culture of the sexual, as yet nonexistent, be elaborated, with each sex being respected."[13] This acknowledgment of difference necessarily implies a kind of "essentialism" for Irigaray; however, this essentialism is anything but naive. Rather, it is an "essentialism which is not one."[14] This essentialism is required precisely because "female" is a gender "which is not one" (meaning, in a patriarchal system, there is only one true gender: "male"); "female," then, is only defined as "not male" under a misogynistic linguistic economy.[15] Thus, when Irigaray "calls" women to "assume the role of women deliberately,"[16] she does so *not* because she believes in a predetermined and universal nature subsequently marked as female, but because she asserts that it is only when a woman ceases "to identify herself as a 'masculine subject' "[17] that she can begin to "convert a form of subordination into an affirmation,"[18] and regain the "specificity of her relationship to the imaginary."[19] And thus claiming an essential difference is the very means by which objectification is "thwarted." By strategically affirming an "essential" difference, woman takes a "gender" as woman, and not just as the "not male," and in doing so she becomes a subject.

This is crucial because "any theory of the subject has always been appropriated by the 'masculine,' "[20] according to Irigaray. When masculine rhetoric is directly and violently misogynistic, when it avows women's essential emotional and intellectual incapacity, women are objectified to suit various male agendas. And yet (critical to the argument here), when women in leadership are praised in a religious context, they have often been perhaps even more objectified, for the praise is often for their approximation toward the masculine.

Women in other historical periods did attempt this type of approxi-mation. Ascetic women of the fourth century, for example, became "male" as a means of attaining particular liberties uncommon for women in late antiquity.[21] A key aspect in this gender metamorphosis was the volitional (strategic) "denial" of the maternal body and maternal respon-sibilities. Similarly, many of John Wesley's female correspondents *found* themselves (figuratively and literally) in (or through) a "single" situation; although an official vow of virginity was not required, Wesley's advice was often quite forceful: God could be better served if a woman was not weighed down with domestic responsibility.[22] Many of Wesley's female intimates followed his counsel, and as a result they too "ascended" to traditionally male ministerial roles as "female brethren."[23]

However, in the case of Phoebe Palmer we see no such defeminizing maneuvers, no call for "women's equality"; such maneuvers are so absent, in fact, that contemporary interpreters have had difficulty decid-ing whether Palmer should be cast as a feminist or as a champion of Victorian ideals of feminine domesticity. Or to expose the real nature of the more abstract scholarly dilemma, can there be such a thing as a "fully" "feminine" "feminist"? I wish to assert that if there has been such a woman, it was Phoebe Palmer. In other words, although Palmer's life does in fact evidence a rather extraordinary transcendence of nineteenth-century social roles, she was never attacked for assuming masculine posi-tionalities. In her writings and through her career, Palmer can be seen as a "strategic essentialist." Which brings me, finally, to my thesis. This essay will explore Phoebe Palmer's "essentialism" through Luce Irigaray's paradigm of female speech and female subjectivity. In doing so, it will give an aspect of the holiness tradition (i.e., its strong affirmation of women) a quite relevant (and certainly not naive) stance in response to the postmodern world and its poststructuralist paradigm.

Phoebe Palmer, Babies, and Bathwater

Forty years ago the need for scholarship on Phoebe Palmer became dra-matically apparent. After decades of silence about a woman who was among the most famous of her era,[24] John Peters, in 1956,[25] and Timothy Smith, in 1957,[26] attributed an entire movement to Palmer's leadership and initiated scholarly interest in her influence. In answer to the call put forth by Peters and Smith more such scholarship has in fact emerged, but slowly. It was 30 years later when full-length treatises of Palmer's life, work, and influence first appeared.[27] Numerous articles have also been published.

A review of such scholarship reveals that there are nearly as many interpretations of Palmer as interpreters. Although no longer neglected, she apparently remains a rather enigmatic figure. Details of her life and thought unquestionably position her as a figure within—indeed, at the very heart of—the nineteenth-century American holiness movement. What she is most known for, and what incites much scholarly consternation and debate, is her articulation of the doctrine of entire sanctification, and her supposed lack of fidelity to the theology of John Wesley. There is a wide discrepancy of analysis regarding the value of Palmer's version of the doctrine among holiness scholars. A second primary point of interpretive conflict about Phoebe Palmer (and one that has attracted scholars outside the holiness movement) has to do with her place as a woman. Was Palmer the epitome of the "cult of true womanhood,"[28] or a premiere feminist?

On this point, Phoebe Palmer has been cited as a key contributor to the nineteenth-century debate concerning the role of women in the church. Donald Dayton, representative of those advocating her placement as a "feminist," succinctly writes:

It was . . . the denominations produced by the mid-nineteenth century "holiness revival" that most consistently raised feminism to a central principle of church life. This movement largely emerged from the work of Phoebe Palmer.[29]

There is no doubt that Palmer stands as an important figure in the development of a religious-feminist enthusiasm particularly evident in the nineteenth-century American holiness movement, an enthusiasm that only gained momentum toward the end of the nineteenth century. Palmer's writings and her direct influence on others through her own traveling and preaching evidence an extraordinary power for a nineteenth-century woman. Anne Loveland writes the following:

The experience of one woman, Phoebe Palmer, belied the confident statements of the "cult of true womanhood." Instead of harmony, she discovered a conflict between the domestic and religious duties, and in the course of resolving the conflict she enlarged the boundaries of woman's proper sphere. . . . [H]er prominence as an evangelist prevents her from being categorized as a "typical" woman.[30]

Palmer led the famous "Tuesday Meetings" that became gender "mixed" under her leadership;[31] she wrote dozens of books and tracts, which made her a very public figure; she edited the most influential holiness magazine of the century;[32] she started an inner city mission and is said to have produced a theological imperative that subsequently made women's charity work commonplace;[33] she was influential in Methodist higher education,[34] and she was a revivalist with the caliber and popularity of Charles Finney himself. Twenty-five thousand were converted, and thousands upon thousands sanctified, under her evangelistic ministry.[35] In many respects, Phoebe Palmer was not the "typical" mid-nineteenth-century woman; she was certainly not bound to the domestic sphere.

And yet despite this type of evidence, Palmer has also been interpreted as a spokeswoman for traditional Victorian values concerning the home, and as a clear supporter of this cult of true womanhood. Theodore Hovet asserts,

> Palmer's unique contribution to middle-class religious culture was to transfer the mystic concept of "the interior life" to the social structure. By sanctifying the domestic sphere, the Christian woman pushed the influence of "the world" out the domestic door and created a sacred sphere within society in which the spirit could unfold itself. . . . Consequently, the sanctified domestic sphere did not imprison the woman, but it protected her from the "unvarying whirl of the world," to use Palmer's phrase, and invested her with the sacred function of nurturer of the spirit.[36]

After a lengthy analysis of Palmer's theology, Hovet concludes by stating, "To see the holiness movement and the teachings of Palmer as a force which helped women break out of the cult of domesticity, there-fore, is to misinterpret the way in which many women in the holiness movement viewed their identity and their freedom."[37]

It could be argued that almost any woman born in 1807 and living in upper-middle-class Victorian America would be shaped by the ideals set forth in the cult of domesticity, by the belief that the home was a most sacred space that utterly depended on womanly virtues for its spiritual sustenance. Phoebe Palmer's rhetoric often supports this ideal of women's sphere. And yet, it is also somewhat "predictable" that the events of her life, and her reverence for early British Methodist women, led ultimately to rhetoric such as *The Promise of the Father*, and to a conceptual enlargement of woman's sphere to include the Church and society. Palmer's spiritual experiences occurred during the "Methodist Century"[38] and also during the "feminization of American culture"[39]— when revivalist spirituality was a dominant force in American society, and when women's spirituality symbolized America itself.[40] It is not surprising, then, that Phoebe Palmer's cultural and ecclesiastical situation would position her as both a traditionalist and an innovator, nor that such a situation would produce ambiguous rhetoric. In other words, Palmer's "ambivalence" arises in part from the chronological fact that she was a *mid*-nineteenth-century Methodist woman.[41]

Despite a wide difference of interpretation regarding Palmer's type of womanhood, there is consensus that her theology of entire sanctification influenced her theology of gender. Elsewhere, I have given a detailed analysis of Palmer's holiness theology and have argued that her understanding of consecration (in the three-step formula known as the "altar covenant") is intricately tied to her own struggle with *idolatry*, and that this struggle led her to reconceptualize domesticity not only as an expected duty for women, but also as a potential threat to their spirituality.[42] "Rather than reciting the traditional litany" of those things that interfered with the spiritual life—selfishness, lack of faith, betrayals of the flesh—Palmer with striking frankness admitted that the primary obstacle to her spiritual growth had been "a large house involving proportionate cares."[43] In other words, Palmer's understanding of sin was not based on an exaggerated sense of self, but on what I have come to call "relational idolatry."[44] It is crucial to note that, while Palmer's "experience of sanctification involved a kind of liberation from earthly affections and domestic obligations," such liberation "did not develop out a discontent with family ties."[45] As Ann Loveland insightfully recognizes, Palmer "was only too willing to make family ties everything, even to the exclusion of religion."[46] This conceptional framing of *sin* allowed her to shift her perception of domestic responsibilities. Margaret McFadden articulates,

> In the "altar transaction," a woman could lay all the details of house and children on the altar and thus be freed from . . . attachments and responsibilities. . . . Additionally, the altar phraseology encouraged the individual to become less emotionally dependent on husband and children, to become spiritually independent and to consecrate the domestic sphere to the inner life of heart holiness.[47]

Hovet recognizes that "the laying of all on the altar served a dual purpose. It not only freed her from attachments to the world in the conventional religious sense but it also provided a means of freeing her religious life from the chains of domestic responsibility."[48] Thus it is possible to interpret Palmer as drastically shifting the meaning of the "home" in nineteenth-century religious life.[49] No longer is the home the means of personal piety; it has now become a potential spiritual hindrance. Yet, while the rhetoric of early asceticism, and even of Wesley himself, implies that "singleness of heart" requires a very practical rejection of maternal responsibility, Palmer does not throw the babies out with the bathwater. She went on to have a very long marriage and three other children.[50] She quite strategically positions herself as a woman who embraced the maternal role—"she was not advocating a radical feminist position."[51] Rather than taking the radical measure of leaving children and husband behind, a radical *internal* shift is instead required. Again, for quite strategic reasons, she "set her readers' minds at ease . . . [and] assured them that 'at this interesting point in her experience' she did not intend to 'neglect' the members of her family, but had only 'resolved that they should cease to be absorbing'—a disclaimer that reflected how aware she was of the domestic implications of her religious actions."[52] This "non-absorbed" posture could have perhaps been the end of Palmer's story—to "return home" with a new *emotional*, spiritually based freedom. However, the implications of Palmer's theology of gender, and her theology of maternity specifically, did not negate the subsequent requisites she demanded for any who would retain the sanctification experience. The last step in the altar covenant formula would write a new chapter in the history of Palmer's life, and in the history of the holiness movement: women must speak in Palmer's paradigm. They must speak in the public sphere even though such public female speech was deemed as undignified according to societal norms. Further, "the world," therefore, although still portrayed as "sinful" in Palmer's own thought, is no longer to be avoided through a retreat back into the safety of the domestic sphere; rather, society becomes, for Palmer, the most explicit place for *expressing* new-found freedom. As Palmer herself declares, "The idea that woman, with all her noble gifts and qualities, was formed mainly to minister to the sensuous nature of man, is wholly unworthy a place in the heart of a Christian."[53] Women had a greater calling. That calling often included a call to preach.

Palmer's work *The Promise of the Father* defends women in ministry, including preachers. And yet, she strategically (very strategically) explains that she is not advocating women's "preaching so-called." What Palmer meant by "preaching so-called," however, was the very technical, highly structured, theologically sophisticated *male* preaching of mid-century. She wanted nothing to do with this very precise type of preaching, by males or females. She never explicitly says so—again, perhaps strategically— but any other type of preaching by women she would and did affirm. In other words, it could be convincingly argued that Phoebe Palmer was savvy enough to know that she could accomplish much more by conscientiously avoiding any offence to the male economy. Rather, she seems to "play" her femininity to an advantage.

Such can be seen in a metaphor she heavily utilizes in *The Promise of the Father*. "Daughter prophetesses," or "prophesying daughters," obviously evokes the "proper" daughterly role of submission under a male authority. However, the function of prophesying overturns that very submission. The prophetess becomes the daughter of God (alone) who (alone) gives her the authority to speak. A woman's complete loyalty and entire devotion to God allows her to overstep (step over) traditional dependency on male authority figures. For Palmer, a woman does not need to "become male" in order to become a subject; rather, by maintaining an essential difference between genders, she pronounces (proclaims, speaks forth) the subjectivity of woman *as* woman, and overturns her place as inessential Other or as "the sex which is not one." The requisites of Phoebe Palmer's theology produced in many women "a space, a path, a river, a dance, a rhythm, a song"[54]—or a sermon. Such women "gave birth to themselves,"[55] *as women* without needing to reject giving birth to others.

Conclusion

Phoebe Palmer offered women access into a specifically *female* subjectivity, while forging particular and novel liberties under the rubric of devotion to God. In other words, Palmer *regendered* the ascetic and Wesleyan theories of subjectivity—which affirmed the necessity of holy women becoming symbolic males—by actually occupying the traditionally female roles of wife and mother, and thus barring a sweeping rejection of her own, and others' maternal bodies. Palmer accepted the basic assumption of the cult of domesticity—that women had more "natural" access to spirituality and sanctity; yet, paradoxically, this enabled her to transcend (and subvert) such a traditional configuration, for although women were "naturally" domestic, in Palmer's estimation, they were also equally implicated in the experience of Pentecost, and thus equally responsible for Christian service outside "women's sphere." They were specifically responsible to speak. Especially in light of Joel's injunction,[56] Palmer believed women to be prophesying daughters of God (not female sons). They were dignified by their calling, while simultaneously considered undignified in society for being speakers at all. Yet for women whose only "lord" was God alone, speech could be both female and dignified.

In a diary entry only a year before she died, Palmer reflects:

> Well do I, as a daughter of the Lord Almighty, remember the baptism of fire that fell upon me, over thirty years since. Not more assuringly, perhaps, did the tongues of fire fall in energizing, hallowing influences on the sons and daughters of the Almighty, when they ALL spake as the Spirit gave utterance, on the day of Pentecost, than I felt its consuming, hallowing, energizing influences fall on me, empowering me for holy activities and burning utterances.[57]

Palmer's burning utterances changed history—not only the religious history of the nineteenth century, but also the individual histories of women who walk in Palmer's footsteps. She not only gave them an example. She gave women *as women* theologically based requisites that demanded that they refuse to keep silent in the churches, and in the world. In light of the fundamentalist backlash against feminism that runs rampant in Wesleyan-holiness churches today, Palmer's type of essentialism could be the most strategic and effective approach to subvert and overturn fundamentalism's presuppositions regarding women's place.

In sum, I am calling for a critical reclamation of Phoebe Palmer and of her theology of holiness as a process for offering persons, particularly women, theological and experiential space for embodied, active, speaking, *subjectivity*. While the "moral psychology" underlying her theology remains inextricably tied to the philosophical structures of the nineteenth century, and while the limits of the cult of domesticity that influenced her have long been broken, I suggest that the implications of her theology have the potential to continue to open spaces for female subjectivity. Likewise, while the requisites she demanded for any who would seek and retain the experience of entire sanctification are tied to a specific historical context, and while these same requisites are obviously limited to a very narrow theological heritage, the "liberation" they instituted (i.e., the freedom to take personal possession of, and responsibility for, one's own spirituality and related praxis) remains theologically and experientially relevant for "holiness women" today. Yet despite any of my possible suggestions as to the significance of Palmer's contribution, a stark reality prevails: holiness scholars today count Palmer as the great pervert/er of their sacred doctrine. Although some have nodded in her direction for her contribution to the "women in ministry" question, her theology is uniformly rejected. She is the greatest Other in the history of the holiness movement—a theologian "who is not one." She, quite ironically and tragically, has been silenced. And yet, because of her pronouncements regarding women preachers, holiness women are still speaking. It is my hope that through a reclamation, not only of these ministerial pronouncements, but also of her very theology, and through a similar type of strategic essentialism in the face of a rather overwhelming opponent, holiness women will not see before them the hard road they have always tread, but a more hopeful future.

Notes

Reprinted with permission: "Two Women Speaking 'Woman': The Strategic Essentialism of Luce Irigaray and Phoebe Palmer," *Wesleyan Theological Journal* 35(1) (Spring 2000).

1. Quoted without citation in Rosi Braidotti, "Of Bugs and Women: Irigaray and Deleuze on the Becoming-Woman," *Engaging Irigaray*, ed. Carolyn Burke, Naomi Schor, and Margaret Whitford (New York: Columbia University Press, 1994), 111.
2. Valerie Saiving, "The Human Situation: A Feminine View," *Womenspirit Rising*, ed. Carol Christ and Judith Plaskow (San Francisco: Harper and Row, 1979), 27. (Reprinted from *Journal of Religion* 40 [1960]: 100–112).
3. Teresa De Lauretis points out there are others who believe that this debate, fought on such terms, has ceased to be productive. "Many have grown impatient with this word—essentialism—time and again repeated with its reductive ring, its self-righteous tone of superiority, its contempt for 'them'—those guilty of it." Teresa De Lauretis, "The Essence of the Triangle or, Taking the Risk of Essentialism Seriously: Feminist Theory in Italy, the U.S., and Britain," *The Essential Difference*, ed. Naomi Schor and Elizabeth Weed (Indianapolis: Indiana University Press, 1994), 1. Naomi Schor furthers the description of the polarized nature of the debate: "What revisionism, not to say essentialism, was to Marxism-Leninism, essentialism is to feminism: the prime idiom of intellectual terrorism and the privileged instrument of political orthodoxy . . . The word essentialism has been endowed within the context of feminism with the power to reduce to silence, to excommunicate, to consign to oblivion. Essentialism in modern-day feminism is anathema." Naomi Schor, "This Essentialism Which Is Not One: Coming to Grips with Irigaray," in *The Essential Difference*, ed. Naomi Schor and Elizabeth Weed (Indianapolis: Indiana University Press, 1994), 42.
4. Gayatri Chakravorty Spivak articulates that "to an extent, we have to look at where the group—the person, the persons, or the movement—is situated when we make claims for or against essentialism. A strategy suits a situation; a strategy is not a theory." Gayatri Chakravorty Spivak with Ellen Rooney, "In a Word. Interview," *The Essential Difference*, ed. Naomi Schor and Elizabeth Weed (Indianapolis: Indiana University Press, 1994), 154.
5. Deborah Rhode summarizes the debate on difference: "[F]eminists generally have taken two approaches, both of which remain critical in contemporary debates over difference. One strategy has been to deny the extent or essential nature of differences between men and women. A second approach has been to celebrate difference—to embrace characteristics historically associated with women and demand their equal social recognition. A third, more recent strategy attempts to dislodge difference—to challenge its centrality and its organizing premises and to recast the terms on which gender relations have traditionally been debated," Deborah L. Rhode, "Theoretical Perspectives on Sexual Difference," *Theoretical Perspectives on Sexual Difference*, ed. Deborah L. Rhode (New Haven: Yale University Press, 1990), 3.

122   *Diane Leclerc*

6. Regenia Gagnier articulates that in a postmodern scheme "microresistances" replace "identities" and are characterized by fluidity—the ability to mobilize and then disperse. See Regenia Gagnier, "Feminist Postmodernism: The End of Feminism or the Ends of Theory?" *Theoretical Perspectives on Sexual Difference*, ed. Deborah L. Rhode (New Haven: Yale University Press, 1990), 23.

7. See Judith Butler's advocacy of understanding gender as pure "performance" in *Gender Trouble: Feminism and the Subversion of Identity* (New York: Routledge, 1990). Elsewhere she argues, "We may seek to return to matter as prior to discourse in order to ground our claims about sexual difference, only to discover that matter is fully sedimented with discourses on sex and sexuality that prefigure and constrain the uses to which that term can be put. Moreover, we may seek recourse to matter in order to ground or to verify a set of injuries or violations, only to find that matter itself is founded through a set of violations, ones that are unwittingly repeated in the contemporary invocation. Indeed, if it can be shown that in its constitutive history this 'irreducible' materiality is constructed through a problematic gendered matrix, then the discursive practice by which matter is rendered irreducible simultaneously ontologizes and fixes that gendered matrix in its place . . . [A]gainst those who would claim that the body's irreducible materiality is a necessary precondition for feminist practice, I suggest that prized materiality may well be constituted through an exclusion and degradation of the feminine that is profoundly problematic for feminism," Judith Butler, "Bodies that Matter," *Engaging With Irigaray*, ed. Carolyn Burke, Naomi Schor, and Margaret Whitford (New York: Columbia University Press, 1994), 143. For a historical overview of gender differentiation, see Thomas Walter Laqueur, *Making Sex: Body and Gender from the Greeks to Freud* (Cambridge, MA: Harvard University Press, 1990).

8. Gagnier reminds, "It cannot be overemphasized that . . . critiques of earlier feminist theorizing are rejecting precisely the stories of oppression that gave earlier feminism its discursive unity, the stories that provided slogans that incited action," Gagnier, "Feminist Postmodernism," 22–23. Karen Offen adds, "The fragmentation of identities [postmodernism] proposes, specifically the dissolution of the category women, threatens the historical feminist project," Karen Offen, "Feminism and Sexual Difference in Historical Perspective," *Theoretical Perspectives on Sexual Difference*, ed. Deborah L. Rhode (New Haven: Yale University Press, 1990), 15.

9. De Lauretis argues, "If 'woman' is a fiction . . . and if there are no women as such, then the very issue of women's oppression would appear to be obsolete and feminism itself would have no reason to exist (which, it may be noted, is a corollary of poststructuralism and the stated position of those who call themselves 'post-feminists')," De Lauretis, "The Essence of the Triangle," 10.

10. Susan Bordo states, "Assessing where we are now, it seems to me that feminism stands less in danger of the totalizing tendencies of feminists than of an increasingly paralyzing anxiety over a fall (from what grace?) into ethnocentricism or 'essentialism,' " Susan Bordo, *Unbearable Weight: Feminism, Western Culture, and the Body* (Berkley, CA: University of California Press, 1993), 225. It can be argued that the intensity of the anxiety over a lost identity is unfounded. Such anxiety fails to acknowledge the tenacity of a "mere" construction; anti-essentialism is unlikely to overthrow or undermine the agenda of feminism, even if feminism itself is seen as a construction.

11. According to Margaret Whitford, "this is not just a personal stance of suspicious defensiveness, but the well-founded realization that one way of neutralizing a woman thinker whose work is radically challenging is to 'reduce' her to her biography," Margaret Whitford, ed., *The Irigaray Reader/ Luce Irigaray* (Cambridge, MA: Basil Blackwell, 1991), 1.

12. The publication of *Speculum of the Other Woman* (1974) led to her banishment from the Freudian school and provoked the fury of the Lacanians. She lost her teaching position at Vincennes as a result.

13. Luce Irigaray, *Je, Tu, Nous* (New York: Routledge Press, 1993), 12.

14. See Schor, "This Essentialism," 40–62. Shor here plays off of Irigaray's most well-known designation of the female "gender" as "the sex which is not one."

15. In the words of Judith Butler, "For Irigaray, that phallogocentric mode of signifying the female sex perpetually reproduces phantasms of its own self-amplification. Instead of a self-limiting linguistic gesture that grants alterity or difference to women, phallogocentricism offers a name to eclipse the feminine and takes its place," Butler, "Bodies that Matter," 12–13.

16. Luce Irigaray, *This Sex Which is Not One*, trans. Catherine Porter with Carolyn Burke (Ithaca, NY: Cornell University Press, 1985), 76.

17. Luce Irigaray, "Any Theory of the 'Subject,' " *Speculum of the Other Woman*, trans. Gillian Gill (Ithaca, NY: Cornell University Press, 1985), 133.

18. Irigaray, *This Sex*, 76.

19. Irigaray, "Any Theory," 133.

20. Ibid.

21. See Gillian Cloke, *This Female Man of God: Women and Spiritual Power in the Patristic Age, AD 350–450* (London: Routledge, 1995).

22. To Elizabeth Richie (November 29, 1775), Wesley writes, "I am glad you were enabled to withstand that plausible temptation [marriage] which few young women have power to resist, particularly when you had to encounter the persuasion of those you esteemed and loved." And elsewhere (February 12, 1779), "Surely it is your wisdom to stand fast even in the outward liberty wherewith Christ has made you free. You are now happily disengaged from caring for the things of this world, and need only care for the things of the Lord." In a letter to Martha Chapman (November 3, 1784) Wesley repeats his theme again, "It is well for you that God did not suffer you to find rest in any creature. He had better things in store for you."

23. Paul W. Chilcote, *She Offered them Christ: The Legacy of Women Preachers in Early Methodism* (Nashville: Abingdon Press, 1993), 103–109. Chilcote cites J. E. Hellier as reporting that several early Methodist women preachers formed a band and called themselves "female brethren." J. E. Hellier, "The Mother Chapel of Leeds," *Methodist Recorder Winter Number* 35 (Christmas 1894): 64.

24. Thomas Oden writes, "Phoebe Palmer, after having been one of the most widely known women of her time in England and America, has remained virtually unknown during the past hundred years." Oden adds his interpretation of Palmer. "[Her] spirituality . . . is deeply rooted in classical Christianity, not on the fanatic, idiosyncratic fringe of centerless enthusiasm. She deserves to be counted among the most penetrating spiritual writers of the American tradition," Thomas Oden, "Introduction," *Phoebe Palmer, Selected Writings*, ed. Thomas Oden (New York: Paulist Press, 1988), 2–3, 8.

25. See John L. Peters, *Christian Perfection and American Methodism* (Nashville: Pierce & Washabaugh, 1956). Perhaps one of the first to call Phoebe Palmer the "founder of the holiness movement" was M. L. Haney. See M. L. Haney, *The Inheritance Restored: or Plain Truths on Bible Holiness* (Chicago, IL: Christian Witness Co., 1904), 215.

26. See Timothy L. Smith, *Revivalism and Social Reform* (Nashville: Abingdon Press, 1957). Smith's thesis is that the holiness movement preceded and anticipated the themes of the Social Gospel movement; Smith believes the holiness movement's social concern partly originated from Phoebe Palmer's Five Point Mission.

27. See Harold Raser, *Phoebe Palmer: Her Life and Thought* (Lewiston, New York: The Edwin Mellen Press, 1987); and Charles E. White, *The Beauty of Holiness: Phoebe Palmer As Theologian, Revivalist, Feminist, and Humanitarian* (Grand Rapids, MI: Francis Asbury Press, 1986).

28. This expression, which is synonymous with "the cult of domesticity," is a commonly used phrase among scholars of the nineteenth century. It represents the belief that women were "naturally" spiritual in both temperament and capacity for virtue. As a result of this natural spirituality, woman were designated as the spiritual leaders of their homes and as those responsible to keep this private sphere safe from the external, "evil" world. For extensive elaboration see Colleen McDannell, *The Christian Home in Victorian America, 1840–1900* (Bloomington, IN: Indiana University Press, 1986).

29. Donald W. Dayton, *Discovering an Evangelical Heritage* (New York: Harper and Row, 1976), 200. Also see Nancy Hardesty, Lucille Sider Dayton, and Donald W. Dayton, "Women in the Holiness Movement: Feminism in the Evangelical Tradition," *Women of Spirit*, ed. Rosemary Ruether and Eleanor McLaughlin (New York: Simon and Schuster, 1979), 225–254. These authors here offer six factors that "account for the holiness movement's consistent feminist thrust." Dale Simmons writes, "by far the greatest [scholarly] interest in Palmer has focused on her incipient feminism. Indeed, it is no coincidence that the explosion of literature on Palmer in the 1970s and 1980s parallels the rise of the feminist movement itself. In this climate, Evangelicals in general have rightly enjoyed using the example of Palmer and others to remind the wider religious community that they were well ahead of the social curve on the issues of women's rights," Dale Simmons, "Phoebe Palmer—Enjoli Woman or Enigma? A Review of the Recent Scholarship on Phoebe Palmer," *Wesleyan/Holiness Studies Center Bulletin* 4 (1996): 1.

30. Anne C. Loveland, "Domesticity and Religion in the Antebellum Period: The Career of Phoebe Palmer," *The Historian* 39 (1977): 455.

31. See George Hughes, *Fragrant Memories of The Tuesday Meeting and Guide to Holiness* (New York: Palmer & Hughes, 1886). Also see Peters, *Christian Perfection*, 109–110. It could be said that these Tuesday meetings are the birthplace of the American holiness movement. The main purpose of these meetings was to promote holiness by providing a place where testimonies to the experience of entire sanctification could be expressed, for the encouragement of both the "sanctified" and seekers after holiness. Many "famous" persons attained the experience in these meetings, including Thomas Upham, Congregationalist minister and philosopher.

32. The *Guide to Holiness* was under Palmer's editorship from 1864 to 1874. During that time circulation reached 40,000.

33. See Smith, *Revivalism*, 169–171.

34. Thomas Oden asserts that "a separate monograph should be written on the ways in which Mrs. Palmer influenced higher education in America." He offers a "preliminary inventory of major American universities and colleges whose early presidents or key leaders [or founders] . . . were significantly influenced, according to their own testimony by her work." Oden lists the following educational institutions: Drew University, University of Michigan, Northwestern University, Evanston College, Boston University, Syracuse University, Wesleyan University, University of Georgia, Oberlin College, Dickinson College, University of the Pacific, American University, DePauw University, Adrian College, Simpson College, and Hamline College. See Oden, "Introduction," Palmer, *Selected Writings*, 4.

35. Ruth A. Tucker and Walter Liefeld, *Daughters of the Church: Women and Ministry from the New Testament Times to the Present* (Grand Rapids, MI: Academie Books, 1987), 263. This was first stated in Palmer's eulogy. See Richard Wheatley, *The Life and Letters of Mrs. Phoebe Palmer* (New York: W. C. Palmer, Publisher, 1881), 633.

36. Theodore Hovet, "Phoebe Palmer's 'Altar Phraseology' and the Spiritual Dimension of Woman's Sphere," *Journal of Religion* 63 (1983): 274.

37. Ibid., 279.

38. See C. C. Goen, "The 'Methodist Age' in American Church History," *Religion in Life* 34 (1965): 562–572; Winthrop Hudson, "The Methodist Age in America," *Methodist History* 12 (1974): 3–15. A. Gregory Schneider summarizes: "This new organization [the Methodist Episcopal Church] became a vessel that both contained and spread a major portion of the remarkable spiritual effervescence that flowed from what is called the Second Great Awakening in America. This Awakening marked the transition from the 'Puritan Age' to the 'Methodist Age' in American church history. There is a simple statistical reason for such a statement. In 1784 . . . the Methodists were small and insignificant sect. By 1850 . . . there were more Methodists in America than any other kind of Protestants. There is also a more sophisticated reason for the statement. When historians speak of the nineteenth century as the Methodist Age in American religious history they refer to a popular religious style that characterizes Methodists but was not limited to them. Indeed, this style of religion penetrated virtually all of Protestant church life and

virtually ever region in America," A. Gregory Schneider, *The Way of the Cross Leads Home: The Domestication of American Methodism* (Bloomington, IN: Indiana University Press, 1993), xx.

39. See Ann Douglas, *The Feminization of American Culture* (New York: Alfred A. Knopf, 1977), for elaboration of this thesis. Douglas' conclusions are extended by Schneider. He writes, "The idea of the family as belonging to a private sphere of affection and moral discipline that was to be set over against a public sphere of competition and self-interest became widespread. This private sphere, moreover, was the proper sphere of Woman, while the worldly sphere belonged to Man. Domesticity became a form of religion with its own sacred symbols and cultus. Womanhood came to be defined as 'naturally' religious. . . . [T]his domestic ideology was the principal way in which the emerging white middle class defined itself," Schneider, *The Way of the Cross Leads Home*, xxii. Also see Barbara Welter, "The Feminization of American Religion: 1800–1890," *Clio's Consciousness Raised: New Perspectives on the History of Women*, ed. Mary Hartmann and Lois W. Banner (New York: Harper and Row, 1974), 137–157.

40. See Amanda Porterfield, "Phoebe Palmer," 1. Unpublished paper presented at the "Women in New Worlds Conference," Cincinnati, Ohio, February, 1980; presently held by the United Methodist Archives, Madison, New Jersey, and used with permission.

41. Stronger voices for suffrage and for the widespread ordination of women sound most loudly only after Palmer's death. Palmer's influence on these emerging voices is yet another question. On this issue, see for example, Lucille Sider Dayton and Donald W. Dayton, " 'Your Daughters Shall Prophesy': Feminism in the Holiness Movement," *Methodist History* 14 (1976): 67–92; Susie Stanley, "Empowered Foremothers: Wesleyan/ Holiness Women Speak to Today's Christian Feminists," *Wesleyan Theological Journal* 24 (1989): 103–116; Susie Stanley, " 'Tell Me the Old, Old Story': An Analysis of Autobiographies by Holiness Women," *Wesleyan Theological Journal* 28 (1994): 7–22; Douglas M. Strong, "The Crusade for Women's Rights and the Formative Antecedents of the Holiness Movement," *Wesleyan Theological Journal* 27 (1992): 132–160. Strong quite effectively argues that Palmer's branch of the holiness movement was not the branch that ultimately led to social activism for women's political rights.

42. See Diane Leclerc, "Original Sin and Sexual Difference: A Feminist Historical Theology of a Patristic, Wesleyan, and Holiness Doctrine" (Ph.D. dissertation, Drew University, 1998).

43. Hovet, "Phoebe Palmer's 'Altar Phraseology,' " 271.

44. This is clearly seen in Palmer's record of her own sanctification experience: "On the morning of this day . . . my thought rested more especially upon the beloved one whom God had given to be the partner of my life. How truly a gift from God, and how essentially connected with my spiritual, as also my temporal happiness, is this one dear object! I exclaimed. Scarcely had these suggestions passed, when with keenness these inquiries were suggested: 'Have you not professedly give up all for Christ? If he who now so truly absorbs affections were required, would you not shrink from the demand?' I need not say that this one dear object, though often in name surrendered, was not in reality given up. My precious little ones, who God had taken to himself, were then brought to my recollection, as if to admonish me relative to making the sacrifice. I thought how fondly I had idolized them. He who said, "I the Lord your God am a jealous God," saw the idolatry of my heart, and took them to himself. The remembrance of how decidedly I had, by these repeated bereavements, been assured that He whose right it is to reign, would be the sole sovereign of my heart, assisted me in the resolve, that neither should this, the yet dearer object, be withheld . . . In full view of the nature of the sacrifice, I said, 'take life or friends away.' I could just have readily have said, 'take life,' as I could have said 'take friends'; for that which was just as dear, if not dearer than life, had been required. And when I said, 'Take him who is the supreme object of my earthly affection,' I, from that moment felt that I was fully set apart from God," Palmer, *Selected Writings*, 114–115.

45. Loveland, "Domesticity and Religion in the Antebellum Period," 460.

46. Ibid.

47. Margaret McFadden, "The Ironies of Pentecost: Phoebe Palmer, World Evangelism, and Female Networks," *Methodist History* 31 (1993): 70.

48. Hovet, "Phoebe Palmer's 'Altar Phraseology,' " 271.
49. For an extensive study of the home as the primary religious symbol in American Methodism prior to 1830, see A. Gregory Schneider (cited above).
50. The death of her first three children was key in bringing her to her experience of entire sanctification.
51. Hovet, "Phoebe Palmer's 'Altar Phraseology,' " 271.
52. Ibid., 271–272. The internally quoted material is from *The Way of Holiness*; Palmer refers to herself in the third person in this work.
53. Phoebe Palmer, *The Promise of the Father* (New York: Walter C. Palmer, 1859. Reprint, Salem, OH: Schmul Publishers, 199–), 345.
54. Luce Irigaray, "Gesture in Psychoanalysis," *Sexes and Geneologies*, trans. Gillian C. Gill (New York: Columbia University Press, 1993), 99.
55. Ibid. The use of this Irigarayian quote in this context should not be construed as any type of Pelagianism when applied to holiness women of the nineteenth century.
56. See Joel 2: 28–29.
57. Phoebe Palmer, *The Life and Letters of Mrs. Phoebe Palmer*, ed. Richard Wheatley (New York: W. C. Palmer, Publisher, 1876), 83.

CHAPTER SIX

Speaking Out: Feminist Theology and Women's Proclamation in the Wesleyan Tradition

LISA BERNAL CORLEY AND CAROL BLESSING

What is the place of women in the Church? Often, secular feminists see little connection between Christianity and feminism because of the way the Church, in its various manifestations and constructions, has marginalized women. Other religious traditions, such as goddess-based worship, Wicca, and other nature-based spirituality embrace female voices and leadership; some women have left the Church in order to discover these alternative ways of envisioning and speaking of the Divine. There is, however, a long connection between Christianity and women's active roles within the Church. Feminist scholarship opens the door for the study of women and their alternative means of proclaiming their relationship with God, from early Christianity to the present. It is a way of recovering an often-overlooked aspect of the Church, of including other voices that dominant religious history may seek to silence or treat as peripheral.

This essay discusses two ways in which Christianity has influenced feminism. The first part explores the contributions of women from the Methodist-Holiness tradition, focusing on the lives of English women Susanna Wesley, Mary Fletcher, and Mary Tooth. They are examples of women who have struggled, defied, and challenged patriarchal practices and structures of the Christian church. They are also models of women who, despite being banned from the preaching ministry of the church found ways to claim the pulpit. The contributions of these women to the history of Christianity and the history of Western society in general are tremendous.

The second part discusses the theoretical contributions of Christian feminists to feminist theory and practice by analyzing the works of contemporary feminist theologians, Elizabeth Schüssler-Fiorenza and Rebecca Chopp. These theologians stand in succession to the Christian women in history who struggled to have their voices heard. Although not "preachers" themselves, their theological works offer contemporary women preachers the tools necessary to secure their place in the Church and in society. Both Schüssler-Fiorenza and Chopp detail how women preachers can shape the message and practices of their community to become emancipatory.

The most important contribution of Christianity to feminism is the women themselves—women who, throughout the history of Christianity have sought to make their voices heard despite strong opposition from ecclesial hierarchy and society. Different institutional restrictions have been put in place to assure that Christian women remain bound to the practices of the Christian church. Canon law also limited the roles that women can take in the exercise of their religious faith.

Perhaps the area most restricted to women in the Church is the pulpit. The Church, from its earliest history has restricted and banned women from the office of "the Word." Women were not allowed to preach in public, and those who attempted to do so faced severe consequences, even the punishment of death. But history also shows that, despite these restrictions, women did find ways to speak of their faith. Some even managed to invent new forms of speech. In third-century Carthage, Christian martyr Perpetua (d. 203) testified to those in prison with her before she was thrown in the arena to be mutilated by a beast. Hildegard of Bingen (1098–1179) recorded mystical visions of God, the Universe, and the body of believers, and composed religious dramas and liturgical praise music to the Trinity and the Virgin Mary, while leading a remarkable community of women in the twelfth century. Catherine of Siena (1347–1380) wrote to princes, kings, and popes calling for reform in the fourteenth-century church and society. Julian of Norwich wrote down, meditated upon, and enlarged upon her visions of God, Christ, Mary, sin, and most emphatically, love, in fourteenth-century England, offering counsel and encouragement for those who sought her advice, and sharing her insights into the Divine with her readers.

In the seventeenth century, there was a host of women writing about issues of education and religion. There were two main reasons for this outpouring and focused concern with women's status and role in society: the seventeenth century's increase of Puritanism and corresponding multiplicities of churches and worship styles, and the growing emphasis on Reason, spawned from the writings of Francis Bacon and concreted by John Locke's works, which was dependent on education in order to develop. The Quaker Margaret Fell, future wife of George Fox, wrote her apologia for women preaching, *Womens Speaking Justified, Proved and Allowed of by the Scriptures* (1666). Fell composes a commentary of select biblical passages, from ones restrictive of women's preaching, to those promoting gender equality. In answer to 1 Corinthians 14:1–35 and 1 Timothy 2:11–12, she urges contextualizing Paul's words within the difficulties of the early Christian church, countering with numerous passages favorable to women. She asserts that, when the Holy Spirit's power is emphasized, women's speaking is allowed, and cites scriptural precedents of women used by God: Deborah, Anna, the Marys, and the women associated with the Apostle Paul (rpt. in Donawerth 60–70).

In 1671, Basthua Makin argued for women's education, in "An Essay to Revive the Ancient Educations of Gentlewomen, in Religion, Manners, Arts & Tongues." Thought to be part of an advertising campaign to promote her own school in Tottenham High Cross, the work lays out a case backed by logic, examples of classical and biblical women, and moral reasoning, for women's schooling. She asserts, "Women ought to be learned, that they may stop their ears against seducers" (rpt. in Rudrum, Black, and Nelson 427–428). Makin appeals to men particularly, citing an educated woman as being a better wife, one who is able to converse intelligently and bring glory to her husband, and says she is not arguing that women should use their education to preach. Nonetheless, she concludes with the injunction that, in Christ, "there is neither male nor female" (rpt. in Rudrum, Black, and Nelson 433).

In 1688, Mary Astell attacked English marriage customs and designed a plan for the first women's college. Her anonymously published works appeared in numerous editions in the late seventeenth and early eighteenth centuries. Because women are the victims of their culture's social customs that allow double standards for male and female fidelity, a point developed further by her friend Lady Wortley Montagu, Astell suggests in her work *Some Reflections Upon Marriage* that women subvert the system by remaining single. In *A Serious Proposal to the Ladies for the Advancement of Their True and Greatest Interest*, she constructs a utopian society for these single women, an Anglican religious community where women can be schooled in the higher arts of philosophy and logic. Answering John Locke, Astell asserts that women are as capable of higher reasoning, of participating in the same educational process men were allowed. Her work is the first developed apologia for a women's college. Although Astell's plans never materialized for that kind of institution, she did begin a Chelsea girl's school, training lower-class females in practical arts. Nonetheless, it is her vision of a community where women can learn and teach, lead and speak of their relationship to God's universe and the Divine that has lived on.

In 1689, poet Anne Finch captures the problems of separate systems for nurturing male and female children, showing that society's restrictions shape women's possibilities, as she states in the introductory poem to her works:

> How are we fallen! Fallen by mistaken rules,
>   And education's, more than nature's fools;
>   Debarred from all improvements of the mind, And to be dull,
>   expected and designed. (rpt. in Fitzmaurice 337)

God, says Finch, has not created women as inferior; it is their nurture and not their nature that makes them so. The double-edged sword constructs a system in which males disallow education for females and then scoff at them for being intellectually inferior.

The arguments for women's education and even preaching capacity heat up at the end of the seventeenth century, shaping the world in which the matriarch, Bible teacher, and educator of her children, Susanna Wesley, was formed. As mother of the Anglican clergyman who would go on to begin the Methodist movement, Susanna Wesley was a significant influence on his view of women. Within the Methodist-Holiness tradition, there was a resurgence of women's activity in the Church, and their ways of communicating pushed the boundaries of restrictions against women's voices. For founder John Wesley's focus on living out the gospel of justice and reconciliation, inclusion of the marginalized was a necessity. The poor, the lower classes, and the oppressed: these were his special interest groups. Within his culture, that would by necessity include women—they were the marginalized of every social class, the ones not represented in government, law, education, or economic systems. Tracing Wesley's discussion of women in his letter and sermons, and studying Wesley's treatment of women, work with women, and use of women in ministry, one may see that he moved to a somewhat more inclusive position as his ministry matured. Was this changing view formed pragmatically and materially, as women helped fund his work and provide a willing work base, or was there something more, rooted in his own concern for inclusion and justice, and even within his own home life?

Susanna Wesley

John Wesley's mother Susanna is considered remarkable in her own day as well as ours. In her husband's absence, Susanna began an in-home prayer meeting that soon grew to 200 participants, still meeting in her kitchen. The effects of a strong female spiritual leader on the future founder of Methodism were profound. According to church historians Davies and Rupp; "These occasions may have enforced in John Wesley's mind the principle that God might well summon sincere Christians to fellowship and worship outside the walls of the parish church and even under the leadership of laymen or even women" (216). Susanna was an influence in breaking down some gender stereotypes. The dichotomy that had traditionally linked males with reason and females with emotions dissolved in the light of her rationalism, which even bordered on skepticism (Davies and Rupp 89). She warned her son John of the dangers of mysticism as he studied Thomas à Kempis in Oxford (Stevens 28). She peppered her journals with references to John Locke and the philosopher Seneca. She educated her 13 children in both academic and spiritual subjects. The daughter of an Anglican minister, Susanna taught both her sons and daughters Greek, insisting that the girls not be taught to sew until they had learned to read.

It was Susanna Wesley's teaching that prepared John for Oxford, that admonished and encouraged him through correspondence while he was there, and that guided his earlier ministry while she was alive and left a profound influence even after her death. In Sermon 96, "On Obedience to Parents," Wesley writes that parental authority does not wane even after the child reaches adulthood. "And when I was between forty and fifty I judged myself full as much obliged to obey my mother in everything lawful as I did when I was in my hanging-sleeve coat" (*Sermons III* 364).

In Sermons 94 and 95, "On Family Religion" and "On the Education of Children," it is clear that John Wesley drew upon his own home life for material, the domestic setting that centered around Susanna. The portrait is of a mother who instructed her children from an early age, who was firm but loving with them, and who prepared them for the world by teaching self-discipline, manners, hard work, and above all, a love of God and knowledge of the scriptures (*Sermons III* 322–360).

Early on, Wesley's attitude toward women preaching was flatly prohibitive, but it gradually evolved somewhat, partly because of the support from women he had received, both in terms of works and finances, and perhaps in part from his mother's example that women could be godly teachers of the Word. In his Sermon 98, "On Visiting the Sick," Wesley condemns those who would demand the silence and passivity of women. He admonishes both sexes to participate in the ministry of visitation, arguing thusly:

Herein there is no difference: "there is neither male nor female in Christ Jesus." Indeed it has been long passed for a maxim with many that "women are only to be seen, not heard." And accordingly many of them are brought up in such a manner as if they were only designed for agreeable playthings! But is this doing honour to the sex? Or is it a real kindness to them? No; it is the deepest unkindness; it is horrid cruelty; it is mere Turkish barbarity. And I know not how any woman of sense and spirit can submit to it. Let all you that have it in your power assert the right which the God of nature has given you. Yield not to that vile bondage any longer. You, as well as men, are rational creatures. You, like them, were made in the image of God: you are equally candidates for immortality. You too are called of God, as you have time, to "do good unto all men." Be "not disobedient to the heavenly calling." Whenever you have opportunity, do all the good you can, particularly to your poor sick neighbor. And every one of you likewise "shall receive your own reward according to your own labour." (*Sermons III* 396)

Wesley would allow women to serve, but in different positions than men. We cannot say Wesley was firmly positive on the presence of women in the pulpit. One of his letters condemns the Quaker practice of women preaching, in a sense, overturning Margaret Fell's earlier argument that attempted to set the scriptural reference in light of early church contexts. He seems, however, to waver in his stance, trying to remain true to the Apostle Paul's injunction against women's preaching, but allowing "exceptional women" to speak. Often, this occurs through his terminology used to denote oral expression—female speaking, exhorting, prophesying, expounding on scripture could be all right, but pulpit preaching was not. Wesley's use of women in ministry was a double-edged sword; on the one hand, giving authority to females to carry out duties as necessary, but on the other, still caught in wanting to uphold St. Paul's injunctions against women's speech. This is a rather typical situation within which

devout females have been, and often continue to find themselves—
reliance on male approval weakens their ability to prove what their obvious giftedness would demonstrate. What is needed is a movement beyond
traditional authority structures and biblical interpretation, to an emancipatory allowance of women's roles, experiences, and most importantly,
voices.

Examples of Women's Voices in Early Methodism

While John Wesley never came out wholeheartedly in favor of women's
preaching, erring on the side of caution, and skirting the issue rhetorically by terming their oral proclamations exhorting, expounding,
prophesying, leading class, and so on, rather than preaching or ministry,
he did create an environment favorable to women in many ways. By
privileging the subjective and emotional through encouraging followers
to develop introspection by keeping journals, writing and sharing conversion accounts and accounts of happy deaths, accounts of dreams, and
letters, all of which emphasized the personal experience over education
and theological prowess, he opened the door for women to play a
leading role. He published many of their conversion and "happy death"
narratives (serene and sanctified deathbed accounts) in *The Arminian
Magazine*, and they continued to be published in *The Methodist Magazine*
after his death. Indeed, although his intentions might not have been to
legitimize female ministry, he provided fertile ground for women to
flourish in leadership and proclamation by encouraging them to write
their stories, which would lead to speaking their story. Susie Stanley's
Holy Boldness contains an important chapter on "How and Why
Wesleyan/Holiness Women Wrote," asserting that they were able to
transcend gender roles through appeal to the work of the Holy Spirit in
their lives (195). *In Methodism: Empire of the Spirit*, church historian David
Hempton goes so far as to state: "Methodism was without question a
woman's movement" (145). A handful of women even received Wesley's
special dispensation to lead in ways not typical of the Anglican church,
which his Methodist movement was trying to reform.

Women's public speaking within Methodism received notice,
acclaim, and disdain in the eighteenth century, and is a subject of many
studies today. Earl Kent Brown's and Paul Chilcote's research have
traced Wesley's attitudes toward women in ministry as it evolved
throughout his work.[1] Chilcote sees the change in Wesley's attitude
toward using women in his work as shaped by several factors. At first, he

was influenced by and tied to the Anglican church, which he wanted to reform, not overturn. His initial conservatism toward women was linked to his desire to avoid creating dissension in this area. As his ministry grew, Wesley was less worried about maintaining this decorum. Wesley was also influenced by Moravian (a Lutheran sect he met in his travel to Georgia) practices that allowed women active roles in the church, as well as by Susanna Wesley, as previously mentioned. (Chilcote, *John Wesley and the Women Preachers* 18–23, 141–142, 237–240) Chilcote also emphasizes Wesley's focus on "personal, religious experience and its power to transform both the individual and the society. . . . He would utilize almost any method to accomplish this divine mission," (*John Wesley and the Women Preachers* 46) including allowing women leaders. Nonetheless, Chilcote seems a bit too optimistic in his assessment of Wesley's acceptance of women's speaking; although guardedly allowing certain women to preach, including the first female Methodist preacher Sarah Crosby, Wesley never flatly condoned the regular presence of women in the pulpit.

Mary Bosanquet was one of the women who had obtained John Wesley's blessing on her ministry. Before her marriage to John Fletcher, she corresponded with Wesley regarding the issue of women speaking in church, using similar arguments to Margaret Fell, based upon women in scripture. Wesley replied with this 1771 letter concerning her work:

MY DEAR SISTER,—I think the strength of the cause rests there—on your having an *extraordinary* call. So I am persuaded has every one of our lay preachers; otherwise I could not countenance his preaching at all. It is plain to me that the whole work of God termed Methodism is an extraordinary dispensation of His providence. Therefore I do not wonder if several things occur therein which do not fall under the ordinary rules of discipline. St. Paul's ordinary rule was "I permit not a woman to speak in the congregation." Yet in extraordinary cases he made a few exceptions; at Corinth in particular.—I am, my dear sister,

Your affectionate brother. (*Letters* V 257)

While this letter at first seems positive, it does raise the issue of the double standard Wesley held to: a woman preaching is anomalous, not a practice Wesley wanted to create or reinforce. Nonetheless, it is clear Wesley felt Mary Bosanquet a gifted woman, one whom he approved to marry his intended successor John Fletcher. Later, however, Wesley would write a letter to George Robinson to censure female leadership, saying "I desire Mr. Peacock to put a final stop to the preaching of women in his circuit. If it were suffered, it would grow, and we know not where it would end" (*Letters* VII 8) Despite Wesley's fears, women's preaching did grow. Through the exemplum of Mary Bosanquet Fletcher's female community, we can see this growth of women's preaching that created anxiety for John Wesley.

Mary Bosanquet had dedicated her life to the service of God at an early age, as recorded here in her 1764 letter to John Wesley:

> From a child I have ever believed, God had appointed me for some Work, in which I should be much blest if I was faithful; but that if I took up with any Thing less than I was called to, I should only be saved as by *Fire* . . .
>
> I plainly see, I have no more to do with the World, than to allow myself the bare Necessaries of Life. And tho' it has pleased GOD, I should not have my Living to work for, That is no Reason my Hands should be idle. I would be as those described by St. Paul, *to bring up Children, to lodge Strangers*, to be ready for the meanest Offices, *to relieve the afflicted, to visit the Fatherless and Widows, and diligently follow after every good Work.* (Bosanquet 9)

As a young woman, Bosanquet cared for orphaned girls in a house school that she ran with the help of Sarah Ryan, a woman also appointed by John Wesley for the task. Bosanquet constructed herself as a person dedicated to the care of others, a person called by the Divine throughout her life. She had left her father's house over the issue of her conversion to Methodism, and formed an alternative family of females. Although she became a preacher's wife, her primary focus was initially and for a long while afterward removed from male presence, as she and famed Methodist minister John Fletcher were only married four years before his death. While they were married, she functioned as a co-pastor with him. Later, Mary Fletcher and the women associated with her, including Sarah Ryan, Sarah Crosby, Sarah Lawrence (whom Fletcher called her adopted daughter), and Mary Tooth, would become some of the most outspoken voices in early Methodism, using a variety of proclamational modes. Both Brown and Chilcote classify the stages of women's speaking within Methodism as including public prayer, testimony, and exhortation; Brown extends those forms in Mary Fletcher's case to include expounding and preaching (Chilcote, *John Wesley and the Women Preachers* 92–107; Brown, *Women of Mr. Wesley's Methodism* 19–25).

In the writings of Mary Tooth, an admirer, helper, friend, and executrix of Mary Fletcher, who was eventually to become a preacher herself, she records being able to hear a public address by Mary Fletcher, which became the primary influence on her own life. It is Mary Tooth, a relatively unknown woman, who gives candid eyewitness views of these English women dedicated to serving the Lord through Methodism. Her unpublished manuscript journals in the Methodist Archives focus on her religious experience, primarily as it centered in the Madeley, Shropshire circle, following the Rev. John Fletcher's death. Mrs. Fletcher continued to remain in the vicarage following John's demise, an unusual allowance that demonstrated her power and respect from the parishioners. Drawing around her a female religious community very similar to that described ideally in Mary Astell's 1688 writings, she formed a gyne–utopia in which women could go beyond societal bounds in terms of female church authority. This group of women was devoted to their idea of serving God, set purposefully apart from male authority and control: in a sense, a reenvisionment of the Church and family. After Mary Fletcher's death, Mary Tooth continued her work for another 28 years.

Although Mary Tooth initially did not live with Mrs. Fletcher, she moved from Birmingham at the age of 16 to work in the home of a woman in Madeley, soon bonding with Mary Fletcher in a relationship that was to be her most important. In one of her earliest journal entries, January 28, 1799, Tooth speaks of returning to "Mrs Fletcher in the evening in time to hear her expound the 20th chapter of Exo. to the 21st at the vicarage. I remained all night."[2] A later journal adds: "All the time I heard the gospel preached at St. Marys [her home church] but my heart never felt the awakening power of God till I came to Madeley, it was in the vicarage Barn (or Mrs Fletchers room)" (Tooth, box 14, vol. b., ms. 23).

The Fletcher-Tooth manuscript collection contains numerous writings of Mary Fletcher she entitled "Watch-Words." They were essentially exhortations Mary Fletcher preached in the "tithe barn" associated with the vicarage. There were two series: the names or words associated with Christ, and the words for the Church. Currently, Methodist pastor the Rev. David J. Frudd is transcribing those works, to be published shortly by the *Asbury Theological Journal*. They are constructed as scriptural exegesis and, according to Frudd's analysis, in everything but name are sermons.

Mary Tooth again provides accounts of precisely what went on in the tithe barn. It became a church in its own right; although in the letter of the law, the tithe barn was not a sanctuary where a woman was preaching, yet in practice it became precisely that. Here is Tooth's entry for December 20, 1796:

> At this time all the protestant worship of God, that was in the Town or Village of Madeley was all held in what was called Mrs Fletcher's Room. Which I do not think I can describe in better words than her own, when writing to a friend the story of it, "It is not very fine, yet it is not as plain as the Stable at Bethlehem. Some Slabs make a good dry wooden floor. A thatched top keeps out the rain & paper shades the cold & dust. The sides & top are lined with Lead [?] & washed with White, so that seven large candles reminds us of the Light & Perfection which the Spirit hath promised to Baptize us with, when our Robes shall be made Whiter than our Walls." (box 14, vol. b, ms. 85)

Tooth adds, "The account of the opening of this Room was preserved by Sarah Lawrence whose account of it is as follows. 'The first Sabbath in July 1788, the Room at the Vicarage in Madeley was opened; it has been for many years a barn, but was now fitted up for Divine Worship' " (box 14, vol. b, ms. 86).

An entry a few days later (December 31, 1796) is even more revealing as to the extent of Mary Fletcher's ministry. For a period of almost two years, she is leading worship more often than the vicar hired to take the late John Fletcher's place fully two-thirds of the time while he speaks at other churches:

> I have now been just one year in Madeley & have found here a people with whom I wish to live & die, the means of grace here are truly sweet to my taste, the church service is only once in three weeks & then held in Mrs Fletchers Room, the other two Lords Days Mr Walters is at either Coalbrookedale or Madeley-wood. While he is at those places Mrs Fletcher speaks to the people in her own Room. This has been the case ever since Sept. 21st 1794 & the people are so well pleased with the arrangement that they are wishing the building of the Church did not go on so fast they do so well without it. (box 14, vol. b., ms. 95)

Mary Fletcher created an alternative sacred space, one in which she is free to interpret and proclaim the Word, and apparently, one to which her parishioners repeatedly flocked. Her active presence in Madeley certainly functioned fully as ministry. In his account of her life, Zechariah

Taft lists the multitudinous occasions that Fletcher (now aged 71) spoke to the people of her parish:

> On Sunday mornings she met the society of Madeley and the neighbourhood; on Sundays in the afternoon, she spoke upon some subject, of which notice had been given the Sunday before, generally upon the names of Christ, or his Church [these were the *Watch-Words*] . . . On Sunday evenings she kept a public meeting, except on Sacrament-days. On Monday night she preached to a crowded house. Generally paraphrases. When we were there the subject was the ninth chapter of John. Indeed she very generally expounded a passage of scripture on Tuesday evening; one week was the intercession, the other a travelling preacher. On Wednesday afternoon she meet the Madeley class. (Taft, *Biographical Sketches* 26)

Backlash Against Women Preaching

By 1802, there was already enough criticism of women preaching to warrant Zechariah Taft's writing and publishing on the subject. Taft, husband of outspoken and controversial female preacher Mary Barritt Taft, and a known supporter of women in ministry, states in his apologia to *Thoughts on Female Preaching*:

> On my occasionally suffering a female to officiate for me, many persons came to ask my thought upon the subject, and as I wish to be ready to give an account of every part of my conduct, with meekness and fear, to all those who may enquire after good; to save time and oblige my friends, on the 16th of November I took up my pen, to collect those passages of scripture that seem to favour the subject, or militate against it, and wrote the substance of the following pages. (n. pag.)

Taft's support of women's proclamation is constructed out of biblical texts; he lists women from the Old and New Testaments who are prophets and exhorters—Deborah, Miriam, Abigail, Huldah, Anna, the women at the crucifixion and resurrection, the four daughters of Philip, Priscilla, and Phoebe (*Thoughts* 2–6). Most importantly, Taft does not distinguish between prophesying, exhorting, or preaching, thus creating a wider scope to legitimize female oral authority (*Thoughts* i–ii) His argument condoning women preaching, claiming that these alternative forms of expression are in fact preaching, is in effect a rhetorical shift that functions to include females' voices.

Female Perseverance

While Taft wrote to support and sustain women in public speaking, Mary Fletcher's circle of women continued tirelessly with their labors. What is somewhat remarkable in Mary Tooth's years of journals is that she never specifically records any opposition to any women's leadership. Her journals are filled with transcribed letters recording positive responses and appreciation from others, including males, for the work of Mary Fletcher, the Sarahs, and her own work, although the Fletcher Methodist Church, Madeley website mentions opposition toward the end of Mary Fletcher's life and somewhat during Tooth's ministry. This female ministry foreshadows many to follow in the Wesleyan holiness tradition, including Phoebe Palmer, called the Mother of the American Holiness Movement, and sister American Frances E. Willard. In 1899, Frances E. Willard, head of the Women's Christian Temperance Union, wrote *Woman in the Pulpit*, a follow-up to Margaret Fell's work and a precursor of Elizabeth Schüssler-Fiorenza's feminist theology. In it, Willard cautions against the biblical texts that silence women: "Whoever quotes to the intelligent and devout women of the American church today the specific instructions given by Paul to the illiterate and immoral women of Corinth does so at the expense of sound judgment, not to say scholarship" (rpt. in Donawerth 248). Willard argues for not only the allowance but also the necessity of hearing female voices: "It is men who have given us the dead letter rather than the living gospel. The mother-heart of God will never be known to the world until translated into terms of speech by mother-hearted women. Law and love will never balance in the realm of grace until a woman's hand shall hold the scales" (rpt. in Donawerth 246). Willard's outspoken arguments anticipate later Christian feminist theologians, such as Rebecca Chopp. Parallel to Chopp's view later in this chapter, Willard sees women's spiritual gift as being able to envision another side, that of compassion for the marginalized, when they read scriptures and present their exegesis. Their proclamation will bring many more to conversion, as Willard states: "The entrance of women upon the ministerial vocation will give to humanity just twice the probability of strengthening and comforting speech, for women have at least as much sympathy, reverence, and spirituality as men, and they have at least equal felicity of manner and utterance. Why, then, should the pulpit be shorn of half its power?" (rpt. in Donawerth 247).

Much of Mary Tooth's and the other Madeley females' ministry went far beyond public speaking to true shepherding of their flock, including visitation of the sick, counseling the distressed, and prayer ministry. Reminding ourselves that Mary Fletcher's initial work was in beginning an orphanage/school for female children, that is, caring for those economically disadvantaged, it is no wonder that her mentee Mary Tooth continued in compassionate work. She also helped begin a teetotaler society for those struggling with alcohol addiction, as well as continued the missionary circle begun by Mary Fletcher. In turn, Tooth mentored a young woman, Sarah Jenkins, guiding her in her spiritual walk, encouraging her to keep a journal of her own, which Tooth reprints portions of in an account of Jenkins's life, and leading her toward ministry as well. Jenkins helped Mary Tooth distribute tracts and although young, became a Methodist Society class leader (Tooth, *Memoirs of Miss Sarah Jenkins* 10). Unfortunately, Jenkins died at the age of 18, cutting short the possibility that she could carry on Mary Tooth's work.

Mary Tooth purposefully placed herself outside of male authority throughout her life in order to carry out her ministry. Twice she received marriage proposals, and twice she refused. The first proposal was from the son of her early employer, Mrs. Micklewright, whose employ she leaves because of the awkward situation. She records the experience with the second man as follows:

> 12th Tuesday [March 1799], a gentleman in this neighborhood came & made a most generous offer which arose from a conviction he said he received in Madeley Church, which was that I was the person that was to be his wife, he said, it was as plain to him as if some one had said, "That is to be your wife." However no such conviction having arrested my mind I saw it right to give a refusal in the most express terms. I plainly see my call at present is to abide <u>as</u> I am, & <u>where</u> I am, with regard to marriage. (box 14, vol. d, ms. 28–29)

Clearly, Tooth sees herself set apart to fulfill a special work, agreeing here with the Apostle Paul that the single state allows her to devote more complete service to God.

The only person to whom Tooth felt a true heart connection only to Mary Fletcher, to whom she referred as either "my beloved Mrs. Fletcher" or "my dear Mrs. Fletcher." Mary Fletcher in fact has counseled her against marriage in both cases. Mary Fletcher's manuscript journals of August 1 and November 13, 1802 show gratitude toward Tooth in accounts that Henry Moore edits out in his 1824 published account entitled *The Life of Mrs. Mary Fletcher.* Calling Tooth "truly a gift of God that I could not do without," Fletcher uses Tooth as her assistant, particularly following the death of Sarah Lawrence, who had functioned in that capacity (Fletcher ms. journals). Tooth saw herself as more than a helper; she learned much from Mary Fletcher in terms of ministry and piety.

Mary Tooth's devastation in losing Mary Fletcher to death in1815 is apparent in her anguished journal accounts and her published *A Letter to the Loving and Beloved People of Madeley, and its Vicinity, Who Have Lost a Friend to Piety in the Death of Mary Fletcher.* She refers to Fletcher as her spiritual mother, guide, friend, and as her most important love next to God. Following Mary Fletcher's death, Mary Tooth must leave the vicarage that had been sold. She again follows what she feels is the will of God, buy a house in Madeley in order to continue her work. She does this in opposition to male advice:

> When I was about leaving the Vicarage & purchasing this House my friend Mr Puritan said to me "was I in your place I would take Lodgings." I replied so would I if I had only myself to consider, but the people where would they have to meet if I have no house of my own? "O! let them go to Madeleywood many walk farther then that for the gospel." But I could not see it right to act in this way, his light was not my light, I have therefore indeavoured according to the ability given unto me to build up God's cause. (box 14, vol. m, ms. 201–202)

Tooth clearly sees the people of Madeley as those to whom she is called to minister. Her perseverance and unflinching vision continue, demonstrating her assurance that she is ordained by God and well-mentored by her spiritual mother. After having spoken in the Tithe Barn of Mary Fletcher's days, Mary Tooth converts a room in her own house for meetings and other gatherings, calling it her Upper Room. Here is a record of one Love-feast, the early Methodist breaking of bread and celebrating the participants' personal stories or testimonies, held in her Upper Room on December 7, 1824:

> This evening the Lovefeast was held in my upper room neither of our Preachers could make it convenient to attend but glory be to a Triune God Jesus was present to break the bread of life to all our waiting souls, the sweet the farest unction of this Holy Spirit was most powerfully felt, the cleanness of the peoples experience & the

simplicity with which they related it made hours pass away as moment. I do see a fulfilment of my glorified friends words, "The residue of the spirit is with the Lord & he will pour it out." Yes, glory be to God he does! (box 14, journal fragments from 1824, ms. n.pag.)

Mary Tooth's journals often mention her reading Mary Fletcher's "Watch-Words," pieces of John Fletcher's sermons, conversion narratives, or letters to the gatherings, leading one to think she had not composed original works. None of her sermons has been published, although her conversion narrative of another woman in ministry, Sarah Jenkins, was. What little that is written on Tooth usually shows her significant primarily in relation to Mary Fletcher. One exception is Dale A. Johnson's informative article "Gender and Models of Christian Activity" that gives an overview of Tooth's work. Opening Tooth's manuscript commonplace books (recording both her own works and quotations from others) shows a thoughtful writer and serious speaker, as she has carefully indexed numerous complete original sermons listed by the dates and places she preached them. She does also use material from the Fletchers, as well as from conversion narratives and happy death accounts. Her work went beyond the town of Madeley, as the volume for 1816 records leading classes and speaking at meetings at 12 different Shropshire towns during the year (multiple times per town). The following sermon preached at Coalport on October 18, 1818 is an illustration of Tooth's no-nonsense approach to convicting and reprimanding her people:

Well, my friends our past lives are a quarter longer & our future lives are a quarter shorter then when we met here last.

Are you proportionally grown in grace & reduced in nature?

You that were in your sins last quarter are you now soundly converted to God?

You that were halting between two & unresolved whether to serve Xt [Christ] or Belial, do you now see it to be your highest interest to comply with the terms of him who as said, "If any man will be my deciple let him take up his cross & follow me."?

You that a quarter past was in a backsliding state, are you now returned to him who weeping over Jerusalem said, "How often would I have gathered thee as a hen gathers her children under her wing but ye would not, mark that word, would not. The Saviour would, the Sinner would not.

O! may it never be so said of you!

May you know in this your day the things that belong to your peace before they are forever hid from you eyes!

If not the candle of the Lord shine upon you, take heed that you turn not again to folly.

Sin is the only object of God's infinite hatred. His love is entended to a great variety of objects, he loves his Angels, his saints, his servants, his creatures, all things he as made he loves. A pious man observes, "Sin is fouler then the foulest Fiend in Hell then the Devil himself for it was sin that made him a Devil & sunk him into Hell, therefore sin is more rank than the Devil, & horrible than Hell itself. Could the Devil be stript of sin he might again enjoy the favours of the most high, for God hates the Devil for nothing else but for sin."

Sin is full of the most fearful effects, I will just tell you a few of the things it will deprive you of if continued in, & then leave you to chose for yourselves whether you will be the servants of sin or not.

It will deprive you of the Favour & Love of God. The only Fountain of all comfort, Peace & happiness.

It will deprive you of your portion in the merits of Xts [Christ's] blood. & you had better have that than all the riches, pleasures & enjoyments that the whole world can afford.

It will deprive you of all communion with the holy spirit, of the holy protection of the blessed Trinity, of a guard of Angels, of all fellowship with the people of God, of the inexpressible pleasures of a peaceful conscience in comparison of which all human glory is but as dust in the balance. For the day is coming when a good conscience will be a better portion then ten thousand earthly concerns. It deprives of all true comfort & right enjoyment of the things of this life.

It will deprive you of an immortal crown of glory, of the unspeakable joys of heaven, of all that endless comfort that is to be enjoyed eternally with the children of God, Patriarchs, Prophets, Apostles, Martyrs, with Xt [Christ] our Saviour that Lamb slain for us, the Prince of Glory.

May you see the dreadful effects of sin & cry to God till you obtain power over it, then will your lives & deaths be both holy & happy.

A man of God that had been confined to his bed some months was one day told his countenance was much altered, & that the time of his departure was at hand. He asked for a looking glass, in which he viewed himself for a short time, & then said, "death as put his mark on my body, but Christ as put his mark on my soul." & the next day he went to be forever with the Lord. (box 26, notebook for 1818, ms. 1–4)

As in this example, many of Mary Tooth's sermons are primarily evangelistic; that is, they are aimed at producing conversion in the audience, a turning from their sin to salvation. This is consistent with the Methodist revival, which focused first on conversion of the listeners and a movement into sanctification, leaving the material and fleshly desires beyond to focus on the heavenly. Despite her tone that sometimes could be rebuking, however, Tooth usually began the sermons with an address to the listeners as friends, placing herself on equal footing and showing her personal concern for her listeners. She does not address the issue of female preaching throughout her manuscripts, nor does she present credentials except to see herself as a carrier of God's message, as in this opening to her April 9, 1815 address to the Madeley parish: "My friends, I feel a desire while God shall give me a voice to speak and his providence shall open a way for my speaking: to deal by you with all plainess of speech" (box 26, vol. 11, ms. 101–110).

Culling through the manuscripts of the Fletcher-Tooth Collection of the Methodist Archives of the Rylands Library, Manchester allows the reader to see an unedited, unapologetic account of a woman's life and ministry in her own words, rarely afforded. The published accounts of most other earlier women preachers are edited, usually by males, such as Henry Moore's account of Mary Fletcher or "The Account of Hester Ann Rogers," another female authorized by John Wesley for exceptional work. Vicki Tolar Collins astutely examines the way Rogers's narrative is reshaped by the males who edit and supplement her diary accounts (7–12).

In addition to her own active role in ministry, Mary Tooth did also idealize and sustain Mary Fletcher's memory, much in the tradition of Isaac Walton's heroic seventeenth-century accounts of preacher poets John Donne and George Herbert. She was also executrix and curator for the Fletchers's belongings, creating in effect a memorial museum to the couple. Tooth's journal entry for October 6, 1841 records giving five ministers a tour of the vicarage, showing them Mary Bosanquet's childhood Bible, the Bible recording their marriage, and some remnants of Mary Fletcher's tithe barn: "They also went upstairs into my upper room where is the communion Table & Cloth Velvet & Curtains of the pulpit that was in the Old Church of Madeley, with Clock & other things brought from the Vicarage Barn" (box 14, vol. n, ms. n. pag.).

In her last years, Tooth, in declining health, notes in her journal that she is frequently feeling violent pains in her head. Nonetheless, she leads as many meetings as she can, including class meetings, missionary meetings, the teetotaler society, sewing circle meetings, and others; counsels the many people who come to visit her, is active in writing correspondence, and records the following: "Time flies very rapidly along, & my mind ever being in presenting work to be done makes me see the necessity of adhering as closely as possibly I can to that excellent rule of Mr. Wesleys '*Never Be Idle*' " (box 14, vol. n, ms. n. pag.). Her last entry discusses working at the parish bazaar.

What is interesting is that the Fletcher circle, particularly in the case of Mary Tooth, goes beyond the roles of women envisioned by John Wesley. While he clung to the letter of the law, as presented in Paul's writings prohibiting female preaching, these women go beyond the restrictions to a freedom within their ministry. Rather than compete with men, these women create their own separate society, one in which women needed no apology and were not seen as exceptional in leadership. Wesley's movement has taken on a life of its own. Whatever these women's public speaking was called, they in actuality did preach and were well received. They envisioned their service as directly to God, rather than placing themselves under the headship of men, especially in the example of Mary Tooth. They may not have functioned in traditional pulpit preaching, but did continue and enlarge upon the tradition of female proclamation, by carving out separate sacred spaces, creating female models of mentoring and ministry, and constructing alternative rhetorical modes of speech.

Christian Feminism and Women's Ministry

The search for female models of ministry and alternative modes of speech continues. Today, the quest is being carried on most emphatically by the Christian feminists. The Christian feminist, be it a man or a woman, envisions a world in which all people are liberated from oppression and injustice, in its various forms. S/he comes from a long line of Christian believers who believe in the power of the gospel to transform the whole of creation: to bring freedom to the oppressed, healing to the broken, and salvation to the lost. It is this promise of restoration that provides the Christian feminist the courage and wisdom to struggle for liberation. It is perhaps not too audacious to say that Christian women in earlier centuries precede the early feminist reformers in their struggle for equality in the society. It is in this august line of women that Rebecca Chopp and Elizabeth Schüssler-Fiorenza stand today.

According to journalist Cullen Murphy (Bergant), the most prominent Second Testament[3] woman scholar is Schüssler-Fiorenza. He recognizes her significant contribution on contemporary feminist biblical interpretation. Schüssler-Fiorenza is the Krister Stendahl Professor of Divinity in Harvard Divinity School. She has done pioneering work on biblical interpretation and feminist theology, and is known for her thesis that the early Christian community was more egalitarian than previously recognized. As a scholar, she wants to reclaim the scriptures for women by formulating a radical biblical hermeneutics. Schüssler-Fiorenza recognizes that the Bible is perhaps the biggest obstacle in the feminist movement since it has been used to justify the subordination of women. Her work then provides critical tools for reading the Bible. It is interesting to note that she is also the first woman scholar to serve as the President of the American Society of Biblical Literature, founded in 1880 with over 6,000 members worldwide. Her work can be briefly described as a feminist hermeneutics of reconstruction.

In contrast to Schüssler-Fiorenza, Chopp examines feminist practice of theology for church life and theological education. Chopp sees feminist theology as comprised of discourses of emancipatory proclamation. *Syracuse New Times* writer Walt Shepperd describes Chopp, on her appointment as president of Colgate University (New York) in 2004, as the new "Gate-Keeper." Colgate is a liberal arts institution founded in 1819. She is the university's first woman president. Before this, Chopp served as dean and professor of theology and culture at Yale Divinity School, and taught religion and women's studies at Emory University, serving also as Provost and executive vice president for academic affairs for three years. Both Chopp and Schüssler-Fiorenza represent Christian feminism at its best and so this section explores their contribution to feminist theology and biblical studies.

Elizabeth Schüssler-Fiorenza:
Re-Writing the Bible for Women

In *Bread Not Stone*, Schüssler-Fiorenza recognizes the political and cultural significance of the Bible in Western societies. She points out the two-pronged direction of this influence. First, it remains the main guide for Christians in the world, for both men and women; and second, it continues to be the major source for Christian ethics and the formation of Christian identity (65). At the same time, it exercises political influence as people continue to appeal to its moral authority to promote social programs, which can result in either liberation or oppression of segments of population (67). Schüssler-Fiorenza comments that conservative social forces have taken advantage of the abandonment of religion by contemporary feminists by claiming the Bible as their own. She believes though that "any social and cultural feminist transformation in Western society must deal constructively with biblical religion and its continuing impact on American culture" (84). She wants to recognize the "positive experiences of contemporary women within biblical religion," without denying the fact that side-by-side with a biblical vision of freedom and wholeness lies its patriarchal content and androcentric language (xiii, 6).

In order to do this, she proposes that discussion about the role of scripture in public life needs to move from a "generalized moral and political discourse in church and society to disciplined theological scholarship"(*Bread Not Stone* 69). This move is necessary if feminists are to succeed in evaluating and judging the impact of biblical traditions and religious texts on contemporary American culture. She proposes two ways to make this shift. First, there is a need for a feminist biblical hermeneutics aimed toward emancipatory praxis, and second, there is also a need for a feminist theology of liberation that seeks "to name theologically the alienation, anger, pain, and dehumanization engendered by patriarchal sexism and racism in society and church" (*Bread Not Stone* 5).

Feminist biblical hermeneutics is an important theological task because there is a need to identify and analyze the ideological functions of the scriptures not only within the Church but in society as well. Schüssler-Fiorenza admits that throughout Christian history, the Bible has been used to arrest the emancipation of slaves and women, on the one hand, and to defend their emancipation, on the other (*Bread Not Stone* 67). So the goal of feminist hermeneutics is to transform how people read biblical texts themselves. At the same time, it is not enough that people are trained to read biblical texts with a critical eye, but it is also equally important that the experiences of women in a patriarchal church—their struggle for self-identity, survival, and liberation—be given voice. Hence, there is a need for a feminist theology that will show how the scripture can become an "enabling, motivating resource and empowering authority in women's struggles for justice, liberation, and solidarity"(xxiii).[4] The elements of these proposals will now be elaborated.

Feminist Biblical Hermeneutics

Schüssler-Fiorenza sees her proposal as an alternate theory, method, or perspective for the understanding and interpretation of biblical texts. This is an indispensable task because traditional biblical hermeneutics viewed scriptures as a "foundational archetype" that provides the Church with timeless, universal principles for teaching and practice. In other words, biblical texts are nothing but the Word of God *himself*, and therefore, its message has the authority of divine revelation. In this traditional approach to biblical interpretation, one only need to read God's Word and apply its teaching to one's life, without much consideration of the sociohistorical situations from which the texts themselves developed. Likewise, in this reading, the patriarchal culture reflected in the texts and the androcentric language through which the texts are communicated do not pose a problem for interpretation. It is often pointed out that with the guidance of the Holy Spirit, the reader will be able to discern the true meaning of the text by simply reading.

In contrast to this approach, Schüssler-Fiorenza offers a critical evaluative hermeneutics. Her approach takes into account the problem of the male-centered biblical language, the sexism embedded in the patriarchal construction of biblical texts, and the absence of positive women's stories in biblical history. She focuses on the analysis of historical texts and literary forms using the experiences of women struggling for liberation and wholeness as the hermeneutical center for interpretation. In other words, for Schüssler-Fiorenza, the experience of oppression and liberation of contemporary communities becomes the criteria of "appropriate" biblical interpretation (*Bread Not Stone* 60). In this method, she follows the insights of critical feminist theory that emphasizes the need for the development of a consciousness that is directed toward the transformation of patriarchal relations of subordination and oppression.

This methodological approach also introduces new elements in biblical hermeneutics. First, it relocates divine authority from the biblical (canonical) texts themselves to the experiences of oppression and liberation. Schüssler-Fiorenza does not have a problem doing this because she sees the Bible not as a "foundational archetype" but rather as a "formative root-model" that provides the readers with visions and models and paradigms (and not absolute commands or teachings). She rejects the idea that we can find or locate universal principles in the texts themselves because she argues that the biblical writers do not either. Instead, in the study of biblical writings, especially New Testament texts, she finds that the writers freely located "revelation" not only in the past traditions but also in their own present (*Bread Not Stone* 35). This means too that for her, only "those traditions and texts that critically break through patriarchal culture . . . have the theological authority of revelation" (Schüssler-Fiorenza, *Memory* 33).

Second, Schüssler-Fiorenza also emphasizes the need for a biblical hermeneutics that can expose the oppressive political import of the Bible. The importance of this step cannot be overlooked because she is aware that scriptures have ideological functions that serve the Church and society well. Thus, students of the Bible must not only be trained how to analyze the texts but to critically reflect on their own presuppositions and prejudices, as well as those of other biblical interpretations. Schüssler-Fiorenza proposes four "reading strategies" to achieve this end. The four reading strategies for emancipatory practice are (1) hermeneutics of suspicion, (2) hermeneutics of remembrance, (3) hermeneutics of proclamation, and (4) hermeneutics of imagination and ritualization (Schüssler-Fiorenza, *But She Said*).[5] This is especially relevant for Church life since she notes that the fear of biblical criticism in religious education is one of the biggest hindrances in the development of critical consciousness among Christian believers. She observes that even those who have studied critical hermeneutics are hesitant to use it for the education of the laity either in preaching or meditation.

Feminist Theology

The development of a feminist theology is essential to women's liberation because the "pastoral-theological paradigm has to formulate its own criterion that cannot be derived from biblical texts but must be draw from Christian communities, to which [the] texts speak today"(Schüssler-Fiorenza, *Bread Not Stone* 4). Schüssler-Fiorenza states that feminist theologians must face squarely a fundamental theological question: "Is being a woman and being a Christian a primary contradiction that must be resolved in favor of one to the exclusion of the other?"(Schüssler-Fiorenza, *Bread Not Stone* 55). Since feminist theology is Christian theology based on the teachings of the scripture, it must respond to this problem.

Schüssler-Fiorenza's answer to this dilemma is a theology operating on a paradigm of emancipatory praxis. Under this paradigm, theological

reflection involves the interpretation and evaluation of biblical traditions
and their political consequences in human history (not just in Christian
or women's history). By addressing the tension found in both biblical
history and contemporary experiences, one need not choose between
being a woman or a Christian, or vice-versa. Instead, a feminist theology
will teach and preach on biblical traditions in terms of liberation. It will
provide a vision of new creation. This approach has far-reaching implications for pastoral-theological practice within the Christian community. For one, she proposes that the interpreter of the scripture must
distinguish carefully between preaching or proclamation and teaching.
The preacher must select biblical texts that address issues facing the contemporary community, using only texts that do not propagate patriarchal
and androcentric views. S/he must employ a "hermeneutic of proclamation" that refuses to anoint patriarchal values embedded in biblical
texts with divine authority and proclaim it as God's *Word*. In practice,
"hermeneutics must insist that all texts identified as sexist or patriarchal
should not be retained in the lectionary nor be proclaimed in Christian
worship" (Schüssler-Fiorenza, *Bread Not Stone* 18).

On the other hand, the task of teaching or catechesis is to preserve the
multiplicity of the early Christian traditions and communities. This
preservation is necessary in order for the readers to remember the struggles that characterized early Christian history. Thus, in teaching, it is
possible to use texts that are characteristically sexist and patriarchal in
order to assess the interaction of biblical texts with contemporary
culture, without giving them divine authority. With the use of feminist
hermeneutics, the reader can reconceptualize critical theological doc-
trines in ways that will promote the emancipation, liberation, and
sustenance of the *ekklesia*-women (i.e., women-church).[6] The "women-
church" does not represent an exclusive gathering of women that
excludes men, but rather a "hermeneutical" constructive articulation
that functions like "binoculars" to show that patriarchal religions have
been exclusive of women (Schüssler-Fiorenza, *Bread Not Stone* 1995).
She bases this idea from her comparative studies of the Pauline texts and
the gospels. She finds that although post-Pauline and post-Petrine texts
support the limitation of women's roles in the communities, the writers
of the gospels of John and Mark present an alternative picture of leadership where women disciples are accorded apostolic and ministerial positions
(Schüssler-Fiorenza, *Memory* 334). In the end, a feminist theology of
liberation evokes multiplicity and freedom and provides a form of discourse that speaks about the Word in light of experience, community,
scripture, and tradition for the world today. According to Rebecca

Chopp, this is what Schüssler-Fiorenza's work offers (Chopp, *Power to speak* 20).

Rebecca Chopp's and the Woman's Power to Speak

Chopp shares with Schüssler-Fiorenza the burden of responding to the feminist critique of biblical religion. She said that there is a need to ask why women stay in Christianity when there seems to be a contradiction between feminism and Christianity. In *Power to Speak*, she notes that oftentimes, Christian feminists are accused of being "adolescents who cannot leave the 'home' of Christianity, even when it curtails or impedes their freedom" (17). Like Schüssler-Fiorenza, she is aware that despite the promise and symbol of radical freedom for all, there remains in Christianity a gendered division between men and women, made more problematic by the "God-male-female-nature" hierarchical scheme. At the same time, Christianity is plagued with practices, teachings, beliefs, and lifestyles that justify the oppression of women in God's name (4). But instead of abandoning the Christian faith, Chopp like Schüssler-Fiorenza, opted to play out Christianity as a source of power for women in the world. She recognizes that Christianity has spoken for women both in and out of the church, and that religion continues to offer a power of interpretation for the world. The task therefore is to challenge the scripture, which is the "primary datum" of Christian faith. She does this by introducing a new discourse that transforms the meaning of women's experience, that is, feminist theology.

For Chopp, theology is proclamation and proclamation involves language. Therefore, her theological method revolves around a new interpretation of the nature and function of language (*Power to Speak* 13). She positions feminist discourse within the "margins" whose goal is emancipatory transformation of the social-symbolic order (15). In Chopp's theology, there is a dialectical relationship between language and the socio-symbolic order. Since language has both reflexive and constitutive capacities, the proclamation of scripture creates realities for women within and without the Christian community. This dynamic however becomes problematic when women are denied access to language, in this case, the Word. Likewise, it becomes doubly complicated when language creates "woman through character of division, a division creating and re-creating the basic division of male and female ordered always on the invocation of God, as the *primal signifier* as the Word from which all words take order and meaning" (25, italics mine).

Thus, according to Chopp, in order for theology (as proclamation) to give voice to women's experiences, there is a need to reinterpret and reconstitute the Word, which remains the primary source of patriarchal teaching within biblical religion (*Power to Speak* 43). This reconstitution and reinterpretation of the Word entails several steps. First, feminist theology needs to analyze how language has been used to exclude women from community and history, and how this exclusion has been justified for the sake of the order of creation. Chopp approaches this by using what she refers to as a "hermeneutics of marginality" (*Power to Speak* 43). Here one asks where and how God is shown to excuse the oppression and abuse of women. These discourses, once found, must be opposed.

The proclamation of the Word also encourages new practices of reading. For Chopp, they include the reading of the Word through "privileging of differences, specificity, embodiment, mutuality, transformation, and anticipation" (*Power to Speak* 43). The freedom of the reader to engage in this celebration of difference is possible because the scripture must be viewed as a "prototype" of "women-church" rather than as a timeless archetypal discourse. Feminist theology uses scriptures as "collections of proclamation, as models of Christian discourses of emancipatory transformation" (41). For Chopp, the Word is a "perfectly open sign" (41) that is directed toward freedom, innovation, and transformation of structures. Chopp shares this view of the scripture with Schüssler-Fiorenza. Both of them want to avoid the view of scriptures as containing universal a priori rules of action. According to Chopp, the Word can transform the social-symbolic order, when it is proclaimed with the goal of changing its institutions, principles, organization, hidden rules, and ideologies (44). The proclamation of the Word becomes concrete in preaching, and preaching for women is a way to reclaim their voice and power, for "to receive and speak is a vision of the nonpersons of history being persons on their own terms" (56). When women who exist in the margins of Christianity and society proclaim the Word, they offer ways to shape their communities' witness and confession. So in feminist theology, true proclamation entails the reordering of the relations in the world, and the correction of relations of sin, oppression, distortion, and suffering (67). For Chopp, it is the role of Christianity to offer this Word to the world (52).

Finally, the emancipatory transformation of language and social-symbolic order must be exhibited in the Church (Chopp, *Saving* 44).[7] If feminist theology is to be more than simply a corrective enterprise, it must be able to proclaim "grace, love, freedom, redemption, and hope in a world of evil and sin" (Chopp, *Power to Speak* 4). The church can achieve this end in three steps: first, the Church must adopt a new "poetics of community" that celebrates beauty and the flourishing of life in Word and words; second, the Church must embrace itself as a community of rhetoric that accentuates the dialogical nature of community life; and third, it must reconstruct its understanding of Christian piety—to embody the gifts of justice, vitality, wisdom, and love (Chopp, *Saving* 4, 73–74). We already see this happening today. In Hispanic churches, the women use liturgies that express resistance and hope in the context of "celebratory self-expression" (Ruether 236); while women within radical African independent (Prophet or Spirit) churches have been given more prophetic/preaching roles. Within communities characterized by these practices, women can truly exercise their power to speak.

Conclusion

One cannot have theory without practice, without it becoming a hollow abstraction; conversely, theory connects practice to a larger idea that holds meaning beyond itself. The earlier examples of Susanna Wesley, Mary Bosanquet Fletcher, and Mary Tooth showcase concrete ways in which women have throughout history found a voice within the Christian tradition, by creating alternative communities and redefining what it means to minister the Word. Although they moved beyond traditional interpretations of scripture that would prohibit women from preaching, they felt their calling and work was legitimate, carrying it on with or without male support. The feminist theological writings of Elizabeth Schüssler-Fiorenza and Rebecca Chopp help contextualize and analyze these past scenarios. Both Schüssler-Fiorenza and Chopp highlight women's ways of reading restrictive verses that re-vision ministry, including the power to speak, within the larger context of scripture's testimony, emphasizing its emancipatory qualities. Both theologians assert as well the need to include community and experience within the testimony of the Word, which the ministries of Mary Fletcher and Mary Tooth within the Madeley community aptly demonstrate. The combination of feminist theology and the examples of past women who would not be silenced opens the doors for future women to speak the Word, by reshaping the very idea of what it means to preach—including place, manner, content, and gender. Theory and praxis in union demonstrate the importance of Christian feminism in celebrating women's words used to proclaim the Word.

Notes

1. See Earl Kent Brown's discussions in "Women of the Word," *Women in new worlds*, ed. H. E. Thomas and R. S. Keller (Nashville: Abingdon, 1981), 69–87 and *Women of Mr. Wesley's Methodism* (Lewiston, NY: The Edwin Mellen Press, 1983). Paul Wesley Chilcote has focused three books on women in early Methodism, and stands currently as the expert on the subject: for detailed coverage, see his works *John Wesley and the Women Preachers of Early Methodism* (Metuchen, NJ: The American Theological Library Association and The Scarecrow Press, Inc, 1991), *She Offered Them Christ: The Legacy of Women Preachers in Early Methodism* (Eugene, Oregon: Wipf and Stock Publishers, 2001), and *Her Own Story: Autobiographical Portraits of Early Methodist Women* (Nashville: Abingdon Press, 2002).
2. Mary Tooth, box 14, vol. a, ms. Fletcher-Tooth Collection, Rylands Library, Manchester, 8. The majority of quotations from Mary Tooth are taken from her manuscript journals and commonplace books in the Fletcher-Tooth Collection, Methodist Archives, housed at the Rylands Library, Manchester, England. I will refer to them by box, volume, and where paginated, page numbers. I owe thanks to Peter Nockles and Gareth Lloyd, curators, for their assistance in accessing the collection. I have tried to retain the original spelling and punctuation from the entries, which reflect both her era's usage and her own dialect and education. Tooth often interchanges commas and periods or semi-colons, drops the period after Mrs. and Mr., frequently eliminates possessives, drops the initial letter h, such as using *as* for *has*, and interchanges *than* and *then*.
3. Also understood as the New Testament.
4. See also Rachel Kohn's interview of Schüssler-Fiorenza in "The Spirit of Things." Radio National, August 17, 2003. Internet. (http://www.abc.net.au/m/relig/spirit/stories/s923231.htm) Accessed: May 20, 2005.
5. These same strategies are applied to Luke 10:38–42 in "The Practice of Biblical Interpretation. Luke 10:38–42," *The Bible and Liberation. Political and Social Hermeneutics*, ed. Norman K. Gottwald and Richard A. Horsley (Maryknoll, NY: Orbis Books, 1993), 173–195.
6. For Schüssler-Fiorenza, *ekklesia-gynaikon* or "women-church" represents a new community not based on individualized and spiritualized biblical interpretations characterizing modern church practice, but "constitutes the practical centre and normative space for the hermeneutical circle-dance of a critical feminist rereading of the Bible for liberation" (*Bread Not Stone: The Challenge of Feminist Biblical Interpretation* [Boston: Beacon Press, 1984], 70).
7. For Chopp, one way to achieve this is through feminist theological education where women are allowed to "write their lives in new ways," by placing themselves in new roles, patterns of meaning, and stories of identity and vocation.

Bibliography

Astell, M. (2002). *A serious proposal to the ladies parts I and II*. Ed. P. Springborg. Ontario: Broadview.
Bergant, D. (1999). Rev. of *The world according to Eve: Women and the Bible in ancient times and our Time*, by C. Murphy. *Christian century*. (April 21).
Bosanquet, M. (1764). *A letter to the Rev. John Wesley by a gentlewoman*. London.
Brown, E. K. (1981). "Women of the word." *Women in new worlds*. Ed. H. E. Thomas and R. S. Keller. Nashville, TN: Abingdon. 69–87.
———. (1983). *Women of Mr. Wesley's Methodism*. Lewiston, NY: The Edwin Mellen Press.
Chilcote, P. W. (1991). *John Wesley and the women preachers of early Methodism*. Metuchen, NJ: The American Theological Library Association and The Scarecrow Press, Inc.

———. (2001). *Her own story: Autobiographical portraits of early Methodist women*. Nashville, TN: Abingdon Press.

———. (2001). *She offered them Christ: The legacy of women preachers in early Methodism*. Eugene, OR: Wipf and Stock Publishers.

Chopp, R. (1989). *Power to speak*. New York: Crossroad.

———. (1995). *Saving work: Feminist practices of theological education*. Louisville, KY: Westminster John Knox Press.

———. (2002). Interview with W. Shepperd. "The new gate-keeper: Colgate University President Rebecca Chopp seeks a balance between tradition and innovation." *Syracuse New Times*. November 27. Accessed May 20, 2005. <http://newtimes.rway.com/2002/112702/cover.shtml>.

Collins, V. T. (1999). "The speaker respoken: Material rhetoric as feminist methodology." *College English*. 61.5. Urbana. (May 1999) 545–574. Bell and Howell Information and Learning. ProQuest Point Loma Nazarene University, San Diego, California, CA. June 28, 2005. <http://proquest.umi.com/pqdweb>.

Davies, R. and Rupp, G., eds. (1965). *A history of the Methodist church in Great Britain*. Vol. 1. London: Epworth Press.

Donawerth, J., ed. (2002). *Rhetorical theory by women before 1900*. Lanham, MD: Rowman and Littlefield Publishers, Inc.

Fitzmaurice, J. et al., eds. (1997). "Anne Finch Countess of Winchilsea." *Major women writers of seventeenth-century England*. Ann Arbor, MI: University of Michigan Press. 333–372.

Fletcher, M. Box 8, Journals, ms. Fletcher-Tooth Collection. Rylands Library, Manchester, England.

Fletcher Methodist Church, Madeley. (1991). Madeley Local Studies Group. July 6, 2005 <http://www.localhistory.madeley.org.uk/buildings/flemem.html>.

Gottwald, N. K. and Horsley, R. A., eds. (1993). *The Bible and liberation: Political and social hermeneutics*. Maryknoll, NY: Orbis.

Hempton, D. (2005). *Methodism: Empire of the spirit*. New Haven, CT: Yale University Press.

Johnson, D. A. (2004). "Gender and the construction of models of Christian activity: A case study." *Church History*. 73.2 (June): 247–271.

Moore, H. (1817). *The life of Mrs. Mary Fletcher, consort and relict of the Rev. John Fletcher, vicar of Madeley, Salop*. Vol. II. Birmingham, England.

Rudrum, A., Black, J., and Nelson, H. F., eds. (2000). "Bathsua Makin." *The Broadview anthology of seventeenth-century verse and prose*. Peterborough, Ontario: Broadview Press. 424–433.

Ruether, R. R. (1998). *Women and redemption: A theological history*. Minneapolis: Fortress Press.

Schüssler-Fiorenza, E. (1984). *Bread not stone: The challenge of feminist biblical interpretation*. Boston: Beacon Press.

———. (1992). *But she said: Feminist practices of biblical interpretation*. Boston: Beacon Press.

———. (1994). *In memory of her: A feminist reconstruction of Christian origins*. New York: Crossroad.

———. (1995). *Jesus, Miriam's Child, Sophia's Prophet: Critical issues in feminist theology*. New York: Continuum.

———. (2003). Interview with Rachel Kohn. "The spirit of things." *Radio National*, August 17. Accessed: May 2005. <http://www.abc.net.au/rn/relig/spirit/stories/s923231.htm>.

Stanley, S. C. (2002). *Holy boldness: Women preachers' autobiographies and the sanctified self*. Knoxville, TN: University of Tennessee Press.

Stevens, A. (1866). *The women of Methodism*. New York: Carlton and Porter.

Taft, Z. (1803). *Thoughts on female preaching with extracts from the writings of Locke, Martin, & c*. Dover: G. Ledger.

Taft, Z. (1829). *Biographical sketches of the lives and public ministry of various holy women.* Vol. I. Leeds.

Tooth, M. Boxes 14 and 26, mss. Fletcher-Tooth Collection. Rylands Library. Manchester, England.

———. (1816). *A letter to the loving and beloved people of the parish of Madeley, and its vicinity, who have lost a friend to piety in the death of Mrs. Fletcher (or de la Flechere) late vicar of Madeley, Shropshire.* Ironbridge: William Smith.

———. (1829). *Memoirs of Miss Sarah Jenkins by Miss Tooth of Madeley.* London: Joseph Bradford.

Wesley, J. (1931). *Letters of the Rev. John Wesley, A. M.* Ed. J. Telford, BA. 8 vols. London, Epworth Press.

———. (1986). *The works of John Wesley. Sermons.* Ed. A. C. Outler. Vol. III. Nashville, TN: Abingdon Press.

CHAPTER SEVEN

Nascent Christian Feminism in Medieval and Early-Modern Britain

HOLLY FAITH NELSON

The Language of Proto-feminism

It is tempting to argue for a distinct female voice in medieval and early-modern religious works by women and to read their texts in light of feminist notions of *écriture féminine* or womanspeak.[1] It would be unwise, however, to give credence to any simplistic account of "feminine writing" in devotional works of the period, for "textual production" involves a "complex process" of "different and conflicting determinants," (Moi 45). Gender is only one of the factors that affect the workings of the spiritual imagination. Nevertheless, many female religious writers in medieval and early-modern Britain operated within an aesthetic of opposition, writing against essentialist concepts of "woman" as a static cultural category—inherently disruptive, spiritually inadequate, physically inferior, and inclined to the bestial.[2] A rhetoric of resistance that exposed gender as a social construct surfaced in their writings, challenging the exclusion of women from the discursive formations of philosophy and religion that defined and transmitted "truth." Ironically, medieval and early-modern women most often discovered their identity and authority in the very discourse of religion that was regularly employed by the clergy and laity to render them secondary, even soul-less, beings. Though a "foundational discourse," religion was not a monolithic language that spoke "with only one voice" (Hinds 7); medieval and early-modern women could employ sacred discourse to promote the notion of the self as a fluid process rather than a fixed object, rereading the scripture to invest the dynamic female body and soul with spiritual and material, private and public, worth. The Christian scriptures, therefore, served as a vehicle through which medieval and early-modern women could engage in the elevation of the female subject, thereby fracturing, if not yet shattering, "the cultural hall of mirrors—the repositories of representation—" and breaking "the silence imposed by male speech" (Friedman 38, 41).

To celebrate the feminine within both the self and the divine, the medieval and early-modern mothers of Christian feminism turned to distinct forms of religious discourse. They gravitated toward those devotional languages that permitted them to transcend the essentialist ontology that rendered them "the devil's gateway," imposed upon them the strictures of silence, chastity, and obedience, and relegated them to the private sphere (Tertullian 14). Catholic mysticism and Protestant radicalism were two such potentially "heretical discourses" that granted incipient Christian feminists the linguistic capital to modify reality by presenting alternative verbal and visual representations of the social and spiritual world (Bourdieu 127–128). These women produced performative utterances that strove to engender transformation in the public sphere. Nevertheless, though religious discourse was a vehicle for spiritual, cognitive, and, in some instances, material liberation, medieval, and early-modern women writers could not entirely escape the language that had defined them as "Other." Their spiritual identity, though resistant to patriarchal culture, was, after all, "built . . . of bits and pieces of that culture, however, they . . . [were] disassembled, criticized, and transcended" (A. R. Jones 374).

The struggle for spiritual worth and authority recorded in the works of incipient Christian feminists prefigures the drive for spiritual freedom and abundance in the oral and written texts of modern Christian women within a range of church traditions. Because of feminism's "pragmatic eschatological orientation," however, contemporary Christian feminists often neglect the voices of their foremothers, failing to forge a history of their movement and alienating themselves from an expansive collective identity (S. Jones 10). Kari Sandhaas writes of the importance of Christian feminists "hearing to speech": "the first steps toward liberation of any oppressed group is that of an uncensored listening and identifying who we are and learning, often re-learning, to articulate that identity in a language that empowers us and liberates us from our oppression" (xiv). By listening "deeply and openly" to the voices of their foremothers, modern Christian feminists access sacred resources through which to authorize the self as spiritual subject, reinterpret established theology, and revitalize existing ecclesiastical formations (Sandhaas xiv).

Medieval Mysticism

Mystical discourse is appealing to women writers because it gives them the option of denying subjecthood altogether, thereby bypassing cultural constructs of womanhood; mystics routinely claim to transcend the material world as they ascend the spiritual ladder to enjoy "complete, self-effacing union with God" (Potkay and Evitt 167).[3] However, neither Margery Kempe nor Julian of Norwich, late medieval English mystics, elected to dissolve entirely the subject-object opposition in the fluid stream of the One. Though Margery and Julian communed with the divine, in each of their works we find "a single, radical and radial energy originating in the subject centre, an aggressive, creative expression of the self" (Olney 15). Mystical faith and pneumatic language, therefore, do not utterly eradicate the female subject.

Fully conscious of her importance as a spiritual subject, Margery Kempe engages in dialogue with the divine object of her desire. In *The Book of Margery Kempe*, Christ declares that Margery is spiritually unique, announcing to her in a vision: "I have told you before that you are a singular lover of God, and therefore you shall have a singular love in heaven, a singular reward and a singular honour" (88).[4] It is for this reason, Christ explains to Margery, that "God loves you specially" (88). Margery's production of a spiritual autobiography demonstrates her recognition of, and appreciation for, her distinct and superior subjectivity. However, she is cognizant that she must forge her identity against the backdrop of contemporary gender stereotypes that limit her access to the divine. The church fathers required females intent on spiritual purification to negate their female biology, generating within them "a profound self-abnegation, self-denial, even self-destruction" (Castelli 88). St. Jerome had declared in his *Commentary on Ephesians* that "[a]s long as woman is for birth and children, she is different from man as body is from soul. But, if a woman wishes to serve Christ more than the world, then she will cease to be a woman and will be called a man" (qtd. in Hubnik 43).

In order to reconstruct her female identity in positive terms, Margery initially rejects the material functions of the female body, in particular coitus and childbirth. The abominable "debt of matrimony," sexual intercourse, becomes unbearable to Margery, an act she compares with the consumption of filth: "she would rather, she thought, have eaten and drunk the ooze and muck in the gutter than consent to intercourse, except out of obedience" (46). Yet paradoxically, Margery is over-whelmed with lecherous desire, inundated with visions of "men's genitals, and other such abominations" (184). In fact, she records, in one vision, a devilish call to serve as a prostitute to various men of religion who reveal to her their naked genitals (184). In order to resist the snare of lechery, she undergoes rigorous bodily penance (49). The sexual act is transformed in Margery's autobiography from a desirable pleasure to a grotesque abomination.

Margery also resists her role as a birthing vessel, which she associates with spiritual annihilation, mental torment, and physical debilitation. She recalls, at the inception of her narrative, that she "went out of her mind" shortly after the birth of her first child, becoming "amazingly disturbed and tormented with spirits" (41). Margery experiences suicidal ideation and becomes, in fact, self-consuming after childbirth when she bites herself and rips her flesh: "She would have killed herself many a time as they [the devils] stirred her to, and would have been damned with them in hell, and in witness of this she bit her own hand . . . [a]nd also pitilessly tore the skin on her body near her heart with her nails" (42). The association of childbirth and mental instability recurs in her text, when Margery approaches a troubled man who explains that he grieves "because his wife had just had a baby, and she was out of her mind" (217). It is no surprise, then, that Margery's self-definition is not connected to the maternal acts of birthing or nursing. Only 1 of her 14 children is briefly mentioned in her autobiography, but only in terms of his adult life.

Margery's rejection of the bodily requirements of wifehood and motherhood in constructing herself as a spiritual subject is certainly a useful strategy in transcending the limitations of a patriarchal family system. However, it compels Margery to reject her female biology, an essential part of her nature. In denying her genitalia and womb, Margery participates in the ecclesiastical configuration of the female body as carnal and grotesque, monstrous and perverse. In order to authorize her speech, Margery believes that she must distance herself from her body, as it is the female form that causes her to be perceived as Other to the normative, authoritative male.

The female roles of wife and mother, however, are not entirely abandoned in her text; they are merely rewritten in spiritual terms. In each instance, Margery transmutes the physical duties of women in the temporal world into spiritual requirements in the transcendent realm of the divine. The alternatively sexually desirable or repulsive male body is replaced with the body of Christ, "for all her love and affection were fixed on the manhood of Christ" (123). Her sensual, orgasmic union with the body of Christ is substituted for the "delectable thoughts, physical lust, and inordinate love" for her husband's body in early life (221). Christ insists on their intimacy in His description of her role as a spiritual wife: "when you are in bed, take me to you as your wedded husband . . . you can boldly take me in the arms of your soul and kiss my mouth, my head, and my feet as sweetly as you want" (126–127). Further, labor pains and parental concern are supplanted by the intense passion that she experiences during visions of the infant and crucified Christ. She recounts, for example, her ecstatic, uncontrollable weeping upon witnessing Christ's "precious tender body, all rent and torn with scourges, more full of wounds than a dove-cote ever was of holes" (106). Margery, in fact, becomes a correlative type of the Virgin Mary, helping to "look after him [Christ] in his childhood and so forth, until the time of his death" (244). Margery succeeds, therefore, at forging a Marian identity for herself in which virginity and maternity unite, donning the white apparel of a nun to demonstrate externally her spiritual authority as the mother and bride of Christ.

Divine love, in Margery's paradigm, is inextricably linked to her womanhood, not merely to her moral character. In the spiritual world, unlike the material world, "female," "mother," "sister," "daughter," "spouse" and "wife" are signs accorded great worth by Christ who employs these terms to commend Margery:

> When you strive to please me, then you are a true daughter; when you weep and mourn for my pain and my Passion, then you are a true mother having compassion on her child; when you weep for other people's sins and adversities, then you are a true sister; and when you sorrow because you are kept so long from the bliss of heaven, then you are a true spouse and wife. (67)

Margery's semiotic practice no longer allows these gendered signs to signify the source of spinning, the solicitor of semen, or the site of embryonic development; rather, they point to the spiritual worth of her gendered self and her intimate union with the divine.[5]

Paradoxically, while Margery validates her identity as woman by re-visioning herself as spiritual wife, mother, daughter, and sister, she employs her newly constructed mystical self to effect material change in the public world. She is, as Ruth Shklar concludes, a political mystic, desirous of ecclesiastical reformation (278). In recounting her interaction with many of the clergy, Margery confronts the dominant medieval conception of womanhood. She is advised by the men of Beverley to "go and spin, and card wool, as other women do." (168), a "great cleric" in the household of the archbishop of York attempts to silence her by citing Paul's verse "that no woman should preach" (164), although she proves her adherence to the articles of faith, and even the Vicar of St. Stephen's at Norwich, who later supports her, cannot help but exclaim upon meeting her: "How could a woman occupy one or two hours with the love of our Lord? I shan't eat a thing till I find out what you can say of our Lord God in the space of an hour" (74). The misogynistic discourse of these men in their public role as God's emissaries, however, is dismissed by Margery who often needs no priestly intermediary between herself and the Godhead. For Margery is on terms of "homely familiarity" with a God who informs her that the priestly function is limited: "There is no clerk in all this world who can, daughter, teach you better than I can do" (80, 197).

Willing, at times, to bypass masculine ecclesiastical authority, Margery is directly authorized by God, who encourages her to participate in, and disrupt, the monologic discourse of the Church. She fashions herself a type of Moses when she "instructed in the laws of God as well as she could" her fellow countrymen (138). She displays the exegetical skill of a cleric when she interprets the biblical phrase *Crescite et multiplicamini* ("be fruitful and multiply") (159). She assumes the role of prophet when she is given knowledge of "those who would be saved," and becomes a neotype of John when she looks within the Book of Life and reads within its margins her name "written at the Trinity's foot" (248). The corporeal world of failed business venture, endless childbirth, sexual temptation, and gendered restrictions are transmuted in her narrative to spiritual acumen through her resignification of the unstable signs that constitute the female identity.

David Aers suggests that by styling herself a vessel of sacred knowledge and a transmitter of divine truth, Margery potentially challenged the "fundamental aspects of gender arrangements and clerical power" in medieval England, and certainly Margery appropriates masculine clerical discourse to expose ecclesiastical abuse (113). When counseled by the archbishop of York not to instruct people on spiritual matters in his diocese, she contends that "the Gospel gives . . . [her] leave to speak of God" and, using the figurative teaching practices of Christ, presents herself as a teller of parables (164). In the parable that she recounts to the clerics, she draws an analogy between the misconduct of a priest and the fecal discharge of a "great rough bear" (165). This scatological interpretation of the corrupt priesthood articulated by an illiterate woman certainly subverts the unquestioned authority of the clergy and challenges the notion of the female as ecclesiastically and doctrinally unsophisticated.

Though Margery participates in religious discourse in the public sphere to render silent the immoral clergy, she also dispenses with language altogether on many occasions. She recalls several instances in which her utterance is not the spoken word but rather the primal cry. Her presence is commonly made known to those around her through a visceral, nonverbal mode of communication. During her vision of the crucified Christ, for example, Margery "fell down and cried with a loud voice, twisting and turning her body amazingly on every side, spreading her arms out wide as if she would have died, and could not keep herself from crying and these physical movements, because of the fire of love that burned so fervently in her soul (106). Her relentless weeping and bodily breakdowns emit "semiotic" pulsations, which, in Julia Kristeva's terms, produce ruptures, absences, and breaks in patriarchal symbolic language.[6] The chaotic threat of her uncontrollable response to the divine disrupts, and at times drowns out, the authoritarian, phallocentric discourse of the medieval Church.

Although Margery's Christian subjectivity involves, at times, her denunciation of clerical abuse and disruption of ecclesiastical monologism, when possible she chooses to remain under the guidance of an established religious institution that bestows upon her spiritual value. She experiences unbearable misery when her confessor is absent, for she feels compelled to participate in confession and the sacrament, in accordance with the practices of the Catholic Church. In their official function as confessors and administrators of the sacraments, priests, in Margery's experience, are indispensable. David Aers explains what he labels this mystical power held by the clergy in pre-Reformation England:

> This is a world in which the Church and the Sacrament it makes has immense magical power, one that is as great "for enchewyng of her bodily perel" as for helping peoples' passage in the afterlife. Margery's form of piety unequivocally confirms such magic and the source of its mediating human agency, the official clergy. (113)

Therefore, on the one hand, mystical discourse allows Margery to produce a radical female spiritual subject who functions as a prophet, a biblical exegete and an ecclesiastical critic who disturbs the Law of the Father; on the other hand, Margery is disinclined to step outside of, or to cast off, the mystical authority of the male priesthood. She cannot reject in its entirety the ritual discourse of members of the priesthood because they are the bearer of the *skeptron* who are "known and recognized as being able and enabled to produce this particular class of discourse" (Bourdieu 113);[7] although the priestly word is only efficacious when "the person subjected to it recognizes the person who exercises it as authorized to do so," Margery cannot or does not wish to function wholly outside the "performative magic" of masculine "ritual functions" (Bourdieu 116).

Thus, Margery both operates within and partially transcends medieval conceptions of gender. Carolyn Coulson discovers in her work the "manifestation of her ever-present awareness of orthodoxy" despite her impulse "to step over the line into heterodox behavior," while Shklar claims that we find in *The Book of Margery Kempe* "both orthodoxy and heterodoxy in . . . dizzying juxtapositions" (Coulson 77; Shklar 278). In certain areas, as Raymond Powell recently demonstrates, Margery's behavior is characteristic of, rather than resistant to, late medieval piety, and we would be wrong to assert, as does Verena Neuburger, that Margery wears a "cloak of holiness" to mask her proto-feminist agenda (qtd. in Powell 2). However, although Margery does not fully escape the dualism of the church fathers—who associate the female with bodily corruption—and often celebrates the feminine in figurative rather than material terms, she successfully deconstructs patristic conceptions of the female as spiritually and cognitively inferior and assumes the identity of a prophet and visionary in the public sphere. At the conclusion of her narrative, she also demonstrates a desire to merge "carnal maternity with spiritual motherhood," as Monica Potkay and Regula Evitt have shown, when she effects the spiritual conversion of her prodigal son, who returns home to receive the blessing of his mother (184, 186).

In her *Book of Showings*, or *Revelations of Divine Love*, the contemporaneous mystic Julian of Norwich shares with Margery Kempe a desire to subvert the conception of the female perpetuated by medieval theologians, despite—as an anchoress—living in a cell attached to the parish church of St. Julian at Conisford. Julian inscribes the typical modesty topos at the inception of her visionary text, "But God forbid that you should say or assume that I am a teacher, for that is not and never was my intention; for I am a woman, ignorant, weak and frail" (135); however, soon after, she negates or neutralizes this expression of female subjugation with a rhetorical question: "But because I am a woman, ought I therefore to believe that I should not tell you of the goodness of God, when I saw at that same time that it is his will that it be known?" (135). Yet rather than fashion the female self as a vessel of spiritual truth by virtue of a God-ordained singularity, as does Margery, Julian forges a spiritual identity through Pauline participative theology, which allows her to diminish the significance of biological sex in the master discourse of religion. While Margery's self-fashioning is rooted in her singularity, Julian's construction of spiritual selfhood involves a mystical union in the Body of Christ, a conception of the Self as plural. In the short version of her *Showings*, Julian writes: "I write as the representative of my fellow Christians," claiming to speak with a collective rather than an individual voice. "If I pay special attention to myself," she insists, "I am nothing at all; but in general I am in the unity of love with all my fellow Christians" (134). The female subject can hide in the mystical unity of the Body of Christ; she is no longer "Other," but part of a fluid, genderless whole.

Having justified with rhetorical skill her need to generate visionary discourse regardless of her sex, Julian, like Margery, remains anxious about her corporal identity. She longs for the "gift" of "bodily sickness" and is rewarded with a near fatal infirmity that renders her a cadaver-like creature (125). Of her illness, Julian observes; "I felt as if the upper part of my body" was "beginning to die. My hands fell down on either side, and I was so weak that my head lolled to one side. The greatest pain that I felt was my shortness of breath and the ebbing of my life" (126, 128). Julian's yearning to experience bodily anguish is not, however, the behavior of a self-loathing woman intent on annihilating her fallen flesh. The desire to crucify the body is a commonplace in the works of ascetics who wish to imitate Christ's agony in order to purify the flesh and spirit. "I intended this," writes Julian, "because I wanted to be purged by God's mercy, and afterwards live more to his glory because of that sickness" (178).

It is through the wounding of her body—her willingness to emulate the physical suffering of Christ—that Julian is regenerated through "God's secret doing" (128) and given the gift of "spiritual revelation" (133). Sandi J. Hubnik rightly concludes that Julian's physical pain rests in "bodily sight," in which her body "attains a facet of God's divine nature"; "rather than becoming invisible," she continues, Julian "becomes a claimant to divinity's manifestation" (49) as she experiences "an actual physiological ebb and flow between Christ's suffering and her own: a symbiotic exchange of pain and joy" (Potkay and Evitt 179). Thus, what initially appears to be a self-imposed eradication of female subjectivity in her mystical writings is, in fact, a means to align herself with Christ, to become a purified subject worthy of a spiritual reward.

This is not to argue that Julian's body is not displaced in the *Showings* by that of Christ, for his body certainly dominates her work, and, in fact, becomes the "text" that she glosses. However, it is Julian's subjective gaze that journeys over the object of her vision, her visual and verbal authority that organizes the text and generates "meaning" for the reader. In Julian's text, we do not experience the male visual entitlement and the objectified female flesh that is evident, for example, in Nicholas's visual response to Alisoun in Chaucer's *Miller's Tale*. The visual entitlement in Julian's *Showings* is a woman's, the body fetishized Christ's, and the authorized voice the female speaking subject.

Yet the object of Julian's visual desire is not, as it is with Margery, the manhood of Christ; in the *Showings*, Julian transmutes Christ's body from male to female. God reveals to her that "[a]ll the lovely works and all the sweet loving offices of beloved motherhood are appropriated to the second person," "our true Mother" (296). The feminine is permissible, even desirable, in the spiritual realm where motherhood connotes divine love, spiritual nourishment, and eternal salvation. Unfortunately, in drawing the analogy between the nature and function of Christ and that of earthly mothers, Julian tends to diminish temporal motherhood, avowing, for example, that "all our mothers bear us for pain and for death," but "our true Mother Jesus . . . alone bears us for joy and for endless life" (297–298). The mortal mother is merely a type or shadow of the anti-type Christ. Nevertheless, in her assertion of the Motherhood of Christ, the configuration of Christ's body as maternal privileges a female body heretofore construed in medieval thought as the locus of corruption and decay.

It is well documented that both male and female mystics conceived of God in maternal terms. Yet Joan M. Nuth rightly argues that Julian "raises the image of Christ's motherhood to a new level of significance, allowing it to summarize her whole soteriology" (65). In the Long Text of the *Showings*, Julian catalogues myriad ways in which Christ can be "read" as Mother. In Julian's theology, Christ, for instance, "carries us within him in love and travail, until the full time when he wanted to suffer the sharpest thorns and cruel pains." (298), and having "borne us so for bliss," nourishes us with his body, "the precious food of true life," and leads us "into his blessed breast through his sweet open side" to reveal to us "the joys of heaven" and "endless bliss" (298). This association of the female body with the salvific functions of Christ assigns spiritual value to the female as biological essence, and displaces orthodox notions of the virulent female flesh.

Julian not only grants the female body a degree of divinity, however; she also foregrounds women's cognitive capacities and affective intuition. Julian is adamant that she must grasp and communicate the "meaning" of her sacred visions, receiving divine images, hearing Christ's words, and interpreting and expounding them in her production of a distinct theology of love. In the process, she fuses rational and affective approaches to epistemology, declaring thus: "For we cannot profit by our reason alone, unless we have equally memory and love" (290). At times, she bases her interpretation on intuition—"[It was] as if he had said" (221), "it seemed to me as if" (163), "for I understood that" (207)—while at other moments, she employs the *distinctiones* and *schemata* of scholastic exegesis. The visions, she pronounces, are "shown in three parts": by "bodily vision," "by words formed" in her "understanding," and "by spiritual vision" (192). She understands "six things" from the vision of Christ's bleeding head (189), perceives "four kinds of fear" (324), discovers "three kinds of longing in God," and so on (326). Like Bernard of Clairvaux, Julian appreciates the epistemological value of the affective knowledge of God, which Bernard describes as "the true and certain intuition of any object, or the certain apprehension of truth" (qtd. in Sommerfeldt 76), but in accordance with the philosophy of William of St. Thierry, Abelard, and Aquinus, Julian defends the employment of reason when she posits that "man's natural reason," "the common teaching of Holy Church," and the "inward grace-giving operation of the Holy Spirit . . . are all from one God . . . [and] work continually in us, all together" (335).

As with *The Book of Margery Kempe*, the *Showings* enact a resistance to medieval gender constructs. Julian employs a series of subtle strategies to authorize herself as spiritual subject. She insists that it is God's will that she speaks regardless of her sex, distances herself from issues of gender by appealing to Pauline participative theology, refuses the silence and passivity demanded of the medieval recluse, highlights the salvific function of the feminized body of Christ, and styles herself a legitimate investigator and articulator of religious truth. In the process she insists on her orthodoxy declaring, "But in everything I believe as Holy Church preaches and teaches . . . I wished and intended never to accept anything which might be contrary to it" (192), managing thereby to reiterate "various ecclesiastical teachings in such a way as to both keep the church's decrees and subvert them" (Hubnik 61). The fluidity of gender in her creation of self and the divine substantiates Caroline Walker Bynum's claim that women mystics "did not have a strong sense of binary opposites grouped around the male/female contrast" (215).

Radical Protestantism in
Revolutionary Times

Women of the early-modern period had access to a wider range of potentially disruptive discursive formations than did their medieval counterparts. The discourse of humanism that flourished in sixteenth- and seventeenth-century Britain presented identity as dynamic, transformable by those with access to educational, resources, and a repertoire of rules. Similarly, the language of the Protestant reformation highlighted the possibility of significant moral improvement in the individual believer through the dedicated study of scripture (Travitsky 4–11).[8] The rhetoric of virtuous education and pious learning challenged essentialist ontology and interrogated the validity of a gender ideology that represented females as soul-less, senseless, static creatures.

Bathsua Makin, educational theorist and tutor to Princess Elizabeth (the daughter of Charles I and Henrietta Maria), relied upon such discursive formations in *An Essay to Revive the Antient Education of Gentlewomen in Religion, Manners, Arts & Tongues* (1673) to defend women's intellectual and moral potential, declaring thus:

> Had God intended Women only as finer sort of Cattle, he would not have made them reasonable . . . Seeing Nature produces Women of such excellent Parts, that they do often equalize, some-times excel men, in what ever they attempt; what reason can be given why they should not be improved? . . . Learning perfects and adorns the Soul, which all Creatures aim at. Nay more, a principal part of God's Image in Man's first Creation, consisted in Knowledge. Sin has clouded this: why should we not by instruction endeavour to repair that which shall be perfected in Heaven? (23–24)

Women with access to a humanist education of some sort who were brought up in the reformed faith rewrote the biblical story to acquit Eve of guilt for the fall (Aemilia Lanyer, *Salve Deus Rex Judaeorum*), decried the divisiveness of the class structure on the female community (Lanyer, "The Description of Cooke-ham"), explored female sexuality, positing woman as a desiring subject rather than the passive object of male desire (Mary Wroth, *Pamphilia to Amphilanthus*), lamented female ignorance and defended women's entrance into "*Eruditions* garden" (Rachel Speght, "The Dream"), projected the female experience into the biblical text during the act of translation (Mary Sidney-Herbert, *Psalms*), and cast aside "a needle" for the "poet's pen" to write on the politics and religion of England (Anne Bradstreet, "The Prologue," "A Dialogue between Old England and New").

However, although the discourses of humanism and Protestant reform permitted women writers of the sixteenth and early seventeenth century to reveal "woman" as an oppressed cultural category and to prove women capable of piety and wisdom, much of their energy was spent on deconstructing misogynistic images of womanhood rather than employing symbolic resources to reconstitute the public world (Beilin xvii). Many of these women would have readily agreed with John Luis Vives's pronouncement, in *The Instruction of a Christian Woman*, that "Nature sheweth, that the males duety is to succour and defend, and the females to follow and to wait upon the male, and to creepe under his aide and obay him, that shee may live better" (226). As Elaine Beilin has argued, the ideal woman of the humanists and reformers was "the domesticated Virgin Mary," who remained "at home to keep the household goods" (xix). Thus, while women authors who wrote within these paradigms held out hope for the cognitive and moral capacity of women, they did not alter society in any fundamental way.

It was the new discursive formation of radical Protestantism that emerged in mid-seventeenth-century Britain that significantly expanded women's access to linguistic capital and the public sphere.[9] With the uprooting of church and state during the civil war years, the patriarchal order was under attack. The Tudor and Stuart monarchs defended the divine right of kings by drawing an analogy between monarchical and familial structures, James I arguing in *The True Law of Free Monarchies*: "By the Law of Nature the King becomes a natural Father to all his Lieges at his Coronation: And as the Father of his fatherly duty is bound to care for the nourishing, education, and virtuous government of his children; even so is the king bound to care for all his subjects" (65). The rebellion against static hierarchy and unquestioned authority affected the patriarchal state, household, and national church; thus, with the "repudiation of monarchical patriarchy" came "[n]ew claims concerning the status and rights of women" (Stone 340).

Radical Protestant discourse permitted hundreds of women—primarily sectarians—to publish works on matters of religion, politics, and economics, claiming that these revolutionary opinions were biblically sanctioned. Stevie Davies vividly describes the scriptural basis of this emerging proto-feminist discursive formation:

> But the revolutionary women . . . were out on the streets protesting, petitioning, demonstrating, preaching. Some heckled

statesmen, roughed up mayors, tossed stools in church, bawled
abuse at ministers. . . . [I]ndefatigably our radical foremothers
wrote, though some began as illiterates who had to teach themselves to read. . . . All learned from radical reading of that incendi-
ary book, the newly affordable pocket Bible—a book which had
for centuries been used to mute and subject them. What they read
there overcame the feminine timidity indoctrinated from birth,
convincing them that their tongues could and must speak. (1–2)

Radical utopian visions of social, spiritual, and sexual equality, however,
required deft rhetorical maneuvering and multiple—sometimes
conflicting—strategies. The revolutionary rereading of scripture was
merely one stratagem in an arsenal of weapons used to combat repressive
and ideological state apparatuses.[10]

Some radical women appealed to more traditional notions of gender,
only to employ them in the service of female empowerment and social
protest. In 1659, 7,000 women, under the guidance of the Quaker Mary
Foster, submitted a petition to Cromwell denouncing enforced tithing
and other "Anti-christian" practices (Garman 59). In the preface to the
reader, the petitioners agree that women are, in some respects, "the
weaker vessel," but subsequently cite scripture to prove that their weakness increases the likelihood of God calling them to public service. "It
may seem strange to some that women should appear in so public a
manner, in a matter of so great concernment as this of Tithes," they
declare, "But let such know, that this is the work of the Lord at this day,
even by weak means to bring to pass his mighty work in the earth."
(Garman 59). The Quaker Joan Vokins, writing at the end of the century, echoes this sentiment, insisting that God "honours his Power
in contemptible Vessels" (Garman 263), a principle recorded in 1 Corinthians
1:27: "But God hath chosen the foolish things of the world to confound
the wise; and God hath chosen the weak things of the world to confound the things which are mighty."

Most radical women, however, rejected the trope of the woman as "the
weaker vessel," describing men and women as equally fallen. Working to
undermine claims of the female as spiritually inferior, Margaret Fell, the
Mother of Quakerism, universalizes the concept of weakness in *Women's
Speaking Justified* by establishing a new binary in which all humanity is
weak and God alone is strong: "And first, when *God created man in his own
image: in the image of God created he them, male and female*: Here God joins
them together in his own image, and makes no such distinctions and differences as men do; for though they be weak, he is strong" (Rudrum 428).

Having established that both men and women were tempted into transgression and disobedience, female sectarians focused on spiritual enlightenment, deflecting attention from the gendered body to the genderless soul. Sacred truth, they claimed, neither derives from patriarchal tradition nor hierarchical institutions, but rather from pneumatic indwelling in the individual believer. The Holy Spirit, or the Inner Light in Quaker terminology, penetrates the soul of the faithful, regardless of biological sex, and the soul knows "no gender-based distinctions" (Trevett 15). To this the Quaker Elizabeth Bathurst attests on the title page of *The Sayings of Women* (1695), where it is written: "The Lord *poured out of his Spirit upon the whole House of* Israel; not only on the Male, but also on the Female; and made them *Stewards of the manifold Gifts of his Grace*" (Garman 430). It is hardly surprising that radical women strove, at times, to distance themselves from their bodily nature, as their flesh was often demonized by members of the establishment, as I. H.'s comments in *A Strange Wonder or a Wonder in a Woman* (1642) demonstrate: "Yet of all WHORES there is no WHORE to a holy WHORE . . . when she turns up the white of her eye, and the black of her tail when she falls flat on her back, according as the spirit moves her. The fire of her zeal kindles such a flame, that the Devil cannot withstand her. Besides she can fit a man with such a cloak for her knavery she can cover her lust with religion" (qtd. in Mack 30). The doctrine of the inner light counteracted such claims of devilish embodiment and facilitated women's assumption of ministerial professions as preachers and prophets, as their genderless souls, "seized upon by the Lord," were compelled to follow the will of the divine (Trapnel sig.A^r).

Though the indwelling of the Holy Spirit encouraged the effacement of selfhood, it provided the female sectarian with an indisputable authorized voice in which God and the self became indistinguishable. The speaker, illuminated by the Inner Light, functioned as "God in the *voice*" (Vaughan 198). Thus, the Fifth Monarchist Anna Trapnel can, in one breath, engage in self-negation and self-assertion in her prophetic work *The Cry of a Stone* (1653): "Oh thy Servant (speaking of her selfe) must now come forth against the great Rabbies of the world: Oh, thou knowest that thy Servant hath often wrastled with thee that thou wouldst employ some other, but thou hast over-ruled her, and hast put her to silence? . . . Oh, it is for thy sake, and for thy servants sakes, that thy Servant is made a voyce, a sound, it is a voyce within a voyce, anothers voyce, even thy voyce through her" (41–42). The religious woman, in this instance, appears as an egoless instrument through which God communicates.

As instruments of the divine, female sectarians claimed that they were called to rebel against ungodly ecclesiastical and political formations and to confront directly heads of church and state. They did so in person and in printed publications, the flourishing of print culture and the "breakdown of censorship and licensing controls in the 1640s" providing women with a wider audience (Crawford 273). In the hand-delivered *Remarkable Letter of Mary Howgill to Oliver Cromwell, Lord Protector* (1657), Howgill, a Quaker, opens by pronouncing Cromwell "a stinking dunghill in the sight of God" (Rudrum 535). Howgill constitutes the world as God's panopticon, in which she as God's eyes and voice must expose Cromwell as a crucifier of Christ who would tread "the blood of the new covenant under his feet"—thereby interrogating the vision put forth by the ruler of the republican Commonwealth (Rudrum 537). Styling herself a biblical prophet with the master-key to unlock the secrets of scripture, Howgill inverts the relationship of Lord Protector and subject of the Commonwealth, investing herself with unlimited authority and stripping Cromwell of his power. Writing against the intolerance of the restored Stuart regime, the imprisoned Margaret Fell inscribes a similar resistance to the state-imposed fictions of Charles II's minions in *A Letter Sent to the King from M. F.* (1666). Fell's biblical exegesis permits her to establish the Quaker community as "God's people" and Charles II as a type of the biblical King Rehoboam who placed a "heavy yoke" on the children of God (Garman 44). Fell predicts the downfall of the king if the state fails to enact the principles of religious tolerance promised at the Restoration.

In their roles as preachers, prophets, and missionaries, sectarian women adopted both masculine and feminine personas, functioning within a fluid concept of gender. At times, radical women defined themselves as spiritual maidens, daughters, and mothers, as did Margery Kempe. The prophetess Lady Eleanor Davies declared that a "Voice from Heaven, speaking as through a Trumpet," appointed her his "meek Virgin," and "Handmaid of the Lord" (Cope 184, 182). Katharine Evans and Sarah Chevers, Quaker missionaries, characterize themselves as "two daughters of *Abraham*" (Garman 171), while Margaret Fell fashions women of God "Mother[s] in Israel" (Fell 16). However, radical women often assume masculine biblical identities because the authorized scriptural discourse they wish to absorb into their prose is spoken by males in the source text. Lady Eleanor presents herself as a second Daniel (discovering the anagram "Reveale O Daniel" in a version of her name), and draws heavily upon the apocalyptic language of the book of Daniel. The Quaker Susannah Blandford pronounces with Peter that "*God is no respecter of Persons*" (Garman 293), while Rebecca Travers, a fellow

Quaker, re-utters the Pauline dictum that God "*hath shined into our hearts to give us Light of the knowledge of the Glory of himself in the face of Jesus Christ*" (Garman 293, 337). The spirituality of sectarian women, therefore, allowed them to move along the spectrum of gender at will, taking advantage of the authorizing strategies employed by members of both sexes.[11]

Sectarian women not only assumed masculine and feminine identities as needed, but also rendered the term "woman" a floating signifier.[12] Elaine Hobby, Phyllis Mack, and Hilary Hinds all take note of the masterful wordplay of Priscilla Cotton and Mary Cole, who accept in *To the Priests and People of England* (1655) "woman" as a derogatory word, only to argue that the term is not fixed; the signifier can be transferred to members of either sex who are spiritually weak:

Women must not speak in a Church, whereas it is not spoke onely of a Female, for we are all one both male and female in Christ Jesus, but its weakness that is the woman by the Scriptures forbid-den . . . Here mayst thou see from the Scriptures, that the woman or weakness whether male or female, is forbidden to speak in the church . . . Indeed you your selves [the priests] are the women, that are forbidden to speak in the Church. (6–7)

Although "woman" retains its negative value, Hobby rightly concludes that this "unyoking of gendered terms from gendered subjects," is one of many rhetorical techniques used to support "an abolition of . . . gender hierarchies . . . and a license for all members of society to think and to speak insofar as their visions can be justified as coming from the true Head, that is, from Christ" (304). Once a signifier has a variable, unspecifiable signified, essentialism based on an irrevocable relationship between signifier and signified becomes difficult to sustain.

The fluidity of gender in sectarian writings also applies to the construction of the divine. As with Julian of Norwich, radical women were inclined to conceive of God in both female and male terms. Rather than present God as a genderless being, Quakers, for example, relied upon the creation story, in which both male and female are created in God's image, to prove the bisexual nature of the Creator. The 7,000 Handmaids of the Lord, as a result, can speak of "Christ Jesus in the Male and in the Female" (Garman 64). This vision of a bisexual or hermaphroditic God furthered the agenda of sectarian women to defy and transcend the orthodox gender ideology that had marginalized and silenced them.

Convinced of the divine authority invested in genderless souls and of their God-given role as agents of a hermaphroditic Christ, sectarian women were unconcerned with religious orthodoxy and the national church. Unlike Margery Kempe and Julian of Norwich, who operated within the Catholic Church and strove to "conform to its precepts," early-modern sectarians were not dependent on priestly counselors and religious rituals because they were willing to operate outside the national church and to establish their own religious movement (Voaden 40). Quakers in particular were accused of founding a "New Religion," but as Elizabeth Bathurst claims in *Truth's Vindication* (1695), they were upholding the "True Religion . . . of great Antiquity," a religion that has no need of the sacraments (Garman 343). According to Quaker doctrine, believers experience mystical union with the divine independent of the sacraments; no delegated clerical spokesperson or ritual discourse is needed as lay men and women are appointed by Christ to speak the authorized discourse previously available only to the priestly class. Quaker women were liberated, thereby, to serve as preachers, prophets, administrators, and missionaries on behalf of their own religious community.

Women in some nonconformist communities managed to balance this active public role with a fulfilling private life, embracing their spousal and parental identity. Given the Protestant denigration of monastic virginity and concomitant celebration of marriage, early-modern British women could embrace marital intercourse and reproduction and remain spiritually pure. Evans and Chevers, while imprisoned in Malta, wrote to their husbands and children with great affection; Evans addresses one letter to "John Evans, my right dear and Precious Husband, with my tenderhearted Children, who are more dear and precious unto me, than the apple of mine eye," figuring her husband in the epistle as a "*Yoak-mate in the Work of our God*" who shares her "*holy Calling*" (Garman 203). In fact, Quaker women in particular, Mack reminds us, "were embedded not only in their own spiritual community but in biological families and physical neighborhoods" at the same time that they were "utterly distanced from traditional forms of female self-definition" as "public prophets," thereby integrating "public and private spheres of existence" (238, 240).

When called by God to serve in a public capacity for a period of time, women were free to set aside private responsibilities to fulfill the divine calling. Despite their domestic attachment to their husbands and children, Evans and Chevers, for example, became traveling servants of God, an action Chevers defends in her letter to her family, "My Dear Husband, my love, my life is given up to serve the living God, and to obey his pure Call in the measure of the manifestations of his Love, Light, Life and Spirit of Christ Jesus, his only begotten Son, whom he has manifested in me." (Garman 206). The discourse of radical Protestantism encouraged women to serve as itinerant preachers and missionaries—frequently without any male attendant—just as the language of mysticism freed Margery to travel to Italy, Spain, and the Holy Land without her husband. The inner light of God demanded that divine vocation, at times, supersede familial obligation while leaving the family structure intact. This freedom may explain the great attraction of women to the Quaker movement.

The ability of Quaker women to balance public and private life was facilitated by the creation of bodies of women who not only attended "all the Sick, the Weak, the Widdows and Fatherless" in the community, but were also granted jurisdiction over marriage, which involved "the authority to instruct and discipline male relatives and neighbours" (Garman 499; Mack 288). Patricia Crawford notes that "[a]fter the Henrician reformation abolished religious confraternies, there were no organizations for women for religious purposes until the 1670s, when separate meetings developed for Quaker women" (275). Although segregation by gender set a dangerous precedent and was not universally supported by the Society of Friends, women's meetings produced a sense of sisterhood or solidarity among likeminded women believers and, as the feminist poet Audre Lorde proclaims: "Without community there is no liberation" (qtd. in S. Jones 126).[13] This spiritual sisterhood is evident in Evans's description of her relationship with Chevers; during their imprisonment, Katharine takes the arm of Sarah and bravely pronounces to the friars who interrogate them: "*The Lord hath joined us together and woe be to them that should part us*," alluding to the biblical passage traditionally used to support the sanctity of marriage in Matthew 19:6: "What therefore God hath joined together, let no man put asunder" (Rudrum 555). Though Margery Kempe and Julian of Norwich do not experience any extended spiritual communion with other women, Margery traveled to meet Julian, who offered her words of encouragement on one aspect of her mystical experience. Margery felt empowered, and was sustained by, a sense of female community in this moment, an experience regularly enjoyed by Quaker women.

Despite the radical view of gender and faith held by the Quakers and other nonconformists, patriarchy was not completely abandoned in these communities. In *Women's Speaking Justified*, Margaret Fell defends women speaking in Church, but does not wholly dismiss the traditional family structure. Responding to 1 Timothy 2, Fell writes: "Here the

Apostle speaks particularly to a Woman in Relation to her Husband, to
be in subjection to him, and not to teach, nor usurp authority over him,
and therefore he mentions *Adam* and *Eve*" (Fell 9). So too, Catie Gill has
shown that Quaker discourse manifested, on occasion, "social conservatism and patriarchalism" (21), pointing to the case of Martha
Simmonds who, when criticized for her forwardness, was advised to
"goe home and follow her calling" (qtd. in Gill 27). Even in sectarian
groups, the notions of the genderless soul and a bisexual God were not
sufficient to undermine entirely long held patriarchal ideology and the
social structures and practices that emerged from it.

Feminism and Faith

In "Women, Religion and Social Action in England, 1500–1800,"
Patricia Crawford remarks that "[t]he problem of finding a voice in which
to speak in a male-dominated area remains for many women even in the
twentieth century" (273). Crawford's observation is borne out in the
work of Natalie K. Watson, who wonders in *Feminist Theology*, whether it
is "possible to write theology in a way that advocates the full humanity of
women in the image of God" and to engage in "feminist reconstructions
of ecclesiology" (27, 44). Watson contemplates the experience of post-
Christian women writers who "have opted against Christianity" because it
is a religion centered on a male God and ultimately supportive of "male-
dominated power structures that suppress women's spirituality" (57–58).
Mary Daly, the author of *The Church and the Second Sex* (1968) encouraged
women, in her 1971 sermon at Harvard Memorial Church, to participate
in a mass exodus from the Christian church:

> We have to go out from the land of our fathers into an unknown
> place. We can this morning demonstrate our exodus from sexist
> religion—a break which for many of us has already taken place
> spiritually . . . We cannot really belong to institutional religion as it
> exists. It isn't good enough to be token preachers. It isn't good
> enough to have our energies drained and co-opted. Singing sexist
> hymns, praying to a male god breaks our spirit, makes us less than
> human. The crushing weight of this tradition, of this power
> structure, tell us that *we do not even exist*. (qtd. in Japinga 133)

Christianity is an intrinsically patriarchal religion, Daly and others
maintain, and thus cannot provide women with a spiritual space in
which to foster a sacramental view of the female body and soul.

Serene Jones, however, in *Feminist Theory and Christian Theology: Cartographies of Grace*, finds hope in the ability of modern Christian feminists "to creatively reimagine a church" that is more inclusive of, and receptive to, female spirituality and in which "women, in all their diversity, can be safe and flourish" (160–161). This was the goal—to varying degrees—of Margery Kempe, Julian of Norwich, and the early-modern women sectarians. These mothers of Christian feminism experienced a deep sense of liberation as a result of the indwelling of Christ. Though they could not completely reconcile their gender and faith, the Christian metanarrative became a vehicle through which nascent feminists subverted essentialist ontology, critiqued patriarchal discourse, generated proto-feminist theologies and ecclesiologies, and fashioned themselves mirrors and agents of the divine. Rather than abandon the Christian church, these women chose to inhabit the paradox of gender and faith and reconstitute the relationship between women, God, and the community of believers.

Notes

1. *Écriture féminine* or "feminine writing," according to the French feminist Hélène Cixous, disrupts binaries and hierarchies, disturbs patriarchal culture, and speaks with the "Voice of the Mother" (Moi, *Sexual/textual Politics*, 114). Though Luce Irigaray claims that "womanspeak" (*parler femme*) is indefinable, she characterizes it as a fluid, plural, tactile discourse that "resists and explodes all firmly established forms, figures, ideas, concepts" (qtd. in Moi, *Sexual/textual Politics*, 145).

2. Diana Fuss defines essentialism "as a belief in the real, true essence of things, the invariable and fixed properties that define the 'whatness' of a given entity" (*Essentially Speaking*, xi–xii). Essentialism, in feminist thought, refers to "any view of woman's nature that makes universal claims about women based on characteristics considered to be an inherent part of being female," a view opposed by social constructivists who claim that "gender" and "the materiality of the (sexed) body" is "linguistically constructed" (S. Jones, *Feminist Theory*, 26; Vasterling, "Butler's Sophisticated," 17,19).

3. For Irigaray, the language of mysticism is the "only place in Western history where woman speaks and acts in such a public way" (qtd. in Moi, *Sexual/textual Politics* 136); paradoxically, despite the self-abnegation that is required of the mystic, mysticism "opens up a space where her own pleasure can unfold" (Moi, *Sexual/textual Politics*, 137).

4. Although *The Book of Margery Kempe* was dictated by the author to scribes, a common medieval practice, the authorial voice is heard in the narrative. Ruth Shklar describes Margery's " 'voice' or subjectivity" as "that most elusive yet noisy figure in the *Book*" (*Cobham's Daughter*, 278).

5. Semiotics, the science of communication, is studied through the interpretation of signs and symbols as they function in a variety of fields. Signs (linguistic or nonlinguistic) are the fundamental elements of communication. Many feminists claim that "the kind of writing that addresses female . . . experience requires a new form of language" (Cameron, *The Feminist Critique*, 8); "we have to invent a woman's word," announces Annie Leclerc (74). The attempt to redefine signs and negotiate meaning in the works discussed in this article demonstrates a desire to subvert sexist language and find an "authentic female voice" (Cameron, *The Feminist Critique*, 3).

6. Kristeva maintains that language has "two modalities": the semiotic and the symbolic. Though the symbolic modality is disposed "towards fixed and unitary definition" allowing for social communication, it "is also driven by an urge to master and control" (Morris, *Literature and Feminism*, 144–145). The semiotic modality—associated with the preverbal stage of the child—is characterized by the "rhythms of heartbeat and pulse . . . the continual flux of physical sensation and libidinal drives" (Morris, *Literature and Feminism*, 144). Some forms of language—mystical and visionary discourses, for example—may permit the semiotic disposition to predominate.

7. The *skeptron* (Hebrew "shebet"; English "sceptre") is an ornamental rod or staff that serves as a symbol of regal or imperial sovereignty.

8. Breaking with the Catholic Church in 1533 after Pope Clement VII condemned his marriage to Anne Boleyn, Henry VIII declared himself the Supreme Head of the Church of England in the Act of Supremacy (1534), thereby laying down the foundation of Protestantism in England.

9. I am drawing a distinction here between the Protestant reformers of sixteenth- and early seventeenth-century Britain and the radical sectarian Protestants of the British civil war period and the Restoration. Sectarians were Protestant dissenters who separated themselves from, and rejected the doctrine and discipline of, the national Church of England.

10. Louis Althusser distinguishes between repressive state apparatuses (e.g., the government, military, police, prisons) and ideological state apparatuses (e.g., the church, family, school, media), all of which can be used to compel "human subjects . . . to submit themselves to the dominant ideologies of their society" (Eagleton, *Literary Theory*, 171), thereby reproducing the existing social structure (Althusser, *Lenin and Philosophy*, 97– 98).

11. Mack has demonstrated that male Quakers of the early-modern period also transcended gender norms when conceiving of themselves, for example, in feminine terms; rejecting a masculine "aggressive and rational egoism," Quaker males experienced an "acute sense of release in identifying with the infantile and feminine qualities of passivity, emotionalism, and loss of bodily inhibition" (Mack, *Visionary Women*, 162). Hilary Hinds contends that the Quaker emphasis on the value of silence reveals the conscious adoption of "a specifically feminine practice" as a "central part of their religious code" (*God's Englishwomen*, 186).

12. According to the linguist Ferdinand de Saussure, every sign consists of a signifier (a meaningful sound or written mark) and a signified (the concept to which the signifier refers). A floating or empty signifier has an indeterminate signified.

13. In *Woman's Consciousness, Man's World*, Sheila Rowbotham stresses the importance of female solidarity in producing social chance: "In order to create an alternative an oppressed group must at once shatter the self-reflecting world which encircles it and, at the same time, project its own image onto history . . . The first step is to connect and learn to trust one another . . . Solidarity has to be a collective consciousness which at once comes through individual self-consciousness and transforms it" (qtd. in Friedman, "Women's Autobiographical Selves," 40).

Bibliography

Aers, D. (1988). *Community, gender, and individual identity: English writing, 1360–1430*. London and New York: Routledge.

Althusser, L. (2001). *Lenin and philosophy and other essays*. Trans. B. Brewster. New York: Monthly Review Press.

Beilin, E. V. (1987). *Redeeming Eve: Women writers of the English renaissance*. Princeton: Princeton University Press.

Bourdieu, P. (1994). *Language and symbolic power*. Trans. G. Raymond and M. Adamson. Ed. J. B. Thompson. Cambridge: Harvard University Press.

Bradstreet, A. (1967). *The works of Anne Bradstreet.* Cambridge, MA: Belknap Press of Harvard University Press.

Bynum, C. W. (1992). *Fragmentation and redemption: Essays on gender and the human body in medieval religion.* New York: Zone Books.

Cameron, D. (1990). Introduction. *The feminist critique of language: A reader.* Ed. D. Cameron. London and New York: Routledge. 1–28.

Castelli, E. (1986). "Virginity and its meaning for women's sexuality in early Christianity." *Journal of feminist studies in religion.* 2: 61–88.

Cope, E. S., ed. (1995). *Prophetic writings of Lady Eleanor Davies.* New York: Oxford University Press.

Cotton, P. and Cole, M. (1655). *To the priests and people of England.* London.

Coulson, C. (1995). "Mysticism, meditation, and identification in *The book of Margery Kempe.*" *Essays in medieval studies.* 12: 69–79.

Crawford, P. (1998). "Women, religion and social action in England, 1500–1800." *Australian Feminist Studies.*13.28: 269–280.

Davies, S. (1998). *Unbridled spirits: Women of the English revolution, 1640–1660.* London: The Women's Press.

Eagleton, T. (1983). *Literary theory: An introduction.* Minneapolis: University of Minnesota Press.

Fell, M. A. (1666). *Women's speaking justified, proved and allowed of by the scriptures, All such as speak by the spirit and power of the Lord Jesus.* London.

Friedman, S. S. (1998). "Women's autobiographical selves: Theory and practice." *Women, autobiography, theory: A reader.* Ed. S. Smith and J. Watson. Madison, WI: University of Wisconsin Press. 72–82.

Fuss, D. (1989). *Essentially speaking: Feminism, nature and difference.* London and New York: Routledge.

Garman, M. et al., eds. (1996). *Hidden in plain sight: Quaker women's writings 1650–1700.* Wallingford: Pendle Hill Publications.

Gill, C. (2004). " 'Ministering confusion': Rebellious Quaker women (1650–1660)." *Quaker studies.* 9.1: 17–30.

Hinds, H. (1996). *God's Englishwomen: Seventeenth century radical sectarian writing and feminist criticism.* Manchester and New York: Manchester University Press.

Hobby, E. (1996). "The politics of women's prophecy in the English revolution." *Sacred and profane: Secular and devotional interplay in early modern British literature.* Ed. H. Wilcox, R. Todd, and A. MacDonald. Amsterdam: VU University Press. 295–306.

Hubnik, S. J. (2005). "(Re)constructing the medieval recluse: Performative acts of virginity and the writings of Julian of Norwich." *The historian.* 67.1: 43–62.

James VI and I. (1994). *King James VI and I: Political writings.* Ed. J. P. Sommerville. Cambridge: Cambridge University Press.

Japinga, L. (1999). *Feminism and Christianity: An essential guide.* Nashville, TN: Abingdon Press.

Jones, A. R. (1985). "Writing the body: l'Écriture féminine." *The new feminist criticism: Essays on women, literature and theory.* Ed. E. Showalter. New York: Pantheon Books. 361–377.

Jones, S. (2000). *Feminist theory and Christian theology: Cartographies of grace.* Minneapolis: Fortress Press.

Julian of Norwich. (1978). *Julian of Norwich: Showings.* Trans. E. Colledge and J. Walsh. New York: Paulist Press.

Kempe, M. (1985). *The book of Margery Kempe.* Trans. B. A. Windeatt. London: Penguin Books.

Lanyer, A. (1993). *The poems of Aemilia Lanyer: Salve deus rex judaeorum.* Ed. S. Woods. New York: Oxford University Press.

Leclerc, A. (1990). "Woman's word." *The feminist critique of language: A reader.* Ed. D. Cameron. London and New York: Routledge. 74–79.

Mack, P. (1992). *Visionary women: Ecstatic prophecy in seventeenth century England*. Berkeley: University of California Press.

Makin, B. (1673). *An essay to revive the antient education of gentlewomen, in religion, manners, arts and tongues*. London.

Moi, T. (1985). *Sexual/textual politics: Feminist literary theory*. London and New York: Routledge.

Morris, P. (1993). *Literature and feminism*. Oxford: Blackwell.

Nuth, J. M. (1991). *Wisdom's daughter: The theology of Julian of Norwich*. New York: The Crossroad Publishing Company.

Olney, J. (1972). *Autobiography: Essays theoretical and critical*. Princeton: Princeton University Press.

Potkay, M. B. and Evitt, R. M. (1997). *Minding the body: Women and literature in the middle ages, 800–1500*. London: Twayne Publishers.

Powell, R. A. (2003). "Margery Kempe: An exemplar of late medieval piety." *Catholic historical review*. 81.1: 1–23.

Rudrum, A., Black, J., and Nelson H. F., eds. (2000). *The Broadview anthology of seventeenth century prose*. Peterborough: Broadview Press.

Sandhaas, K. (2001). "Hearing to speech." *The wisdom of daughters: Two decades of the voice of Christian feminism*. Ed. R. H. Finger and K. Sandhaas. Philadelphia: Innisfree Press. xiv–xv.

Shklar, R. (1995). "Cobham's daughter: *The book of Margery Kempe* and the power of heterodox thinking." *Modern language quarterly*. 56.3: 277–304.

Sidney-Herbert, M. (1998). *The collected works of Mary Sidney Herbert, Countess of Pembroke*. Ed. M. P. Hannay, N. J. Kinnamon, and M. G. Brennan. Oxford: Clarendon Press; New York: Oxford University Press.

Sommerfeldt, J. R. (1976). "Bernard of Clairvaux: The mystic and society." *The spirituality of western Christendom*. Ed. E. R. Elder. Kalamazoo: Cistercian Publications, Inc. 72–84.

Speght, R. (1996). *The polemics and poems of Rachel Speght*. Ed. B. Lewalski. New York: Oxford University Press.

Stone, L. (1977). *The family, sex and marriage in England 1500–1800*. New York: Harper Torchbooks.

Tertullian. (1994). "On the apparel of women." *The Ante-Nicene fathers: Translations of the writings of the fathers down to A. D. 325*. Ed. A. Roberts and J. Donaldson. Vol. 4. Edinburgh: T & T Clark; Grand Rapids, MI: Wm. B. Eerdmans Publishing Company. 14–25.

Trapnel, A. (1654). *The cry of a stone, or a relation of something spoken in Whitehall, by Anna Trapnel*. London.

Travitsky, B. (1981). "Introduction." *The paradise of women: Writings by Englishwomen of the renaissance*. Westport: Greenwood Press. 3–13.

Trevett, C. (1995). *Women and Quakerism in the 17th Century*. New York: The Ebor Press.

Vasterling, V. (1999). "Butler's sophisticated constructivism: A critical assessment." *Hypatia*. 14.3: 17–38.

Vaughan, H. (1995). "Holy scriptures." *Henry Vaughan: The complete poems*. Ed. A. Rudrum. Harmondsworth: Penguin. 197–198.

Vives, J. L. (1592). *A verie fruitfull and pleasant booke called the Instruction of a Christian woman*. Trans. R. Hyrde. London.

Voaden, R. (1999). *God's words, women's voices: The discernment of spirits in the writing of late-medieval women visionaries*. Woodbridge: York Medieval Press.

Watson, N. K. (2003). *Feminist theology*. Grand Rapids, MI: William B. Eerdmans Publishing Company.

Wroth, M. (1983). *The poems of Lady Mary Wroth*. Ed. J. A. Roberts. Baton Rouge: Louisiana State University Press.

CHAPTER EIGHT

Biblical Literalism and Gender Stability: A Christian Response to Gender Performance Theory

CHRISTOPHER NOBLE

In March 2005, I was invited to participate in a forum on Christianity and feminism sponsored by a student-run organization on the campus of Azusa Pacific University, where I teach in the English department. Since I cover feminist theory in my course on literary criticism, I was eager to accept the invitation. Joining me on the panel of respondents were two students, a professor of biblical studies, and an Episcopal priest, the Reverend Wilma Jakobsen, who is known for her work on women's issues in her native South Africa. Following some introductory remarks by the panelists, questions were solicited from the roughly one hundred members of the audience. After a few tentative opening comments and questions from students around the room, a woman near the front posed the crucial, inevitable question: "If you are claiming to be biblically-based feminists, how do you explain those passages in scripture which speak out against placing women in positions of religious leadership?" Without hesitation, Reverend Jakobsen responded, "I don't think you can be a feminist and take the Bible literally."

As Jakobsen expanded on her position, she expressed frustration with Christians who enlist biblical support for feminism. Such Christians typically deny that the Bible is patriarchal, preferring instead to laud biblical heroines as feminist poster girls. In Jakobsen's view, it is far more honest to acknowledge that patriarchal perspectives are endemic to scripture, and to focus selectively on biblical passages amenable to contemporary values of equality and social justice. Such a view usually depends on a theology of progressive revelation: although we cannot "take the Bible literally," we understand it to be an inspired, indispensable agent of religious-cultural consciousness. In this vein, for instance, Kari Elisabeth Børresen has maintained that "a fruitful and healthy theology . . . must be inspired by the Roman Catholic understanding of the coherence between scripture and tradition as parts of an ongoing revelation" (4). According to views like Børresen's, we cannot take the Bible "literally," though we take it seriously; as new cultural concerns arise, scripture providentially produces new meanings appropriate to the particularity of the historical circumstances, including meanings appropriate and relevant to twenty-first century Christian readers.

For many participants in the predominantly evangelical audience, however, reading the Bible literally was a nonnegotiable article of faith. For them, to renounce the concept of literal interpretation entailed a total abandonment of scripture's truth claims. To suggest that Christians read "non-literally" implies that if biblical references to women's roles could not be taken literally, then neither could references to miracles or to Christ's resurrection.

Taking It Literally: The Limits of
Christian-Feminist Debate

At first glance, resolving the impasse between these two interpretive stances—literalism and progressive revelation—appears unlikely. Participants on each side typically dismiss the arguments of the other without inquiring more thoughtfully into the assumptions informing them. Indeed, such paralyzed exchanges sometimes replay themselves so predictably in Christian academic settings that we might begin to regard the Christian-feminist debate as a stubborn filibuster rather than a vibrant dialogue.

In this essay, I argue that this rivalry between literalism and progressive revelation constitutes a false dilemma that stifles a fuller and more balanced Christian-feminist discourse. By allowing the literalism/ progressive revelation question to set the terms of debate, Christians are prone to overlook surprising correspondences between theology, biblical scholarship, and developments in feminist theory. In particular, recent studies of gender in the book of Genesis can be enriched through an engagement with a branch of contemporary feminism known as gender performance theory. Inaugurated by the publication of Judith Butler's *Gender Trouble* in 1990, this theory defines gender as a social performance, rather than as a biological reality or fact. Because it raises very fundamental questions, Butler's work remains controversial even for secular feminism. Although more traditional versions of feminism have survived or even flourished over the past 30 years in the work of Christian scholars, particularly in theology, gender performance theory has generally been regarded with suspicion or even open hostility. This hostility, I propose, is due to the fact that gender performance theory appears to threaten both biblical literalism and progressive revelation by dismantling the assumptions about gender on which they rely. This hostility also suggests that biblical literalism and progressive revelation are not as diametrically opposed as they first appear. The engagement of Christian-feminist scholarship alongside gender performance theory can reveal blindness and insight in each; further, it may offer Christians a way to rethink feminist questions without retreating into these two familiar stalemates.

How precisely does the literalism/progressivism paradigm derail Christian-feminist debates? As an example, consider a prominent literalist proof text, Paul's words in 1 Timothy 2:11–14 (NIV): "A woman should learn in quietness and full submission. I do not permit a woman to teach or to have authority over a man; she must be silent. For Adam was formed first, then Eve. And Adam was not the one deceived; it was the woman who was deceived and became a sinner." As a woman in a position of religious authority over men, Jakobsen would likely insist that she does not think these verses should be taken literally, since such a literal reading fails to address the religious/cultural circumstances of present-day Christians. Some would, on the contrary, demand that the passage be taken literally, in the interests of preserving the authority of scripture. Culture, they would argue, must adjust itself to accord with scripture, not the other way around.

But this stalemate leaves a crucial question unanswered: what does it actually mean to take 1 Timothy 2:11–14 literally? To those unfamiliar with speech-act theory and the philosophy of language, this question may initially seem counterintuitive, obstructionist, or even nonsensical.[1] After all, despite their many differences, literalists and progressivists agree that one literal meaning does in fact exist for passages like the one quoted above, and that this one literal meaning is equally obvious to everyone. They differ only in the importance and meaning they assign to the literal. And yet their shared premise—that one literal meaning exists—is surprisingly difficult to justify.

What might the one literal meaning be? Let us consider three possibilities. First, one might propose that, taken literally, the passage means women should not be placed in positions of religious leadership over men under any circumstances. This reading continues to determine the standard practice in many American churches today. It may be a justifiable practice, but it is not justifiable on the basis of a "literal" reading of 1 Timothy 2:11–14, for Paul nowhere explicitly states in this passage that his comments should be taken as a timeless and universal command. Quite to the contrary, he localizes his restrictions: "*I* do not permit." And so, second, if we are to read only the "letter of the law" and nothing else, one might propose that, taken literally, the passage is a mere statement of Paul's personal preference. But of course if we begin to take things *that* literally, we will severely limit scripture's contemporary relevance. Third, to take the passage literally might also mean to recover Paul's original intent. On this reading, we would need to know more about the historical circumstances of Paul's letter in order to reconstruct the motivations behind the writing of the epistle. For instance, we would need to know whether historical evidence exists of a small group of disruptive women threatening the unity of the church at the time of Paul's writing, and we would then try to determine whether Paul might be writing specifically in response to such a disruption.

I do not here advocate any of these three interpretations. The important point is that they show just how various the concept of the "literal" can be. This is not to say that literal meanings are illusions or that the term is utterly meaningless; it is only to say that people actually have very different interpretive procedures in mind when they use the term "literal."[2] In the first example, "literal" means directly transferring Paul's instructions from Timothy to ourselves. In the second example, "literal" means restricting the passage's meaning to the letter of the law (thus viewing it as a mere statement of fact about how Paul advised Timothy to regulate male/female relations). In the third example, "literal" means attempting to recover the biblical author's original intent. Ironically, "literal" does not itself appear to have a literal meaning. Unfortunately, however, the word "literal" does possess tremendously powerful rhetorical connotations for a variety of possible readings and positions. When the word is used, it usually indicates an attempt to seize the interpretive high ground by asserting an indisputable foundation. As the three previous 1 Timothy examples show, however, such a rhetorical appeal to the stability of literalness is far less certain than it may appear to be.

As such, the Christian-feminist debate should seek to change its terms by abandoning the simplistic distinction between literalism and progressivism. Ultimately, a much more precise critical terminology is required to describe the interpretive strategies being used to evaluate the validity of feminist claims. The debate should not be whether to take a given passage literally, but instead whether "literal" is ever an appropriate term to use when discussing the complexity and profundity of biblical meaning.

Gender performance theory offers the Christian-feminist debate just such an alternate path. By identifying assumptions held in common by supposedly "opposite" positions, it offers Christians a new set of vocabulary and concepts for reinterpreting biblical sites of feminist controversy. At the same time, however, gender performance theory may itself require revision in the light of scriptural revelation.

How does a consideration of gender performance theory advance the terms of Christian-feminist debate beyond its literalist/progressivist boundaries? In short, it does this by questioning essentialist assumptions about language and gender that both biblical literalism and progressive tradition take for granted. Literalists and progressivists ask questions such as "Does the Bible support equality between men and women?"; a gender performance theorist, by contrast, might ask "How are the gender identities of men and women in the Bible constructed and established in various situations and events?" Broadly conceived, such theoretically challenging questions—found in works such as Donna Haraway's "A Cyborg Manifesto" (1985) and Judith Butler's books *Gender Trouble* (1990) and *Bodies That Matter* (1993)—oppose "gender essentialism," the idea that gender identity (masculinity or femininity) is narrowly determined by the facts of biological sex (male or female), and challenges the notion that this identity is stable, unchangeable, and universal. For example, the proposition that men are naturally more rational or independent and that women are naturally more emotional or relational is an essentialist notion. By contrast, Haraway and Butler deny that sex determines gender, and propose instead that "men" and "women" come into being as gendered entities through social and even technological performances rather than emerging from an ordained essence. In Haraway's case, neither the term "man" nor the term "woman" suffices to describe gender identity. She envisions a new entity—the cyborg—a being that reveals the insufficiency of our concepts of gender by blurring the line between nature and technology. Indeed, many of the challenges issued by gender studies are attacks on Enlightenment concepts of nature. Whereas "literal meaning" can be understood as the "natural" sense of things, traditional conceptions of gender identity might be understood as the "natural" identities of men and women. Haraway and Butler, in different ways, oppose the idea that men and women have static or universally gendered meanings. Christian scholars interested in feminism, such as Susan Gallagher, have generally resisted an engagement with gender performance theory, perhaps because they see no hope for rapprochement. Consider, for instance, a passage from Gallagher's evaluation of feminist literary theory, published in 1991, just after Butler's first groundbreaking book:

> The various ethical dimensions of feminist literary criticism may provide some models of ways to apply religious beliefs while reading literature. Like feminist critics, the Christian critic regards beliefs about life rather than an interpretive technique as the distinguishing characteristic of literary study. While feminists ground their criticism in the belief that women are unjustly oppressed, Christians ground their criticism in basic beliefs about the nature of God, human beings, and language. Like feminist criticism, Christian criticism must be committed criticism. It should not merely explore a hypothesis; it should attempt to serve God and humanity. (247)

Gallagher's conclusions are undeniable when applied to traditional essentialist feminism. When applied to gender performance theory, however, the ethical basis of comparison dissolves. Butler and Haraway, though deeply invested in feminist projects, certainly do not "ground their criticism in the belief that women are unjustly oppressed" (Gallagher 247). Indeed their thought persistently critiques the stability of the very categories ("oppression" and "women") upon which traditional feminism is based.

Gender performance theory, therefore, presents the Christianity-feminism discussion with both promises and problems. On one hand, it promises fresh approaches to understanding the relationship between biblical revelation and gender identity, approaches no longer haunted by literalist or progressivist concerns. On the other hand, however, it refuses to acknowledge God (or, indeed, anything) as the origin or foundation of gender since, for gender performance theorists, gender is defined as an *event* or a *technology*, not as an essential attribute possessed by people. Just as Gallagher sought to establish common ground between Christian criticism and traditional feminism, my purpose here is to seek common ground between Christian perspectives and gender performance theory. Although it is obvious that a complete synthesis between these two is neither possible nor perhaps even desirable, nevertheless each contains valuable insights for the other. The first such insight evaluates the current state of feminist debate over a key biblical passage on gender identity—the image of God as described in Genesis 1:26–28—and suggests how recent interpretations of that passage might benefit from a consideration of gender performance theory. The second insight reviews several key arguments made by gender theorists, which can be considered for understanding the Christian self in a world where technology is making all identity (including gender identity) constantly more fluid and unpredictable.

The Elusive Image of God and Gender Identity in Genesis 1

Was Adam androgynous? Most contemporary biblical scholars reject this reading of the first chapter of Genesis. For instance, Phyllis Trible, using rhetorical analysis, contends that the "shifts [in Genesis 1: 26–28³] from singular to plural disallow an androgynous interpretation of *hā-'ādām*. From the beginning humankind exists as two creatures, not as one creature with double sex" (18). Yet the fact that the question can even be seriously posed—Trible is responding to minority views in Hebrew tradition and modern scholarship—is a telling reflection on the tantalizing elusiveness, compactness, and complexity of the *imago Dei*. Though it rarely finds support in scholarly interpretations, the Hebrew myth of the androgynous *'ādām* (in Hebrew *'ādām* can function both as a proper name and as a collective noun for humanity) serves as a powerful reminder of the astonishing range of interpretations Genesis 1:27 has received. Consider this midrashic account from Genesis Rabbah 8:1:

> R. Jeremiah b. Leazar said: "When the Holy One, blessed be He, created Adam, he created him androgynous, for it is said, *Male and female He created them* (Genesis 1:27) *and He called their name: Adam.* (Genesis 5:2)." R. Samuel b. Nahman said: "When the Lord created Adam He created him double-faced, then He split him and made him of two backs, one back on this side and one back on the other side." To this it is objected: But it is written, *And he took one of his ribs (tsela)* (Genesis 2:21). This means: one of his *sides*, replied he, as you read, *And for the other side (tsela) of the Tabernacle* (Exodus 26:20). (qtd. in Teugels 109)

This midrash serves as an excellent example of the dangers of assuming that a "literal" reading of gender issues in scripture will render a single, universally obvious meaning—for the rabbis are certainly paying as close attention to the letter of the passage as would most conservative literalists today. Although few modern scholars reach the same conclusion about Adam, their disagreements about the gendered significance of the image, along with their characterizations of the image of God as an "empty" space, suggest that a biblical view of human gender identity shares with gender performance theory a nonessentialist, dynamically evolving view of the human subject.

As we might expect, contemporary readings of Genesis 1:26–28 diverge sharply. In his commentary on Genesis, John Hartley concludes that the reference to "male and female" is integral to the image of God:

> The Hebrew emphasizes the phrase "male and female" by placing it before the verb. This third and final part of the verse contains four important ideas. (a) It ascribes sexuality to God's design for humans. Thus, an essential aspect of human nature is quite different from God's nature. An implication of this is that we need to draw on the outstanding qualities found in each gender to have a full view of God. If we imagine God as predominantly male or female, our picture is partial and distorted. (48)

Hartley is discussing a passage that presumably shows how we are *like* God—thus, since the image is "male and female," we must draw on the "outstanding qualities" of both in order for the image to be accurate and complete. But in the same analysis Hartley asserts that "sexuality" has nothing to do with God's nature. Thus, strangely, humans are indeed very *unlike* God in the same passage that purportedly establishes our likeness to God. Further, what might the "outstanding qualities" of each gender be exactly? Do they include sexuality? Are there "outstanding qualities" of maleness and femaleness that transcend sexuality? Against Hartley's assertion, Phyllis A. Bird argues that sexual differentiation has no bearing on the divine image. In Bird's reading, no logical connection is to be assumed from the mere proximity of the phrase "male and female" to the phrase "the image of God." Rather, in Bird's view, sexual differentiation is linked to the fertility and dominion blessings in the subsequent verse (Genesis 1:28), rather than to the God-human resemblance:

> The idea that God might possess any form of sexuality, or any differentiation analogous to it, would have been for P [the Priestly author of Genesis 1] an utterly foreign and repugnant

notion. . . . Consequently, the word that identifies *adam* by reference to divine likeness must be supplemented or qualified before
the blessing of fertility can be pronounced; for the word of blessing
assumes but does not bestow the means of reproduction. The
required word of qualification and specification is introduced in vs.
27b. *Unlike* God, but *like* the other creatures, *adam* is characterized
by sexual differentiation. (11)

Here we encounter a view precisely opposite to Hartley's, a view that
insists that gender identity must be read as a limitation on humanity's likeness to God, rather than as an essential attribute of it. Bird's account is perhaps logically more consistent than Hartley's, but not as rhetorically
satisfying. Her account does nothing to clarify what the resemblance
between God and humanity actually is. It merely excludes sexual distinction from consideration. Rather than contemplating God's nature as both
male and female, as Hartley does, Bird contends that the Priestly author
endorses neither attribute as divine resemblances. This move boasts certain
tactical advantages for egalitarian-feminist readings, since the hierarchy
between God and humanity has so often been inscribed on the
male/female relationship, using Genesis 1:27 as a justification.[4] And yet
this still does not explain why the phrase "male and female" is framed in a
parallel poetic construction with "the image of God." Although Genesis 1:27
makes no explicit connection between sexual distinction and the *imago*,
the implicit connections are extremely difficult to ignore. As Phyllis Trible
shows, the pronouncement concerning the image in the first creation
account is contained in a highly structured poetic verse form, which uses
chiasmus and parallelism to emphasize both the centrality of God's creative
role and the link between sexual differentiation and the image:

> Clearly, "male and female" correspond structurally to "the image
> of God," and this formal parallelism indicates a semantic corre-
> spondence. Likewise, the switch from the singular pronoun "him"
> to the plural pronoun "them" at the end of these two parallel lines
> provides a key for interpreting humankind (hā-'ādām) in the first
> line. The plural form reinforces sexual differentiation within the
> unity of humanity. Altogether, the third line, in straight parallelism
> to the second, opens up meanings that are highlighted yet hidden
> by the inverted parallelism of lines one and two. (17)

Is this parallel correspondence, used at the founding moment of Hebrew
and Christian anthropology, merely a coincidence? It is difficult to see

the link as arbitrary.[5] From a formalist or rhetorical point of view, then, the *imago* seems to be inextricably linked to sexual difference; from a logical or historical point of view, the *imago* seems to be radically severed from it.

Theology informed by essentialist feminism offers little chance of resolving this conundrum. The traditional feminist reading (of which Ruether's work provides an example) assumes that the identities of men and women are discrete, predetermined, natural essences, residing in bodies and distinguished by biological difference alone. The primary concern, then, for traditional feminism, is to extract from Genesis an egalitarian interpretation—one that honors the "essential attributes" of both sexes and which rescues Eve from subordinate status. But the interest in establishing biblical equality between male and female tends to obscure a much more basic issue: the paradoxical relationship of gender itself to the divine. It makes little sense to pursue equality between "male and female," when it is the blending or free combination of those identities that best seems to describe the human-divine likeness. If Hartley is correct that "outstanding qualities" of each gender give us a fuller view of God, and if the *imago Dei* establishes human likeness to God, then would it not be plausible to conclude that a fuller view of each human being requires that we draw on a multiplicity of gender characteristics?

Taking our cue from gender performance theory, suppose we regarded God as the creator of our gender identity as well as the creator of physical sexual difference? In this view, the mystery of the *imago Dei* passage—the paradox that we are both like and unlike God—is a key to understanding identity rather than an obstacle. If, as some theologians believe, the *imago Dei* is linked to sexual difference, and yet at the same time the Priestly account in Genesis 1 preserves the absolute otherness of God as a paramount value, then perhaps we should interpret the human-God resemblance as implying a *capacity for otherness* in human identity.

Interpreting the *imago* as a "capacity for otherness" bridges the gap between Hartley's and Bird's views. It respects the parallelism of verse 27αβ and verse 27b, as well as the silence between them. We are like God, not because God possesses masculine and feminine attributes, but because there is something about the human, gendered experience of being male and female that resembles God's transcendence. God's absolute otherness becomes for us a limited otherness. In this view, human gender is set apart and performed by God in Genesis 1:27 as a special category, in dominion over the animals whose sexual difference is deterministically linked to nature, rather than artistically placed in it. Bird protests that "the specifying clause, 'male and female he created them' must not be understood as distinguishing humans from other creatures or as giving to human sexual distinction a special meaning" (22). Her reason for so arguing appears to be that "male and female"—*zākār ûnĕqebâ*—are biological rather than social terms, used elsewhere in the Bible (Genesis 6:19) to refer to animals. But this only demonstrates the seductive coercion of essentialist assumptions. Bird takes the nature/culture distinction itself on faith—it is an assumption of her philosophical framework taken utterly for granted. She is likely accurately emulating, to the extent possible, the mindset of the ancient Near East. But this implicit faith in nature as a simple, objective, ahistorical category obscures an important question of twenty-first century interpretation. Why—if *zākār ûnĕqēbâ* are such physical, biological, nonsocial terms—would the Priestly author grant them such parallel proximity to the image of *'ĕlōhîm*? If we take the nature/culture distinction for granted, then the "obvious" answer is that the Priestly author "mentions [male and female] only out of necessity" (Bird 22).

Read this way, sexual distinction is an embarrassment to the image. But does not the text permit a wholly different construal? Could not verse 27aβ and verse 27b constitute a literary paradox, signaling from the outset of creation that the human relation to biological nature is fundamentally different from the animal? Bird sees her scholarly role as an attempted reconstruction of the Priestly author's intent, but she leaves open the possibility that scripture may be meaningful on grounds different from, and even opposed to, the human author's purported intentions. She says:

> My argument in summarizing the Priestly writer's view analyzes the intentions and assumptions of the author as inferred from the text in its ancient setting. However, the text itself permits an egalitarian reading, I would argue, despite the fact that it must be viewed as unintended and unforeseen by the ancient author. It not only permits such a reading, it encourages it, by the "emptiness" of its key terms, the structure of its pronouncements, and its restraint from specifying social roles and responsibilities. (24)

If we believe that God, not P, is ultimately the author of Genesis, and if we believe, furthermore, that the Holy Spirit is instrumental in interpretation, then the Priestly author's intent, no matter how accurately construed, is not where the hermeneutical buck stops. Nothing in Genesis 1 constrains us to accept the "capacity for otherness" interpretation; but, likewise, nothing in Genesis 1 precludes it. It is, at the very least, as plausible as other attempts to interpret this foundational passage, urging but not forcing the Christian-feminist discussion toward a rejection of gender essentialism.

Like Bird, biblical scholars frequently remark on the "emptiness" or ambiguity of the image. The Priestly author of Genesis 1 makes an astonishing pronouncement—humans are like God—and then, in the wake of this announcement, the Priestly author unaccountably neglects to specify the nature of the resemblance, leaving it blank, sparse. In *Church Dogmatics*, Karl Barth surveys the variety of content with which Christian thinkers, historically, have sought to fill the image (III. 1. 192–194), implying that humans abhor an interpretive vacuum, or perhaps that the image was providentially intended as a flexible category, capable of accommodating human change. For her part, Bird observes that the image "as a metaphor for likeness is concrete, formal, holistic—and 'empty,' lacking specific content, and thus an ideal term for P, who employs it with changing connotations in changing contexts" (8). This emptiness is profoundly compelling, because it invites us to view our God-given identities as forever capable of development, not as bound and fixed essences. If, like God, we possess a capacity for otherness, then renewed, dynamic identities are always possible.

Barth sought to account for this otherness by abandoning the image as *analogia entis* (analogy of being) and instead reading it as *analogia relationis* (analogy of relationship) (III. 1. 184–185; 195–196). As feminist theologians have pointed out, however, this change does not sufficiently preserve God's absolute otherness. For if the relationship between male and female is said to mirror or to represent (1) relationships in the personhood of God and (2) the relationship between the divine and the human, then our theology remains fundamentally anthropomorphic, viewing God in the light of our humanity rather than viewing ourselves in the light of God's otherness. Furthermore, as Ruether notes, an analogy of relationship inevitably implies patriarchal hierarchy in the male–female relationship (284). And yet, a feminist critique often exhausts itself in the quest for an egalitarian reading of the Bible, failing to see that the concept of equality is bound to the same Western, rationalist, essentialist tradition as representation. If the Christian-feminist debate is to engage meaningfully with gender studies, then Christians will need to rethink essentialist assumptions, and to take both divine and human otherness more seriously. The image, then, is not an analogy but an aporia,[6] a paradox and a beginning.

In the final section of this essay, I wish to explore the similarity between the "otherness" or "emptiness" of this biblical aporia and the constructionist[7] view of gender espoused by gender performance theory. While this comparison reveals a second possible insight gained from Christians engaging gender performance theory, it also requires a critique of certain aspects of gender performance theory that are not compatible with a Christian worldview.

The Nature of Nature: Gender
Construction and the Christian Self

In 1993, the Brown University geneticist Anne Fausto-Sterling published an intentionally provocative article in *The Sciences* citing "natural" evidence for the existence of not two, but five human sexes: male, female, true hermaphrodites, male pseudo-hermaphrodites, and female pseudo-hermaphrodites. In her article, Fausto-Sterling admits that taboos surrounding the three "additional" sexes make it extremely difficult to verify the actual number of "intersexuals" (human beings who are neither exclusively male nor exclusively female), but estimates that they may account for as much as 4 percent of live births. That estimate, as Fausto-Sterling reports in a later article, is likely to be very high: her best approximation of the intersexual birthrate in the year 2000 was 1.7 percent. But the actual percentage—whatever it is—does not materially diminish Fausto-Sterling's key point: "If the state and the legal system have an interest in maintaining a two-party sexual system, they are in defiance of nature. For biologically speaking, there are many gradations running from female to male" (21). Of course, one might want to raise the objection that hermaphrodites don't upset the two-sex model because they shouldn't be allowed to count as legitimate exceptions. They are a statistical minority, a genetic aberration.[8] At the very least, however, we would have to allow that Fausto-Sterling's argument conclusively shows the two-sex model to be a technical oversimplification of nature. As a matter of biological fact, not every human being is definitively male or female.

Do such persons, then, have a share in the image of God? If the answer is yes, then a Christian understanding of the human-divine likeness—the theological basis of human identity—cannot rely on gender essentialism. This is because gender essentialism remains fundamentally static and dualistic; it proposes that permanent, universal, and "natural" gender characteristics attach to two biological sexes in a mutually exclusive and formulaic way. Thus, a gender essentialist might view men as *naturally* more logical and women as *naturally* more emotional.

A Christian gender essentialist reading the book of Genesis will often conclude, therefore, that God is ultimately responsible for implanting these gender characteristics into the essence of each biological sex, so that as created beings our gender has been stabilized and finalized as soon as our biological sex is determined. Only God, it is supposed by essentialist thinking, partakes of the "outstanding qualities" of both genders. But if this is the case, then what are we to say of the hermaphrodite's gender identity? Has God *naturally* implanted both male and female gender characteristics into androgynous human beings? (If so, the interesting result would be that hermaphrodites bear a closer resemblance to God than do either males or females.) And what of male and female pseudo-hermaphrodites? How would gender essentialism propose to distinguish their gender identities? In short, the trouble with gender essentialism is that its dualistic bias proves incapable of accounting for the variety that actually exists in social and biological reality. It oversimplifies, and thus obscures, the complexity of both gender and biological sex.

By contrast, the "performative" reading of Genesis I have proposed suggests that our likeness to God justifies a more fluid, multiple understanding of gender within a Christian worldview. Because we are like God, we are capable of experiencing a broad spectrum of gender characteristics, regardless of biological sex. This is a critical point—a point that can very easily be misunderstood. I am not arguing for a radical and absolute disjunction between gender and biological sex. I am merely arguing that biological sex does not determine gender. In any given cultural/historical situation, significant correlations may emerge between biological sex and social gender roles. For instance, in twenty-first century America, care-givers (nurses, baby-sitters, etc.) are more likely to be female than male. But this statistical fact is a far cry from proving that women are "naturally" more caring than men. As any logician knows, correlation alone does not prove causation. And even if it could be shown that women are *naturally* more caring than men, this would certainly not be enough to justify such a state of affairs from a Christian standpoint. Surely, from a biblical perspective, caring is an attribute of Christ that people of all sexes should imitate. For the Christian who has abandoned gender essentialism, the spiritual identity of intersexuals no longer poses a great problem, since the image of God (upon which this identity is based) is no longer thought of as being bound by "natural" facts.

Over the past 20 years, writers such as Fausto-Sterling have been questioning the essentialist picture of nature in many fields, particularly in medical science, social history, and feminist theory. This trend should not be taken lightly, nor should it be regarded with unthinking revulsion. Christian writers sometimes commit both errors. For instance, in his book, *The Right Questions*, Phillip E. Johnson ridicules an inaccurate caricature of gender studies. Johnson begins his discussion with a carefully constructed morality tale about a professor's son who decides to dress in a "transgendered" fashion. The moral of Johnson's story is clear: he believes gender studies to be inherently untenable from a Christian standpoint. The following passage is symptomatic of his stance:

> The notion that sexual difference is merely one of "gender," something that humans imagined and that can be changed whenever they like, is foreign to the Bible. Today people are rebelling against the Bible's teaching, imagining that it is up to us and not (a supposedly imaginary) God to decide what the fundamental division of humanity should be. (140)

Johnson's argument stands as an example of the collusion between misguided biblical literalism and gender essentialism. Although the Bible does indeed indicate that God created humans "male and female," this implies nothing in itself about the truth of gender performance theory. A much more serious problem with Johnson's view, however, is that the definition of gender he attacks bears only the flimsiest resemblance to the actual claims of contemporary gender studies. Gender, defined as "something that humans imagined and that can be changed whenever they like," is foreign not only to the Bible, but to everyone. Not even the most radical gender theorists propose such a definition. For a theorist like Judith Butler, whom Johnson dismisses as "trendy" (128), gender is vigorously material (as opposed to "imagined"), seldom under human control, and certainly not a matter of an individual subject's whimsical choice. In short, Christian critiques like Johnson's fail to understand the very theory they are opposing.

My purpose in criticizing Johnson's position is certainly not meant to imply that no conflicts exist between gender performance theory and a Christian worldview. These conflicts, however, deserve careful consideration rather than thoughtless dismissal. My position is that Christians should reject gender essentialism, but not that they should therefore embrace all the claims of gender performance theory. The many aspects of my Christian faith, its scriptures, and its traditions dissuade me from viewing human identity as a static quantity. In fact, quite to the contrary, the powerful images used by Christ and the Apostle Paul, respectively, to describe the life of faith, "born again" (John 3:3) and "new creation" (2 Cori. 5:17) testify to a dynamic and progressive model of human identity. Gender performance theory's critique of essentialism is therefore a powerful conceptual tool for Christians who believe that essentialist categories limit the expression of the *imago Dei*.

The claims of gender constructionist theories, however, go well beyond a straightforward critique of essentialism. Though Johnson is incorrect when he characterizes these theories as asserting that gender can be "whatever [we] like," it is true that gender performance theories tend to sever human identity from metaphysical origins, and it is this tendency that is most obviously at odds with a Christian worldview. Viewed from a Christian perspective, constructionist gender theory's great strength is to be found in its freeing of gendered characteristics from biological anchors: courage should not be thought of as a male virtue; nurturing should not be thought of as a female virtue. Furthermore, it offers powerful insight into how our subjectivity is constructed through the performance of these virtues rather than preexisting them. Conversely, gender theory's greatest weakness, from a Christian viewpoint, is its denial of gender's metaphysical origins. Not content to separate gender from biological sex, gender constructionists go further by separating gender from *any* cause. Or, rather, they see gender itself as the cause and view individual identity as the effect (this is Butler's position). Strangely, then, Johnson and gender theorists are actually in complete agreement that gender is not something that humans imagined and can be changed whenever they like. Gender performance theorists would concur with this statement because, for them, gender itself is the social force that does the choosing, not individual human beings. It is not humans who choose their gender, but rather the social performance of gender that regulates human identity. The effect of this move, then, is the deification of gender, which consequently creates opportunities for Christian modifications. In order to explore these opportunities, we must examine gender theory itself in greater detail, particularly that of two influential gender theorists—Donna Haraway and Judith Butler—in order to gauge their potential for application in Christian-feminist debates about human identity.

The first constructionist theory I wish to evaluate was proposed by Donna Haraway in her 1985 article, "A Cyborg Manifesto: Science, Technology, and Socialist-Feminism in the Late Twentieth Century." Haraway's stated goal in this much-anthologized essay is to "build an ironic political myth faithful to feminism, socialism, and materialism" (424).

"Faithful" is a carefully chosen word, for Haraway views feminism as akin to a religious institution, and knows that in challenging gender essentialism she has become a blasphemer against holy doctrine. Haraway would agree with Susan Gallagher's comment, cited in the first section of this essay, that feminist criticism is "ethically committed" criticism. For Haraway, however, feminism's commitment is pointedly not to women: "There is nothing about being 'female' that naturally binds women. There is not even such a state as 'being' female, itself a highly complex category constructed in contested sexual scientific discourses and other social practices" (429). Strange words indeed from a feminist: here is a feminist who does not believe in being female. Haraway's ethical commitment, therefore, is not to an essential and universal category called "women," but rather to a potentially utopian freedom of identity from all such proscribed categories.

To embody this vision of constructionist feminism, Haraway abandons women (as an ontological category) and embraces the cyborg, "a cybernetic organism, a hybrid of machine and organism, a creature of social reality as well as a creature of fiction" (424). Drawn from science fiction, the cyborg functions—both as metaphor and as material reality— to dissolve the accepted boundaries between "natural" and "artificial." Cyborgs are both at once. A cyborg's gender therefore cannot be determined by nature. In theory, even its biological sex is mutable. On the other hand, because it is also an organic being, the cyborg cannot be dismissed as a "mere machine." A cyborg is severed from natural determinism. He/she/it is therefore potentially "free"—not as a unitary, Cartesian self, but as an identity spliced together from technology and flesh.

The central objection Christians should raise in response to Haraway's vision is not to its gender constructionism per se, but rather to its materialism and its utopian ambitions. These points are logically separable. In other words, it is possible to affirm Haraway's mistrust of the way the category "woman" has been constructed and culturally performed while refusing to accede to her contention that "salvation" will come through technology. Haraway's greatest usefulness to Christian scholars and theologians, however, lies in the warning her essay gives us, that theology has not kept pace with the speed at which technology is influencing gender identity, and indeed human identity in general.

Despite the conflicts between Haraway's position and a Christian worldview, her insights into the relationship between technology and identity are powerful indeed. Cyborgs, as Haraway defines them, are not merely daydreams or figments of science fiction. They are material realities. Increasingly, perhaps inevitably, human identity is subject to technological influence and manipulation. This is not to say that we should expect the world to devolve into a dystopia like the one envisioned by Ridley Scott's *Blade Runner* (1982). Nor does it mean we will have to contend with killer robots running amuck. Twenty-first century cyborgs are bland by the standards of fiction, but they are no less real for being ordinary. Perhaps a few examples of contemporary cyborg technology will suffice to make this point: pacemakers, Carticel (a product that genetically replaces damaged knee cartilage), lens implants, artificial organs, performance-enhancing drugs, genetically altered food. Recently, one of my students came to class with a computer hard drive integrated into his sunglasses. With the completion of the human genome project, it is only a matter of time before Christians will have to confront "cyborg" ethics in profound theological, philosophical, historical, and literary ways. Feminism and gender identity are inextricable from these ethics.

Many would perhaps like to simplify matters by utterly rejecting technological incursions into territory previously held by "nature." Reactions to human cloning are a case in point. But it is likely too late for strategies of simple avoidance. Many reading this essay either qualify as cyborgs already under Haraway's definition or have become so acculturated to cyborg thinking (without realizing it) that a rejection of cyborg identity would entail an equally acute rejection of a great deal of current medical technology. Perhaps, alternately, there are those Christians who believe that medical or technological alterations in the body do not affect identity in any way. After all, the person who receives a pacemaker implant is presumably the "same" person before and after the surgery: but what if this "same" person's leg were replaced with a prosthesis, or if this "same" person's face were completely disfigured in a fire, or if this "same" person underwent sex reassignment surgery, or if this "same" person were altered at the genetic level? Christians who believe in the material effects of the fall and in resurrection cannot afford to dismiss the body's involvement in identity, even as we continue to affirm moral, emotional, and spiritual dimensions of personhood. Even anticipated, "natural" changes in the body (such as adolescence or aging) affect identity. If the body has no impact on identity, then Christians should be indifferent about becoming cyborgs, since changes to the body are merely cosmetic, without moral significance. If, on the other hand, the "natural" body holds deep spiritual and moral significance, then why do twenty-first century Western Christians offer so few objections to modifying and enhancing it? In 2001, a patient received the first completely implanted artificial heart, replacing his "natural" heart, the one God designed. Should that patient have been allowed to die? Perhaps medical intervention in the body is morally justifiable only to correct a systemic malfunction? If so, Christians, then, should decline all elective surgery, and especially plastic surgery, and circumcision would be out of the question.

Perhaps medical intervention in the body is to be viewed as God's gift of creative imagination, its purpose being to ameliorate the corrupting effects of the fall, to render our bodies partially regenerate in anticipation of the resurrection? In that case, who is to say how far we are fallen, and how much we may regenerate? What genetic alterations and mechanical implants might be necessary for us to live as long as Methuselah? If our bodies have lost so much of the divine image, then perhaps even what we now know as "male" and "female" are shadows of their former selves. Christians have yet to face cyborg ethics squarely: at what point do technological bodily enhancements become spiritually significant? Haraway's essay cannot resolve this question for Christians. Whereas some brands of earlier feminism sought to deify women (an understandable reaction to patriarchal slights), Haraway anticipates a future in which technology frees gender from all hierarchies and theologies. Despite the fact that Christians cannot accept Haraway's answer, she presents us with a question we cannot ignore.

The gender performance theory of Judith Butler, presents a similar quandary. Butler's *Gender Trouble* (1990) made it impossible for essentialist feminists to ignore constructionist challenges, and inaugurated the model of performative gender that persists to this day. It is not my purpose here to retrace all of Butler's steps, especially since her work is well known and widely available. Rather, I reference her work in order to clarify how her central insight—the theatricality of gender—bears on the rejection of "essential" or "natural" categories. In reviewing Butler's thought, one notoriously common misunderstanding must be defused from the outset. When she characterizes gender as performative, Butler is not claiming that we can change our gender whenever we like, or that we can decide to be masculine one day and feminine the next. This is a typical misreading of Butler's work. Instead, what Butler proposes is that gender is a performance that exceeds and precedes individual choice, desire, or intention. In fact, according to *Gender Trouble*, the performance, far from being "chosen" by a preexistent performer, actually produces the performer:

> In this sense, *gender* is not a noun, but neither is it a set of free-floating attributes, for we have seen that the substantive effect of

gender is performatively produced and compelled by the regulatory practices of gender coherence. Hence, within the inherited discourse of the metaphysics of substance, gender proves to be performative—that is, constituting the identity it is purported to be. In this sense, gender is always a doing, though not a doing by a subject who might be said to preexist the deed. The challenge for rethinking gender categories outside of the metaphysics of substance will have to consider the relevance of Nietzsche's claim in *On the Genealogy of Morals* that "there is no 'being' behind doing, effecting, becoming; 'the doer' is merely a fiction added to the deed—the deed is everything." In an application that Nietzsche himself would not have anticipated or condoned, we might state as a corollary: There is no gender identity behind the expressions of gender; that identity is performatively constituted by the very "expressions" that are said to be its results. (24–25)

Those who castigate gender studies for its performative gender models typically misunderstand this crucial argument. Performativity and theatricality do not imply conscious choice. In Butler's view, gender identity simply does not exist prior to a given performance—gender *is* the consolidated repetition of everyday activities: wearing lipstick, putting on a tie, bowing or curtseying, cutting hair short or long, and the like. In Butler's account, then, we do not wake up each day and "decide" to be masculine or feminine. In innumerable social ways, that decision has already been made for us, and indeed has *made* us. This is hardly a new idea. As early as 1929, the psychoanalyst Joan Riviere postulated that femininity was a "masquerade" to which women unconsciously resorted because of social and psychological pressures. Even popular clichés—"the clothes make the man"—reverberate with constructionist thought. What Butler produced in *Gender Trouble*, however, was a thorough tracing of this constructionist thought to its logical and radical conclusions. If the clothes do indeed make the man, then the *act* of dressing becomes prior to "being" masculine. Butler therefore argues that physicality cannot be interpreted apart from social performance. For Butler, then, feminism should not even undertake to represent "women," understood as "universal female essences." For her, as for Haraway, feminism does not primarily concern women. It is a theoretical and political imperative to interpret and parody the gender performances that constitute all humans.

Christian objections to Butler's gender performance theory are likely to be very similar to their objections to Haraway's, with one important difference. Butler's theory does not herald a utopian future in which gender will be freed from all constraints. Although she might wish for such a future, Butler is not so sanguine. Rather, she believes that gender will always be constrained to imitate a set of socially acceptable norms and that its only "freedom" consists in repeating or parodying those norms. This less optimistic perspective actually makes Butler's position slightly more amenable to Christian viewpoints, since, by setting limits to the range of possible gender performances, she does not deify gender as Haraway does.

In a much more significant way, however, Butler's theory is readymade to be appropriated by Christians interested in gender identity. For when she states that "there is no being behind the doing," she is merely denying an essentialist view of the self, by replicating Nietzschean assumptions that prevent her from considering other alternatives. When Butler insists on "no being behind the doing [of gender]," she means that human gender identities are constituted by the performances (wearing suits, cutting hair, etc.) we enact unconsciously every day. She means that human beings do not really exist until they are performed. At this point, however, Christians need not raise an objection since they do not (or should not) view themselves as the source of their own being. Christians, on the contrary, are comfortable with the idea that they are not the creators of their own identity. In order for Butler's gender performance to be useful for Christian thought, then, we need only modify her proposition as follows: there exists no *human* "being" behind the "doing" of gender. By imagining our identities, including our gender identities, as God's artistic performance, we can both evade the problems of essentialism and appropriate performance theory in a way Butler is not likely to have anticipated. Like most secular gender theorists, she falsely assumes that theology requires essentialist thinking; this, however, is manifestly not the case. If, as suggested in the previous section, the image of God can be meaningfully understood as a "capacity for otherness," for unnaturalness, then the significance of the *imago* would be to dislodge the performance of gender from nature within a theological framework. Butler's presuppositions may disqualify her from considering God as the source of gender performance; Christians, however, need not suffer from such impediments. Furthermore, if this reading of the *imago* is correct, then Christians need not fear becoming cyborgs—beings detached from nature—for in a sense we have always been so.

Notes

1. For a more general philosophical review of the question of literal meaning, see J. L. Austin, *How to Do Things With Words* (Cambridge, Harvard University Press, 1962); Stanley Fish, *Is There a Text in this Class?* (Cambridge, Harvard University Press, 1980); Stanley Cavell, *Must We Mean*

What We Say?: A Book of Essays (New York: Cambridge University Press, 2002); Jacques Derrida," Signature Event Context," *Limited Inc* (Evanston, IL, Northwestern University Press, 1998).

2. Stanley Fish is particularly incisive on this point: "It may seem confusing and even contradictory to assert that a text may have more than one literal reading, but that is because we usually reserve 'literal' for the single meaning a text will always . . . have, while I am using 'literal' to refer to the different single meanings a text will have in a succession of different situations" (*Is There a Text in this Class?: The Authority of Interpretive Communities* [Cambridge: Harvard University Press, 1980], 276).

3. Genesis 1:26–28, "Then God said, 'Let us make man in our image, in our likeness, and let them rule over the fish or the sea and the birds of the air, over the livestock, over all the earth, over all the creatures that move along the ground.' So God created man in his image, in the image of God he created him; male and female he created them. God blessed them and said to them, 'Be fruitful and increase in number; fill the earth and subdue it. Rule over the fish of the sea and the birds of the air and over every living creature that moves on the ground.' " (NIV)

4. On this point, see Rosemary Radford Ruether, "*Imago Dei,* Christian Tradition and Feminist Hermeneutics," *Image of God: Gender Models in Judaeo-Christian Tradition,* ed. Elisabeth Børresen (Minneapolis: Fortress Press, 1995), 282–284.

5. Bird, of course, is not ignorant of the structural parallelism. Rather, she extends her structural analysis to the whole of verses 26–28, in order to propose that "male and female" must be understood as referring to fertility in the physical world. And no doubt it does. But this compelling contextualization still does not explain away the striking poetic characteristics exhibited by verse 27. Bird accuses Trible of "a faulty syntactical analysis which isolates verse 27 as a unit of speech/thought" ("Sexual Differentiation and Divine Image in the Genesis Creation Texts." *Image of God: Gender Models in Judaeo-Christian Tradition,* ed. K. E. Børresen [Minneapolis: Fortress Press, 1995], 23). But one need not isolate verse 27 as a syntactical "unit" in order to argue for a correspondence between the image and sexual difference. Indeed, one can accept both conclusions—they are not mutually exclusive. Why parallel "male and female" with "in the image of God" at all, if fertility is sexuality's only context?

6. Rhetorically, "aporia" refers to the idea of a "blocked passage" that we nevertheless cross over—as when a writer begins an essay by claiming that he or she does not know what to write. In failing to begin, a beginning is nonetheless made. The concept of the aporia has been theorized by deconstruction over the past several decades. I am here suggesting that the *imago Dei* is such a "blocked passage." By asserting that we are like God, but refusing to specify that likeness, Genesis 1 encourages us to explore the nature of human identity while at the same time preventing us from ever settling on a final set of characteristics that compose it.

7. "Constructionist" is a term often opposed to "essentialist." It implies that identity is an ongoing and communal process, rather than a static and individual substance.

8. It is well worth pointing out that, before the seventeenth century, women were frequently viewed as biological aberrations from the male "norm." For a wealth of historical evidence on this, see Thomas Laqueur, *Making Sex: Body and Gender from the Greeks to Freud* (Cambridge: Harvard University Press, 1990).

Bibliography

Austin, J. L. (1962). *How to do things with words.* Cambridge: Harvard University Press.

Barth, K. (1958). *Church dogmatics.* Ed. G. W. Bromiley and T. F. Torrance. Edinburgh: T. & T. Clark.

Bird, P. A. (1995). "Sexual differentiation and divine image in the Genesis creation texts." *Image of God: Gender models in Judaeo-Christian tradition.* Ed. K. E. Børresen. Minneapolis: Fortress Press.

Blade runner. (1982). Dir. R. Scott. Perf. H. Ford, R. Hauer, S. Young, E. J. Olmos, D. Hannah.

Børresen, K. E. (1995). "Introduction: *Imago Dei* as inculturated doctrine." *Image of God: Gender models in Judaeo-Christian tradition.* Fortress Press: Minneapolis.

Butler, J. (1990). *Gender trouble.* New York: Routledge.

———. (1993). *Bodies that matter: On the discursive limits of "sex."* New York: Routledge.

Cavell, S. (2002). *Must we mean what we say?: A book of essays.* New York: Cambridge University Press.

Derrida, J. (1998). "Signature event context." *Limited Inc.* Evanston, IL: Northwestern University Press.

Fausto-Sterling, A. (1993). "The five sexes." *The sciences.* (March–April): 20–25.

———. (2000). "The five sexes, revisited." *The sciences.* (July–August): 18–23.

Fish, S. (1980). *Is there a text in this class?: The authority of interpretive communities.* Cambridge: Harvard University Press.

Gallagher, S. (1991). "Feminist literary criticism: A chorus of ethical voices." *Contemporary literary theory: A Christian appraisal.* Ed. C. Walhout and L. Ryken. Grand Rapids, MI: Eerdmans.

Haraway, D. (1991). "A cyborg manifesto: Science, technology, and socialist-feminism in the late twentieth century." *Simians, cyborgs and women: The reinvention of nature.* New York: Routledge.

Hartley, J. (2000). *Genesis.* New international Biblical commentary. Old Testament Series 1. Peabody, MA: Hendrickson Publishers.

The Holy Bible: New international version. (1978). Grand Rapids: Zondervan Bible Publishers.

Johnson, P. E. (2002). *The right questions: Truth, meaning, and public debate.* Downers Grove, IL: InterVarsity Press.

Laqueur, T. (1990). *Making sex: Body and gender from the Greeks to Freud.* Cambridge: Harvard University Press.

Riviere, J. (1929) "Womanliness as masquerade." *International journal of psychoanalysis.* 10: 36–44.

Ruether, R. R. (1995). "*Imago Dei*, Christian tradition and feminist hermeneutics." *Image of God: Gender models in Judaeo-Christian tradition.* Ed. K. E. Børresen. Minneapolis: Fortress Press.

Teugels, L. (2000). "The creation of the human in rabbinic interpretation." *The creation of man and woman: Interpretations of the Biblical narratives in Jewish and Christian traditions.* Ed. G. P. Luttikhuizen. Boston, MA: Brill.

Trible, P. (1978). *God and the rhetoric of sexuality.* Philadelphia: Fortress Press.

ABOUT THE AUTHORS

Linda Beail is Professor of Political Science and Director of the Margaret Stevenson Center for Women's Studies at Point Loma Nazarene University in San Diego, California, where she teaches gender politics and feminist theory. She has published articles on maternal images in popular culture and the role of religion in America.

Carol Blessing is Professor of Literature at Point Loma Nazarene University in San Diego, California, where she teaches Medieval and Early Modern Literature, Women Writers, and Literary Theory. She has written extensively on women on early women writers, Elizabeth I, and women in the Church.

Lisa Bernal Corley is an Assistant Professor of Theology and Ethics at the School of Theology and Christian Ministry, Point Loma Nazarene University in San Diego, California. Her research is in social justice issues.

Allyson Jule is Associate Professor/Senior Lecturer in Education at the University of Glamorgan, Wales, United Kingdom, where she teaches educational theory and methods. She is also the author of *Gender, Participation and Silence in the Language Classroom: Sh-shushing the Girls* (2004), and editor of *Gender and the Language of Religion* (2005).

Diane Leclerc is Professor of Historical Theology and Preaching at Northwest Nazarene University in Nampa, Idaho. She has published several articles and is the author of *Singleness of Heart: Gender, Sin, and Holiness in Historical Perspective* (2001).

Holly Faith Nelson is Assistant Professor of English at Trinity Western University, Langley, Canada, where she teaches early-modern literature. She has coedited *The Broadview Anthology of Seventeenth-Century Verse* *and Prose* (2000), *Of Paradise and Light: Essays on Henry Vaughan and John Milton* (2004), and *Eikon Basilike* (2005).

Christopher Noble is Associate Professor of English at Azusa Pacific University in Azusa, California, where he teaches nineteenth-century British literature and literary theory. His current research focuses on gender and mourning in Victorian literature.

Bettina Tate Pedersen is Professor of Literature at Point Loma Nazarene University, San Diego, California, where she teaches nineteenth- and twentieth-century British literature and literary theory. She has authored articles on nineteenth-century women writers and pedagogy.

Elizabeth Powell is a Graduate Student at Regent College, Vancouver, British Columbia, Canada, where she studies Intersections of Christianity and Culture. Her research focus is feminist philosophy and contemporary theology.

INDEX

abolition, 70, 173
abortion, 12–13, 32
activism, political, 4, 12, 14, 32, 68,
    70, 125
Aers, David, 162–163
American Holiness Movement, 115,
    124, 139
American Society of Biblical
    Literature, 146
analogia entis, 192
analogia relationis, 192
Anthony, Susan B., 70
Anzaldua, Gloria, 5–6, 8
Arobin, Alcee, 64
Astell, Mary, 129–130, 136, 154
authority
    feminist biblical hermeneutics and,
        147–150
    male, 119, 136
    protofeminism and, 157–158
    Wesley and, 131–133
    women and, 24, 38–39, 138–140,
        161–164, 172, 174–176
Awakening, The (Chopin), 63, 79, 80

Bacon, Francis, 129
baptism, 74, 120
Barnhill, Carla, 69, 72
Barry, Kathleen, 14–16, 33
Barth, Karl, 192
Barthes, R., 42
Bathurst, Elizabeth, 171, 174

Beauvoir, Simone de, 7, 81–95, 98,
    101–104, 106–107, 108, 109
    gender-construction and, 83–87
    reinterpretation of, 91–95
Beilin, Elaine, 169
Bernard of Clairvaux, 167
Beloved (Morrison), 70–71, 79
Bible
    interpretation of, 28–29, 133,
        148–149, 154, 181–182, 185,
        191–192, 195
    Reformation and, 20–22
    see also literalism; scripture
Bird, Phyllis A., 188–192, 202
Blandford, Susannah, 172
Blessed Mother, 7, 59, 61, 63, 65–67, 69,
    71–73, 75, 77, 79
Bodies That Matter (Butler), 122, 123,
    128, 159, 173, 174, 175, 177, 185
Book of Showings (Julian of Norwich),
    164–167
Borderlands/La Frontera: The New Mestiza
    (Anzaldua), 5–6, 8
Børresen, Kari Elisabeth, 182, 202
Bosanquet, Mary, 134–135, 144,
    153, 154
Bradstreet, Anne, 169
Bread Not Stone (Schｷssler-Fiorenza),
    146–150, 154
Brontë, Charlotte, 9
Brontë, Emily, 25
Brown, Earl Kent, 133, 135, 154

CPSIA information can be obtained at www.ICGtesting.com
Printed in the USA
LVOW040822180112

264358LV00005B/1/P